Adrian Gilbert is the author or co-author of 10 books, including several *Sunday Times* bestsellers. He attended St Edmund's College, the oldest Catholic school in Britain, and read Chemistry at the University of Kent in Canterbury. His books are characterized by scrupulous research coupled with an easy, narrative style that has wide appeal for readers. He is married and lives with his wife and daughter in Kent.

THE BLOOD OF AVALON

THE SECRET HISTORY OF THE GRAIL DYNASTY FROM KING ARTHUR TO PRINCE WILLIAM

ADRIAN GILBERT

WATKINS PUBLISHING
LONDON

Map 1: England and Wales

Motto of the Chair of Tir Iarll:

Nidda lle gellir Gwell

"Nothing is truly good
that may be excelled"

This edition first published in the UK and USA 2013 by
Watkins Publishing Limited
PO Box 883
Oxford, OX1 9PL
UK

A member of Osprey Group

For enquiries in the USA and Canada:
Osprey Publishing
PO Box 3985
New York, NY 10185-3985
Tel: (001) 212 753 4402
Email: info@ospreypublishing.com

1 3 5 7 9 10 8 6 4 2

Typeset by Jerry Goldie

Printed and bound by CPI Group (UK) Ltd, Croydon, CR0 4YY

A CIP record for this book is available from the British Library

ISBN: 978-1-78028-570-2

Watkins Publishing is supporting the Woodland Trust, the UK's leading woodland
conservation charity, by funding tree-planting initiatives and woodland maintenance.

www.watkinspublishing.co.uk

CONTENTS

ILLUSTRATIONS

CHAPTER 1

Two Royal Weddings

It was a sunny day at the end of April and, following an exceptionally long winter, Regent's Park was once more in full bloom. At ten-yard intervals along The Mall, the avenue leading from Trafalgar Square to Buckingham Palace, members of the Brigade of Guards stood at attention; their understated purpose, as always, was to protect the monarch from would-be assassins. The mood of the crowd, though, was anything but hostile. Mobile phone cameras at the ready, its members were desperate to take pictures of Britain's Queen and send them back instantly to Berlin, Cape Town, Peking, Los Angeles or wherever else they had family and friends to impress. Indeed, some people had camped out all night just for the opportunity to be part of this royal occasion: the wedding of Prince William of Wales to his long-time girlfriend Kate Middleton. When, flanked by the Household Cavalry, the Royal procession eventually came into view, a great roar erupted.

The Queen, dutiful as ever, gave away no hint of the deep anxiety that, for months now, had been eating away at her. Accompanied by the Duke of Edinburgh and waving to her admirers as she trundled past in her horse-drawn carriage, she hid her concerns behind a fixed smile. Soon they arrived at Westminster Abbey, the nation's primary shrine to the cult of royalty. As they entered the venerable church, the Duke two steps behind her, the Queen's thoughts could not help but stray back to memories of a very different and sadder occasion. Nearly 14 years had passed since then, but the memory was still raw: the funeral of her former daughter-in-law – Diana, Princess of Wales.

It was not the last time that Queen Elizabeth had been in the Abbey, but it felt like yesterday. Walking through the Great West Door brought it all back: the pain, the embarrassment, but above all the sense of betrayal by those who should have known better. The Queen knew only too well that, over and above her civic duties such as Trooping the Colour and opening Parliament, she was also a religious leader. She was the head of the Church of England, and therefore of the wider Anglican Communion. It was both who she was as a person, and the oath of service she had taken at her Coronation. That Diana had not come up to the mark both shocked and saddened her. It had also meant that, for a time, the monarchy itself had been in danger, a potential calamity that few people understood outside a tight circle of 'initiates'.

The one point of light to illumine such dark thoughts was that, so far, Diana's oldest son, William, seemed not to have inherited the wilder aspects of his mother's character. The stars evidently predicted that he had great potential, but this would come to naught if he behaved like a fool. The Queen could only hope that his bride would not break under the strain like Diana, even though she lacked a royal or even aristocratic upbringing. The monarchy had many enemies – some of them practitioners of the black arts who would stop at nothing if they felt it would advance their cause. For the world's sake, as well as her own family's, it was important that Kate should keep William anchored so that he could manifest what should be a truly great destiny. Above all, it was important that she should bear him an heir, someone who would preserve William's very special genetic inheritance.

Diana died quite unexpectedly in bizarre – and rather sordid – circumstances. Recently divorced from her husband, Prince Charles, she was visiting Paris on her way home to London after a protracted holiday in the Mediterranean. It was the night of 31 August 1997, and she was sitting in the back of a Jaguar saloon. Sitting next to her was her current lover, Dodi Fayed, who many regarded as a playboy. Exactly how the accident came about – if it was an accident – is uncertain. At any rate, travelling at great speed through the road tunnel at Place de l'Alma, the car swerved and crashed into a concrete pillar. Dodi and the driver died instantly at the scene of the accident, while Diana survived for a short time, passing away over an hour or so later in hospital. The only survivor of the crash was their bodyguard who had had the common sense to put on his safety belt.

The poignancy of the moment was further increased when the pathologists discovered that Dodi was carrying a diamond engagement ring in his pocket. Although Diana had only been going out with him for a few weeks and it did not seem to outside observers that she took the relationship all that seriously, he evidently thought differently: the ring implied that he had intended to propose to her over dinner that very night. It was almost as if the crash was God's way of preventing such an eventuality. For although Diana was wild at times and behaved quite inappropriately for the mother of a future king, it was as if she had been protected in some mystical way – until that fateful moment. Could it be that she had indeed agreed to marry Dodi and this had in some strange way sealed her fate?

When the revelation of Dodi's marriage proposal came out, it was a great embarrassment to the Queen and all the royal family. Dodi's father, Mohammed al-Fayed, was a sworn enemy of theirs, especially of the Duke of Edinburgh. Had the couple married, it would have made Dodi stepfather to the Queen and Duke's two grandsons: Princes William and Harry.

In the event, although the circumstances of the accident raised awkward questions, the Queen and Duke were spared the embarrassment of having Mohammed al-Fayed as an in-law member of their extended family. Nevertheless, there was speculation at the time (and this was later repeated in court by Mohammed al-Fayed) that Dodi and Diana were murdered by agents of MI6, the British secret intelligence service. It was – and presumably still is – al-Fayed's belief that the Duke of Edinburgh had personally given the orders. The Duke, of course, strenuously denied such allegations, and it is hard to believe that, even if he had wanted to, he would have had the power. However, it cannot be denied that, although on a personal level, the

Queen and Duke were sorry for Dodi's untimely death, they were undoubt-edly relieved that any future ties with the al-Fayed family were severed.

Yet, as I have looked further into this matter, I have found something else: a secret at the very heart of Britain's establishment so deeply veiled that very few outside of a tight cabal of initiates even suspect it exists. This secret unites a group of interlinked, elite families that form, as it were, an aristocracy within the aristocracy. Knowingly, or more likely unknowingly, Diana's destiny had been to enact a plan going back centuries. What this plan was, and what it means for the rest of us today, is the focus of this book. However, one thing is certain: Diana was indeed special, as she carried the 'Blood of Avalon' in her veins.

CHAPTER 2

The Cinderella Princess

Diana was 36 years old when she died and still in her prime. Healthy, fit and beautiful, she seemed at last to be getting over what had been an extremely trying time for her. It all seemed so different sixteen years earlier when, at the tender age of 20, she almost floated up the steps of London's St Paul's Cathedral, her long train following like the folded-back wings of a virgin queen bee. Her wedding, which took place on 29 July 1981, was watched on television by an estimated global audience of some 750 million people – a record for such an event. The build-up to the wedding had been pure Disney, with Diana playing her part to perfection. For although in looks her groom was hardly a Hollywood 'Prince Charming', she had, like Cinderella, spent much of her life in the shadows of two older sisters and a hated stepmother.

'Lady Di', as she was then referred to by the press, came from a broken home. Her mother and father, Lady Frances Shand Kydd and Lord John Spencer, Viscount Althorp (later the 8th Earl Spencer), divorced when she was only seven years old. It was an acrimonious split, and afterwards Diana and her younger brother, Charles Spencer, initially lived in London with their mother. Later, after their father was given custody of all the children, they went back to live with him at his stately home – Althorp in Northamptonshire.

While Diana missed her mother, she certainly enjoyed living in one of England's greatest country houses. There, she could dance on the patio and go swimming in its famous Oval Pond: something she missed while living in central London. This idyll came to an abrupt end when, in July 1976, her father remarried. The Earl's second wife, Raine McCorquodale, had herself just gone through a bitter divorce. The four Spencer children, including Diana, did not take to their new stepmother, referring to her as 'Acid Raine'. This antipathy became much worse after the Earl suffered a stroke in 1978. With her husband largely incapacitated, Countess Raine took over the running of Althorp House and started a programme of renovations. To the horror of the Spencer children, she not only displayed extremely poor taste in her choice of décor for the old house, but also sold off many family heirlooms in order to pay for these unwanted changes. This was something for which she would never be forgiven.

Lady Raine – the wicked stepmother to Diana's Cinderella – was the daughter of the colourful Dame Barbara Cartland, who would turn into Diana's Fairy Godmother. Dame Barbara, something of a society belle herself in her youth, is best remembered today for wearing pink at all times and for her prodigious output of romantic fiction. She was a close friend of Prince Charles' grandmother, the Queen Mother. She may have not had aristocratic heritage, but as the author of more than 720 novels that have sold more than a billion copies worldwide in 36 languages, she certainly earned the right to call herself the 'Queen of Romance'.

Barbara Cartland was also a close friend of Charles' favourite uncle and mentor: Lord Louis Mountbatten, who was a great-grandson of Queen Victoria and second cousin to the Queen's father, George VI. Like his father, Lord Louis joined the Royal Navy and, in 1940, led a fleet of destroyers in the Battle for Norway. The Prime Minister, Winston Churchill, liked him and promoted him to senior positions in the army and air force as well as the navy; eventually he appointed him head of SEAC (South East Asia Command). In conjunction with General William Slim, at the time probably Britain's most able field marshal, Mountbatten oversaw the liberation of Singapore and Burma. In 1947, he was appointed Viceroy of India, the last person to occupy that office prior to that country's independence. For his services to the Crown, he was rewarded with the hereditary title Earl Mountbatten of Burma.

Mountbatten was the brother of the Duke of Edinburgh's rather eccentric mother, Princess Alice of Battenburg, who ended her life as a Greek Orthodox nun. Always close to his nephew Philip, there is little doubt that Mountbatten had a hand in organizing the latter's courtship of the future Queen Elizabeth II. Then, as mentor to their eldest son, Prince Charles, he saw it as his duty to instruct the heir to the throne in the ways of sex and marriage. He advised Charles to sow plenty of wild oats while he was young and even provided him with a guestroom for the purpose in his own house, Broadlands.

Nevertheless, he was adamant that when he did marry, the Prince should choose a virgin for his wife. He explained it would be easier for a prospective Princess of Wales to settle into her eventual role as Queen if she had had no prior experience of sex with other men. In this he may have been influenced by his own experience. His wife, Countess Edwina Mountbatten, was a notorious bisexual (as he too may have been), and had a number of scandalous liaisons, including, it was rumoured, affairs with the singer Paul Robeson and with Jawaharlal Nehru, independent India's first prime minister. Keenly aware of how the marriage of Edward, Prince of Wales, and the American divorcée Mrs Wallis Simpson had very nearly destroyed the monarchy in the 1930s, he insisted that Charles should choose a wife without a colourful past.

Mountbatten discussed his matchmaking plans with his old friend Barbara Cartland. She, however, had ideas of her own on this subject and raised with him the possibility of the Prince marrying one of her step-granddaughters. The girl in question was one of Diana's elder sisters, Lady Sarah Spencer; consequently she and Charles started dating. Unfortunately, any romance that there might have been came to an abrupt end when she told journalist Andrew Morton that she had had 'thousands' of previous boyfriends, suffered from anorexia and would never marry someone she didn't love. She was probably exaggerating, but by her own admission it was evident that she was not the sort of blushing virgin that Mountbatten had advised the Prince of Wales to marry. Charles beat a hasty retreat.

The girl Mountbatten had in mind was his own granddaughter, Lady Amanda Knatchbull. Charles might indeed have married her had not fate, destiny, or whatever you want to call it, interfered once again in a most cruel way to put a stop to a potential marriage. In 1979, Lord Mountbatten was blown up by a terrorist bomb while on a boat off the northwest coast of Ireland. It was an ignominious end for a former First Sea Lord, admiral of the fleet and Viceroy of India, although he would have no doubt thought it fitting that he should die at sea. He, along with Lady Amanda's brother Nicholas, was killed by the blast, while another brother and her parents were injured. Thus, although Charles proposed to Amanda the following year, she was in no mood to be a royal bride and turned him down.

By 1980, with Mountbatten dead and the heir to the throne still unmarried, things were starting to look a bit desperate. At this point, Barbara Cartland, who was still keen to play the role of fairy godmother to Charles' Prince Charming, once again waved her magic wand and pointed in an unexpected direction. She reminded her old friend the Queen Mother that while Sarah had maybe proved unsuitable, her youngest sister, Diana, was only 18 and almost certainly a virgin. Available and lacking an embarrassing past, she might make a good wife for the Prince of Wales. By now under intense family pressure to hurry up and marry someone, Charles took her for a weekend's sailing at Cowes, aboard the Royal Yacht *Britannia*. After formally introducing her to the Queen and Prince Philip, he proposed to her in early February the following year. To the huge relief of the entire Royal family, this Spencer girl did not spurn his advances, but immediately said 'yes'.

The story of Charles and Diana's courtship and wedding has a fairytale character that could itself have come out of a Barbara Cartland novel. Although not exactly dressed in rags, Diana was certainly the Cinderella of her family. Her education, such as it was, was minimal even by the standards of aristocratic girls expected to do no more in life than provide heirs; for even though she sat her exams twice, she left school at age 16 without so much as a single 'O' level. What she enjoyed – and indeed excelled in – were ballet and swimming. Unfortunately, her height (she grew to 5' 10") barred her from her desired career as a dancer with the Royal Ballet, while her swimming, though good, was not up to Olympic standards. Thus it was that by the time she was 17, she found herself back at her mother's flat in London wondering about her uncertain future. For her 18th birthday she was given a flat of her own, in Earl's Court, which she shared with two friends. Since she had an affinity for children, she took a part-time job as a kindergarten assistant, while, in true Cinderella style, she supplemented the meagre income this generated by doing cleaning and baby-sitting work for her sister Sarah and her friends. Given her lack of qualifications and the dead-end career in which she found herself, it is hardly surprising that she leapt at the opportunity offered by Charles. Instead of cleaning and child-minding, she would become Princess of Wales and, eventually, or so it was expected, Queen of Great Britain, Canada, Australia, New Zealand and many other countries and territories. It was a destiny she could not have even dreamed of even a few months previously.*

This fairytale marriage, however, was fated to have an unhappy ending. The wedding itself was a joyous occasion, but Diana's life within the Royal household turned out to be anything but happy. Although she quickly produced the required 'heir' (Prince William) and 'spare' (Prince Harry), it was soon apparent that her husband was not – and perhaps never really had been – in love with her. Their interests too were worlds apart. She liked dancing and high fashion, while he was passionate about classical architecture, conservation and organic gardening. This lack of mutual interests denied them the cement that, in the absence of love, could yet have helped them to turn their marriage into a life-long commitment.

It turned out that Charles' real love was a former girlfriend of his, Mrs Camilla Parker-Bowles, with whom he conducted a clandestine affair.

---

* See Chart 1: Courtship, First Marriage and Progeny of Prince Charles, page 224

Realizing that her marriage was a sham, Diana too began to have secret affairs. It was a situation that invited gossip and one that could not continue without risking severe damage to the reputation of the monarchy. As lack of love for one another turned into active dislike, it became clear that the only realistic solution to their marital problems would be a clean break. Thus, in 1996, and with the Queen's blessing, they divorced. Diana would be dead a year later, but by then she had already fulfilled her destiny by changing the genetics of the British royal succession.

CHAPTER 3

Funeral for a Princess

The death of Diana shocked the world. Curiously, it provoked a show of emotion, at times hysteria, rare for the British. The reasons for this were not at all obvious, but may be linked in some mysterious way to her hidden destiny. It was as though people knew instinctively that someone with a rather special role had gone out of all our lives and, as a consequence, those of us left behind were so much poorer.

The mood of the nation was well captured by Tony Blair, Britain's newly elected Prime Minister. In a total breach of protocol for such an occasion, he delivered an impromptu speech to the BBC. At times with a quivering voice, he eulogized the Princess almost as if she were a saint. He reminded the nation and the world that her paparazzi image was only one facet of her character. Behind the glossy pictures there was a real woman: the mother of two vulnerable boys; the patroness of numerous charities that did valuable work, everything from the disposal of landmines to caring for the sick and hungry in Africa. For those in need she always had time and displayed, over and over again, her compassion and a feeling of common humanity. She also, he said, possessed a strange charisma so that just a look or gesture from her made people feel better.

Blair offered no answer to the question as to how she might have come by such a power, but in what many interpreted as a dig at the Royal Family, he referred to her as 'The People's Princess'. By awarding her this unofficial title (Diana had recently been stripped of her formal appellation of 'Her

Royal Highness'), he was perhaps reminding her now-divorced husband that an unloved monarchy has no future. He implied that by not making a success of his marriage to 'The People's Princess', the Prince of Wales had shown a failure in judgement that could yet cost him the throne.

At first, the Queen tried to distance herself from a tragedy that she saw as being clearly of Diana's own making. However, following Blair's speech and the chord it evidently struck with the public, it became clear that such a hard-hearted attitude did not accord well with the public mood. Realizing this, she ordered that the Royal Standard, the monarch's personal flag that is raised over Buckingham Palace when she is at home, be flown at half-mast. She also felt compelled to deliver her own eulogy for a young woman who she must secretly have wished had never become involved with her family at all. Nevertheless, and perhaps surprising even herself, she too was affected by the sense of unfolding destiny. She referred to the dramatic emotional impact Diana had had on her and reminded her subjects that she herself was a grandmother as well as being their queen. She paid tribute to Diana's wonderful qualities: her compassion, her dedication to her two sons and her ability to keep on smiling through adversity. With some ambiguity, she said that no one who had met Diana would ever forget her. She also acknowledged, though she didn't say what these were, that there were lessons to be learnt both from her life and from the people's reaction to her death.

On 6 September 1997, just six days after the accident, Diana was given a state funeral: something that, prior to Blair's speech, few would have expected. By now, the gates of Buckingham Palace and also those of Kensington Palace were piled high with floral tributes. From the latter, her coffin, draped in the Royal Standard as befitting a member of the Royal Family, was taken to Westminster Abbey on a horse-drawn gun carriage with mounted police and soldiers in attendance. At The Mall, Prince Charles, Diana's brother Charles Spencer and her two sons joined the funeral cortege. When it arrived at the Abbey, it was taken off the gun carriage and carried into the church by eight sturdy members of the Prince of Wales Company, 1st Battalion of Welsh Guards.

The Abbey church was packed for the service that followed, and the Royal Family, which had clearly been caught on the back foot by all that had happened, could be forgiven for thinking that they had weathered the storm. It was then that Diana's brother Charles dropped a bombshell of his own. Speaking with eloquence and passion, he delivered a superb funeral oration for his sister. However, his eulogy proved highly controversial: for both in tone and language, he implied that she had been betrayed by her husband's family – the Windsors. As head of the Spencer family – he was now the holder of the ancestral title of Earl Spencer – he promised to make sure that her values rather than theirs would be passed on to her two sons. He also vowed to protect them from the fate that had befallen her. He did not say what had caused his sister's anguish, but then he didn't need to. It was common knowledge that the cold, formal nature of the Windsor household, emotionally repressed and still living in the Victorian age, was at least partly to blame for her divorce and untimely death.

Then, in another dig at the Windsors, he declared that her 'blood family' would see to it that the boys were educated in the sort of loving and imaginative way that she would have wanted: a way that would enable their 'souls to sing openly'. Exactly why the Spencer family's blood was special again he did not say, but the implication was that from their souls' point of view, especially with regard to 'emotional intelligence', it provided them with possibilities over and above their inheritance from the Windsors.

Following the funeral, Diana's body was transported back to her old home – the family seat of Althorp in Northamptonshire. There, much to the amazement of those present, the Earl ordered the removal of the Royal Standard, which, from the time it left Kensington Palace to its arrival at the gates of Althorp, had remained draped over the coffin. In its place he ordered that a flag bearing the arms of Spencer should be spread. A further surprise, at least for those with some knowledge of heraldry, was that these arms were almost identical to those of the medieval family of le Despencer whose repeated rises and falls are woven into the very fabric of English history. The implied symbolism of the Earl's act – or at least the way that it was interpreted by the media – was that the unfeeling Windsors (symbolized by the Royal Standard) were being left at the gate. In death, Diana was returning to the warm bosom of her own family, the Spencers. The implication was that their blood was every bit as good as the Windsors and maybe, in some unspecified way, even more special. Then, also somewhat surprisingly, the Earl announced that her body would not be placed in the family mausoleum, but rather buried on an island in the middle of Althorp's Oval Pond. Here, away from the prying lenses of the paparazzi and the souvenir-hunting hands of her millions of admirers, her body would be able to rest in the peaceful surroundings of the lake she used to swim in as a girl.

Diana's place of burial is marked by a plaque, but her most important legacy is her two sons, the elder of whom, God willing, will one day be crowned King of Great Britain. This is not an empty title, for the succession to the throne matters greatly for psychological as well as political reasons. In Britain, the monarchy is associated with a half-remembered golden age when King Arthur sat on the throne. According to the legends, he ruled over Britain during the period of chaos that overwhelmed the country following the collapse of the Western Roman Empire. A formidable warrior himself, he is said to have rallied the ancient Britons in their desperate struggles against the invading Anglo-Saxons.

The source of Arthur's power lay in his magic sword, Excalibur, which was given to him by a mysterious water fey, the Lady of the Lake. Using it, he won a series of 12 battles culminating in a decisive victory at 'Badon Hill' (generally thought to be Solsbury Hill near Bath). This victory, for which he was credited with slaying 900 of his foes by his own hand, brought about a period of peace that lasted for some 30 years. During this time he ruled over the island of Britain – or at least the western parts of it – from a magnificent fortress-city called Camelot. Here, he set up a Christian Brotherhood, an order of chivalry whose members sat around a Round Table. Noted for their high standards of honour, valour and discipline, these 'Knights of the Round Table' policed the Arthurian kingdom, protecting women and the weak from the predations of lawless foes. However, all was not perfect. Arthur's wife, Guinevere, proved unfaithful, while his nephew Mordred (the son of his half-sister Morgan-le-Faye), who was also his son according to some versions of the story, plotted against him. Meanwhile, the majority of his knights perished in a forlorn quest for a sacred cup, the 'Holy Grail', which was said to have been used by Jesus Christ at the Last Supper. According to other legends, this cup was later used to collect some drops of his blood as it poured from his wounds while dying on the cross. Because of this link with the Blood of Christ, the Holy Grail was said to have powerful, healing energies associated with it. Indeed, it was so powerful that it could prolong the life of its custodian almost indefinitely. Unfortunately, by the time it was found by an exceptionally saintly knight called Perceval (in some versions of the story it is Galahad who finds it), Arthur's kingdom was close to collapse.

In the final chapters of the story Arthur is betrayed by Mordred, who usurps the kingdom while Arthur is away in Brittany. Furious, he returns to Cornwall with his remaining knights to confront Mordred and his Anglo-Saxon allies. The two armies clash in the Battle of Camblan, with disastrous consequences for both. Tradition says this battle was fought near a bend in the River Camel, not far from the town of Camelford, but it could have been somewhere else entirely. By the end of the battle, Mordred is dead and Arthur too is mortally wounded. He is taken by barge to 'Avalon' (usually identified as Glastonbury in Somerset), while a faithful knight, Sir Bedivere, is tasked with throwing Arthur's magic sword, Excalibur, back into the Lake from where it came. The myth finishes by saying that Arthur is not dead, but merely asleep; one day, at Britain's hour of greatest need, he will return as the 'Once and Future King'.

The story of King Arthur (with its associated legend of the Holy Grail) is the most important myth to come out of Britain. Ever since his death there has been a yearning for the return of the island's greatest hero-king. Arthur was popular in the Middle Ages not just because he was victorious in battle, but rather because he symbolizes all those virtues expected in a Christian monarch that are often sadly lacking: courage, justice, chivalry, leadership, magnanimity and, above all, triumph over the forces of darkness.

Despite the yearning for his return, Arthur has proved a hard act to follow. So it is perhaps not surprising that there have been no kings of this name since the old Kingdom of Logres was renamed England and the remnant of the native Britons surrendered the title of over-king to the Anglo-Saxon English. Nevertheless, so powerful is Arthur's legend that even though he fought against the Anglo-Saxons, he has been effectively anglicized; today most people in England think of him as an English king.

There is no doubting that Diana was fond of Althorp and also its pond; however, there may have been reasons other than security for the Earl's curious choice for her burial site. She was born under Cancer, the sign of the astrological zodiac that is ruled by the Moon and is particularly associated with lakes, ponds and other stationary bodies of water. In Greek mythology, Diana, the huntress sister of Apollo, was similarly associated with wild places and again the Moon. Whether or not Earl Spencer knew of these associations or had any interest in astrology, his choice of a river island for Diana's final resting place seemed inspired and, from a symbolic point of view, wholly appropriate. Without reading too much into it, it links her tragic story to that of the 'Lady of the Lake': the mythical fairy-queen whose outstretched hand gave King Arthur his magical sword Excalibur and received it back after he died.

In death as in life, Diana was to receive mythic status. This was appropriate, for as I was discovering, she was not just *anyone*. Indeed, in some ways it can be said that she was even more royal than the Queen, and the way I came to understand this was a long journey of the mind which, given her title 'Princess of Wales', begins appropriately enough in Glamorgan.

CHAPTER 4

Arthur, King of Glamorgan and Gwent

Diana's death was still in the future when, in 1995, I paid my first visit to a ruined chapel on a windy hilltop. At the time she was still married to the Prince of Wales, and I had no inkling that this chapel could be in any way connected with her. On the contrary, as far as I knew, the Principality of Wales – especially South Wales – was a backwater. It had little archaeology worth mentioning, or so I thought, apart, that is, from the wreckage of its former coal industry and the ghosts of steel works that had long been closed. It shortly became apparent how wrong my assumptions were.

Accompanying me, acting as my guide, was Alan Wilson – one of the very few people in recent times to champion the traditional, ancient history of Britain. A stocky man in his sixties, with a shock of hair tied back in a ponytail, he reminded me of the late Professor J R R Tolkien, author of *The Lord of the Rings*. Wilson had previously made his living in the shipbuilding industry, but now that he was retired from that profession, he was at last able to put to good use the degree in History and Archaeology that he had earned at Cardiff University in his youth. His passion was the legend of King Arthur, who, he informed me, was from Wales and not England, as I thought. It quickly became clear that I was going to have to relearn a lot of history.

Wilson, along with Tony 'Baram' Blackett, a research colleague, had first come to my attention about six months earlier when I read about them in a Sunday newspaper. The article concerned their discovery of what they believed to be the true burial place of the legendary King Arthur. I knew that, according to the legends, he was born at Tintagel in Cornwall and was eventually killed not far from there, at a bend in the river Camel. This was the first time anyone had suggested to me that he was buried in Wales! As I understood it, he was interred at Glastonbury in Somerset.

Wilson and Blackett disputed this account in almost every detail and claimed to have the evidence that the famous King Arthur of legend was actually from Wales. However, he was not as isolated a character as the legends imply. According to them, there had been not one but two Dark Age kings called Arthur; we don't realize this today because their stories have been muddled up. Arthur I, they said, lived in the late 4th to early 5th centuries and fought against the Romans. He was the eldest son of Magnus Maximus, a well-documented personage who, at the head of an army from Britain, invaded Gaul (France) in AD 385. There, he defeated and killed the Emperor Gratian, usurping, for a time, the Western Roman Empire. Their 'Arthur I' was evidently called Andragathius by the Romans, and he was a General as well as being Maximus' eldest son. In fact, it was he, they said, and not his father who killed Gratian after pursuing him from Soissons (where the Battle of Sassy took place) to Lyons.

Victory over the Romans was to prove short-lived, for three years later the usurpers were themselves defeated by a huge army sent by the Eastern Emperor Theodosius. Magnus Maximus was beheaded at Ravenna, but what became of Andragathius is far from clear. According to Wilson and Blackett, he returned to Britain to his power-base in Warwickshire. However, hard evidence for any of this was thin on the ground.

The second Arthur they mentioned lived in the 6th century and is much better documented than the first. According to them, his power-base was the Glamorgan–Gwent area of South Wales, which was then called Siluria. He was not just a local king, though: he was also a 'Pendragon'. This meant he was the head (*pen*) military leader (dragon) of all the Britons who were then fighting the Anglo-Saxons. Neither he nor the first Arthur was buried at Glastonbury as is generally supposed. In reality, they said, the first was most likely buried near Atherstone in Warwickshire, while the second was interred in Wales, in the vicinity of the ruined church I was now visiting.

At first sight, Wilson and Blackett's theories concerning not one but two Arthurs seemed preposterous. For one thing, I had visited Glastonbury on many occasions and had even stood on the spot in the Abbey ruins where, prior to the Reformation, there was an elaborate shrine to King Arthur. In addition, I knew that this romantic, mysterious town is also closely connected with other legends concerning the Holy Grail and Joseph of Arimathea, which explained why King Arthur (singular) had been buried there. Joseph is described in the Bible as having been a member of the Sanhedrin or Jewish Council of elders, while also being a secret follower of Jesus Christ. Because of his high status, he was able to obtain permission from Pontius Pilate, the Roman Governor of Judea, to take down Jesus' body from the cross and have it buried in his own prepared tomb. The corollary to this story is that Joseph used a cup from the Last Supper to collect some drops of blood from the still-bleeding body of the Christ. Then, after the Resurrection and Ascension of Jesus, he took this precious relic (the Holy Grail) to Britain. Here, he and his companions were given land at Glastonbury, where they built a church, the Vetusta Ecclesia, and dedicated it to the Virgin Mary. It was on the site where this church had once stood that the monks of Glastonbury built the Lady Chapel of their later abbey in Norman times. That the Britons would have wanted to bury King Arthur in such a holy place seems obvious, and, indeed, while digging in their graveyard, the monks even found the bones of a tall man along with a lead plaque identifying him as Arthur.

Faced with such a powerful legend, Wilson and Blackett's claim that there were two Arthurs and that neither of them were buried at Glastonbury seems highly suspect. Nevertheless, this was not just idle speculation on their part. The article revealed that they had carried out meticulous research over many years; they also made use of all manner of historical records, a large proportion of them ignored by earlier writers and researchers as they were written in Welsh. Furthermore, following clues contained in these texts, I found that they had actually bought the ruined church I was now to visit and had organized an archaeological dig to look for his remains.

This dig, conducted by professional archaeologists and under the auspices of CADW (the Welsh Heritage Agency), took place in 1990. Though Arthur's remains were not found, they ascertained that the derelict church was only the latest in a sequence of buildings on that site that seemed to go right back to the 1st century AD, the very dawn of Christianity in Britain. One of the succession of buildings – provisionally dated to the fifth or sixth century – had been a round 'beehive' structure. Given its shape and age, they thought it was probably a hermitage rather than a church. What was

more interesting was that, at the very centre of this round building, the archaeologists found a votive cross. It was about eight inches long and had been cast from an amalgam of mainly silver with some copper and small amounts of other metals as impurities.

The percentage proportions of metals in the cross – 79.5% silver, 14.6% copper, 2.03% lead, with just traces of other elements – was consistent with it having been cast during the Dark Ages. As if to confirm its Arthurian credentials without ambiguity, it also carried a Latin inscription: PRO ANIMA ARTORIUS, meaning 'for the soul (of) Arthur'.

Figure 1: The King Arthur votive cross.

This was not the only Arthurian relic to be found on the site. The reason the dig had been conducted in the first place was because of an earlier discovery by Wilson and Blackett: a large, L-shaped stone in the graveyard. This too had a Latin inscription, which read: REX ARTORIUS FILI MAURICIUS. Leaving aside the poor Latin grammar (it should more properly have read *Rex Artorius filius Mauricii*), the meaning was clear enough: 'King Arthur the son [of] Maurice'. They knew from various sources that there had been a 6th-century king of Glamorgan called Maurice ('Mauricius' in Latin, *Meurig* in Welsh) and that he had been succeeded by his eldest son who was, indeed, called Arthur ('Artorius', *Athrwys*). Thus, the discovery of this stone and the buried silver cross in the centre of the beehive structure seemed pretty good evidence that this 'King Arthur' was probably buried in the vicinity of this church. Faced with this evidence, on the ground as well as in libraries, I felt compelled to think again and reassess all that I knew about King Arthur, Wales and the history of the Dark Ages in general. First, though, I needed to take another look at the Glastonbury legends that claimed that Arthur was buried in Somerset and not Wales at all.*

---

* See Chart 2: Saints and Kings of Glamorgan, page 225

CHAPTER 5

The Glastonbury Legends

In the popular imagination, the story of King Arthur is inextricably bound up with the ancient town of Glastonbury in the Somerset Levels. Accordingly, at first sight, the idea that he might actually have been Welsh and a King of Glamorgan seems ludicrous. Yet as I began to dig a little deeper below the surface of the Glastonbury/Arthur legend, it became clearer and clearer that it was an elaborate hoax. In this chapter we shall examine this hoax in detail. I ask the reader to be patient and open-minded about this as I attempt to put the claims of Glastonbury into context. I do not do this from any sense of spite or desire to undermine the status of the town. As a matter of fact, I am very fond of its abbey ruins and chose to be married in the Catholic church across the road. Nevertheless, what matters much more than sentiment is the truth. To reach this sometimes requires painful sacrifices and the slaughter of sacred cows. Alas, the Glastonbury legends form a whole herd of these that, if not removed, will continue to block any further progress down this chosen road. They must be slain without sentiment or remorse. Then not only are we able to make further progress towards unravelling the true mysteries of Britain, but we can form a truer appreciation of Glastonbury's real marvel: its one-time Abbey.

Glastonbury Abbey was once an incredibly rich institution: so much so that it was said that if the Abbott of Glastonbury married the Abbess of

Shaftesbury Convent (also a very wealthy institution), they would be the richest couple in all of England. That may have been so in their heyday, but like so many other religious houses, both fell prey to the Reformation. Today, Glastonbury Abbey is a romantic ruin set in parkland behind high walls. There is hardly a trace to be seen of its supposed early history. Stripped bare of anything valuable, with the bones of its stonework left open to the elements, it looks, in fact, much like any other Benedictine abbey of the era. What we see now, however, is only the physical remains of this once great abbey. During the Middle Ages, it had unique pretensions that went far beyond the Benedictine order. Notwithstanding its out-of-the-way location, it claimed to be of apostolic foundation. As we have seen, it also claimed that, in the company of many illustrious saints, King Arthur was buried in its churchyard. In short, it claimed to be the most sanctified spot in all of Britain if not, indeed, in the whole of Europe.

These claims went back to before the Norman invasion of England, but in the early 12th century nobody was really quite sure exactly how old they were. In 1125, William of Malmesbury, probably the most famous historian of the period, spent some months in Glastonbury. He stayed as a guest at the Abbey, making use of its extensive library while researching his magnum opus *Gesta regum Anglorum* – 'Deeds of the kings of the English'. While there, he was happy to repay the monks' hospitality by carrying out some researches on the history of their church. He subsequently published his findings in a shorter work entitled *De Antiquitate Glastoniensis Ecclesiae* or 'Concerning the Antiquity of Glastonbury Church'. Documentary evidence, however, for the church's great antiquity turned out to be elusive even in his day. Consequently, he was forced to resort to generalizations and rumours instead of chapter-and-verse quotations. Thus he writes:

> *'I shall trace from its very origin the rise and progress of that church*
> *[Glastonbury] as far as I am able to discover it from the mass of*
> *evidence. It is related in annals of good credit that Lucius, King of*
> *the Britons, sent to Pope Eleutherius, thirteenth in succession from*

St Peter, to entreat that he would dispel the darkness of Britain by the splendour of Christian instruction.'

Exactly what these 'annals of good credit' were he doesn't say, but the story of Eleutherius' mission is also contained in *The Anglo-Saxon Chronicle*, which tells us, in the year AD 167, 'Eleutherius received the bishopric in Rome, and held it worthily for fifteen years. To him Lucius, King of the Britons, sent men with letters, asking that he be baptized, and he soon sent back to him; after this they remained in the true faith until Diocletian's time (*viz* 284–305).'

We can deduce the hand of a later scribe when William reveals his knowledge of the devastating fire that destroyed the old church (*vetusta ecclesia*) at Glastonbury. In actuality this occurred in 1184 – some 40 years after his death.

In his book *Gesta Regum Anglorum* (Deeds of the Kings of the English), which was completed in 1125, William also includes a section that brings together many tidbits concerning the legends of the Abbey's foundation. As we have seen, he was of the opinion that the church of St Mary at Glastonbury had been founded by missionaries sent to Britain by Pope Eleutherius (*c.*AD 175–189) on the invitation of a British king called Lucius. Again, what seems to have been a later hand (perhaps the same one) tells us, in great detail, that these missionaries were St Phagan and St Deruvian. Pseudo William informs us that they didn't so much found the church of St Mary as restore it; it had, in fact, been built over 100 years earlier. Disciples of Christ had been sent to Britain from Gaul by St Philip, one of the Twelve Apostles. These disciples are not named, but we are told they were led by St Joseph of Arimathea, the wealthy man who, the Bible informs us, took the body of Jesus down from the cross and laid it in his own tomb. Joseph and his companions then arrived in Britain in AD 62–63 and 'preached the faith of Christ in all confidence'. The story continues:

'The King [unnamed] gave them an island on the borders of his country, surrounded by woods and thickets and marshes, called

Yniswitrin. Two other kings in succession, though pagans, granted to each of them a portion of land: hence the Twelve Hides have their name to the present day. These saints were admonished by the archangel Gabriel to build a church in the honour of the Blessed Virgin. They made it of twisted wattles, in the thirty-first year after the Lord's Passion and the fifteenth after the Assumption of the glorious Virgin. Since it was the first in that land, the Son of God honoured it by dedicating it to His Mother.'

To explain how it was that the church of St Mary at Glastonbury required refounding, William (or more likely his later impersonator) tells us that, after the death of these first settlers, it became derelict. As we have seen, he claims that it was restored by saints Phagan and Deruvian at the time of Pope Eleutherius. According to him, the restored church then became a magnet for such important Celtic saints as Patrick, Gildas and David. The first two, he says, were buried there, while relics of the last, along with those of St Columkill (a Scots-Irish saint who converted the Picts and died on the Island of Iona), St Benignus (an Irish disciple of St Patrick), plus the remains of numerous other saints, were supposedly taken and reburied at Glastonbury. We don't know what the source of this information was as, if it existed at all, it perished in the fire.

Moving from the Celtic to the Saxon period, William of Malmesbury records that King Ina of Wessex, who reigned from AD 688–726, gave various land donations to the church at Glastonbury while, at the same time, exempting it from all taxes. Ina's gift is described in great detail, so it is rather surprising that there is absolutely no mention of his benefactions towards Glastonbury in the *Anglo-Saxon Chronicle* or, indeed, in any other writing prior to 1125. However, the Domesday Book, which was compiled in 1085 and published the following year, does say that the Manor of Glastonbury was free of taxes, so this was presumably still the case when William was writing nearly 40 years later. Nevertheless, it seems unlikely that it was Ina, who exempted the Abbey from taxation. It is much more probable that it was King Edgar.

William also writes of 'warlike Arthur'. He calls him 'a man worthy to be celebrated not by idle fictions, but by authentic history'. He tells us that:

'He long upheld the sinking state, and roused the broken spirit of his countrymen to war. Finally, at the siege of Mount Badon, relying on the image of the Virgin which he had affixed to his armour, he engaged nine hundred of the enemy, single-handed, and dispersed them with incredible slaughter.'

Later on he informs us:

'The sepulchre of Arthur is nowhere to be seen, whence ancient ballads fable that he is still to come.'

This evidence at least seems unequivocal: in 1125, the whereabouts of Arthur's grave was unknown, although it was generally assumed he was buried at Glastonbury.

William of Malmesbury makes no mention of the Holy Grail, but John of Glastonbury, another monk writing some three centuries later, informs us that, on his mother's side, King Arthur was descended from none other than Joseph of Arimathea himself. Indeed, he gives us what is clearly a bogus genealogy to this effect. As for the derivations of the various names for Glastonbury, according to William, 'Avalon' comes either from the Welsh word *aval*, meaning 'apple' coupled with *on* (a corruption of *ynys*, meaning 'island') – hence 'Island of apples'. Alternatively, he says, it is derived from someone's name, although he doesn't tell us whose. An alternative name for Avalon is apparently *Ineswitrin*. This again is supposed to derive from *ynys*, the Welsh for 'island', this time coupled with *witrin*, deriving from either the Latin *vitrum*, meaning 'glass', or the Welsh *gwydr*, with the same meaning. Translated into vernacular English, this would become glass-(t)on-bury, or Glastonbury.

As we will see later, the derivation from someone's name is the truth. These other supposed derivations are inventions: in reality, there is no connection with either glass or apples. William of Malmesbury's explanations for these names are clearly inventions after the fact and not genuine etymologies. They have, nevertheless, successfully confused the issue for the best part of 1,000 years, thereby obscuring the real mystery concerning Glastonbury: that it was somewhere else entirely.

Meanwhile, the monks of Glastonbury, who had everything to gain from linking the hitherto modest Abbey with the illustrious King Arthur of legend (and thereby making it a major place of pilgrimage), were all too keen to exploit matters further. Following the disastrous fire of 1184, they conveniently discovered the alleged bones of King Arthur and Queen Guinevere in their graveyard. These 'Arthurian' relics subsequently received the approval of none other than King Edward I himself – the same King who had brought Wales under his own crown. In 1278, not long back from his first invasion of north Wales, he visited Glastonbury to see the bones for himself. He knew all about King Arthur, of course, from Geoffrey of Monmouth's famous book *The History of the Kings of Britain*, which was first published in 1135. Geoffrey concludes his account of Arthur by saying that he was taken to the Island of Avalon to have his wounds attended to. There is no mention of Arthur's actual death, so a legend developed that he was not dead but sleeping and would one day return to lead the Britons in a great rebellion against their English overlords. When that happened, they would re-establish the true bloodline of the Kings of Britain as rulers over the whole island.

Edward I was keen to scotch such rumours. It suited his purposes, therefore, to declare that the bones found by the monks were genuinely King Arthur's and to order the building of a special shrine in which they should be housed. After all, having an Arthur who was safely dead and buried, with his acknowledged remains under the control of friendly monks, reduced the chances of any future Welsh leader being able to claim his mantle as the 'Once and Future King'. As it suited his purposes, he was also happy to go along with the monks' claim that Glastonbury Abbey was founded by Joseph of Arimathea in the 1st century AD. If this were true, then it would certainly be the oldest church in Britain – if not in the whole world. The question we have to ask ourselves is: does this legend stand up to scientific analysis or is it a hoax as well? In the 20th century, this was put to the test by an unlikely examiner, an architect with a penchant for spiritualism.

CHAPTER 6

The Company of Avalon

In the early 20th century, the Glastonbury legends were finally put to the ultimate test by using the then rather novel science of archaeology. Between 1908 and 1919, a series of digs was carried out at the abbey ruins by the Somerset Archaeological Society. This was done under the guidance of a 'Director of Excavations' called Frederick Bligh Bond. He was a Fellow of the Royal Institute of British Architects and also the Diocesan Architect for Bath and Wells. He was also well read on the subject of the Abbey's history, knowing what traditional historians such as the 12th-century William of Malmesbury and the 15th-century John of Glastonbury had written. He was therefore as well qualified as anyone at the time to interpret the meaning of what was found.

Bligh Bond knew all about the Glastonbury legends and repeated some of them in *An Architectural Handbook of Glastonbury Abbey*, the book he subsequently published detailing his findings. In this book we can sense his excitement at being given the task of carrying out an archaeological dig on such hallowed turf. However, without the knowledge of the church authorities, he also engaged the help of the spirit world in his quest. To this end, he made use of the services of a friend, John Alleyne, who was adept at 'spirit writing'. What this meant in practice was that Alleyne would hold a pen or pencil in one hand, while Bond placed one of his own hands on top. In a process somewhat similar to the better-known Ouija board, they would ask questions of the spirit world, and the pen, presumably directed by their unconscious minds, would draw random marks on the paper. They would then think and talk about other things, while the pen, guided by their hands, would move randomly on the paper.

Sometimes it would draw pictures, while at other occasions it would spell out words or even whole sentences. Using this method, they were able to communicate with a group of spirits, mostly former monks, who called themselves 'the Company'. They told Bond stories from their lives and, more importantly from an architectural point of view, gave him instructions as to where to dig for evidence of certain former chapels.

The story of how he had used spiritualism as an aid in his work was eventually revealed in a book Bligh Bond wrote entitled *The Gate of Remembrance*, which was first published in 1918. Needless to say, the Church authorities were not pleased with this revelation, and, in 1921, he was stripped of his post as Diocesan Architect. The reason for his loss of favour, however, was probably only in part because he dabbled in spiritualism. After all, the Bishop must have known that Bond was a Freemason and a member of the SPR (Society for Psychical Research).

What probably upset him rather more was that, in the course of his archaeological digs, which were extensive, Bond found no evidence at all for any buildings on the site that predated a small, memorial chapel built by Dunstan in *c.*AD 975 to receive the remains of King Edgar. Of the *Vetusta Ecclesia*, supposedly built by the Saxon King Ine in the 7th century, or the even older wattle-and-daub church built by Joseph of Arimathea, restored at the time of Pope Eleutherius and allegedly visited by saints such as Gildas, David and Patrick, there were absolutely no traces whatsoever – not even foundations. Although Bond was loathed to admit it openly, the evidence on the ground indicated that Glastonbury Abbey was no older than the 10th century and had clearly been founded by Dunstan on a virgin site. This was in accord with what Osbern, a Canterbury monk, had written in 1070 in his *Life of St Dunstan*. Here, he actually writes that Dunstan was the first Abbott of Glastonbury, but because nobody wanted to believe this, his work is ignored.

I have written before about the 'Glastonbury Hoax' in *The Holy Kingdom*, the book I co-authored with Wilson and Blackett. It was they who first suggested to me that the Glastonbury legends were, for the most part, forgeries. At first I did not want to believe this. The ruins of this great abbey were a favourite haunt of my wife and myself, and we had even been married in the Catholic church of St Mary that faces them on the opposite side of the road. Sure, there was plenty about modern-day Glastonbury that I found repugnant – in particular, the way its alleged spirituality was being used by cranks and fraudsters as a justification for extorting money from the sick. However, it was one thing to dismiss the faux prophets and magicians who haunt the town today, and quite something else to declare that even the medieval abbey was founded on a deception. I decided, therefore, to take a long, hard but dispassionate look at the known history of not just the abbey itself but the whole area. In doing so, I discovered some further uncomfortable truths that were being studiously ignored by those who claimed to be experts on Glastonbury's Arthurian connections.

The first thing I discovered was the remarkable omission of any mention of either Glastonbury or the Island of Avalon in Asser's biography of Alfred the Great. This King who truly deserves the title of 'Great', was to all intents and purposes the founder of Saxon England. The youngest of four brothers, he was a hero in every sense of the word. During his reign, what is now England was very nearly conquered entirely by the Vikings, and they, at that time, were pagans. The climax of the Viking invasion occurred in AD 878. By then, they had already overrun the rest of England and either driven into exile or martyred the rulers of its various petty kingdoms – Northumbria, East Anglia, etcetera – and now it was to be the turn of Wessex.

Alfred was peacefully celebrating Christmas at his palace of Chippenham when they attacked. Taken by surprise, his forces were routed, and he himself was forced to flee for his life to the Fenlands of Somerset. Here, on the marshy island of Athelney (where he famously burned some cakes), he planned his fight-back. He sent out word to the men of his kingdom that they should meet him at Egbert's Stone, a monolith near Shaftesbury. His new army then won a great victory over the Vikings in what became known as the Battle of Edington, a hilltop near Westbury in Wiltshire.

This was not the end of the war, but it did provide the turning point. Alfred succeeded in hanging on to his kingdom and in later years even extended it to include Kent, London and Essex. His successors – notably Athelstan and Edgar – extended the rule of the Wessex kings to include nearly all of the rest of England. Alfred's legacy therefore was a powerful, Christian kingdom that, having resisted invasion, was to become a centre of learning, too.

Asser, Alfred's biographer, was Welsh and perhaps the most learned man in Britain in his day. He divided his time between helping Alfred raise the standard of education in Wessex and his own duties as Bishop of St David's in West Wales. In the biography he tells us how, following Edington, Alfred signed a peace treaty with Godrum, the leader of the Vikings, at Wedmore. As part of the agreement, Godrum agreed to be baptized, with Alfred standing in as his godfather. Anxious to give thanks to God for his deliverance, Alfred then founded a convent at Shaftesbury and a monastery at Athelney – the marshy outpost where he had hidden during the winter of AD 878. While the convent, which had his daughter Aethelgifu as its first Abbess, prospered, the monastery failed and was soon abandoned. Few men, it seems, wanted to live in such an inhospitable place. Other projects, however, were more successful. Alfred learned Latin and translated several books, including St Augustine's *Soliloquies*. He also commissioned the *Anglo-Saxon Chronicle*, the first part of which mainly concerned the semi-legendary founding of the Kingdom of Wessex, extending to his own times. This project was undoubtedly inspired by Asser, who as Bishop of St David's would have been only too aware that the Welsh had been keeping equivalent chronicles of their own for centuries.

Now what is very odd about all of this is that both Wedmore (to the northwest) and Athelney (to the south) are less than ten miles from

Glastonbury. However, a monastery at Glastonbury is not even mentioned by Asser, although it would surely have been the most obvious place to hold Godrum's baptism. Even more curiously, there is no record of Alfred showing the slightest interest in Glastonbury, which seems strange behaviour given that it was in his Kingdom of Wessex and he was an extremely devout Christian. If Asser had known anything of any legends linking Glastonbury with Joseph of Arimathea or such Welsh saints as David, Patrick and Gildas, he was remarkably silent on this subject, too. In fact, Glastonbury Abbey doesn't even get a mention in the *Anglo-Saxon Chronicle* until over a century after Alfred's death (in AD 906). The entry for 1016 includes the following: 'Then on St Andrew's Day King Edmund passed away, and is buried with his paternal ancestor Edgar in Glastonbury.' There is, however, a brief mention in the entry for year AD 956 that '...Abbot Dunstan was driven over the sea'. Again, it doesn't mention Glastonbury Abbey, but if Dunstan was an Abbott at this time, this would have been his monastery. Taken together, all the evidence points to Glastonbury Abbey having been founded by Dunstan in about AD 940, and therefore some 50 years after Alfred's victory at the Battle of Edington.

This conclusion raises further questions. If Dunstan were the true founder of Glastonbury, what then, one might ask, of the earlier legends connecting it with King Lucius and the mission of Saints Phagan and Deruvian? What, too, of Joseph of Arimathea? For the moment, I had no firm answer to these questions. Nevertheless, I had my suspicions, and, in due course, I discovered that the real story of 'Glastonbury' was much more interesting and better documented than William of Malmesbury realized. His problem was simply that he had been looking in the wrong place. If he knew that Glastonbury was a fraud (and I rather think he did), he also knew that for political and ecclesiastical reasons it was expedient for him to hold his tongue. For this reason, his history of Glastonbury, though recording the most extraordinary and unlikely legends, was unable to provide documentary proof for a foundation prior to *c*.AD 940. The downside was that, unwittingly, he had placed a huge block in the way of genuine Arthurian research, and had obscured the story of the Joseph of Arimathea mission to the point where it was now regarded as no more than a myth. Rescuing the real history from these events would prove to be a Herculean task, but first I needed to investigate the story of King Arthur's Camelot.

CHAPTER 7

The Quest for Camelot

I n his book *The History of the Kings of Britain*, Geoffrey of Monmouth tells us that King Arthur was crowned by St Dubricius at Caerleon – formerly a city, but today just a village in South East Wales. That the Arthur of legend is usually identified with the South West of England seems curiously at odds with this simple statement: if Arthur came from that part of Britain, why was he not crowned at Exeter or Winchester or even London? Furthermore, Geoffrey's Arthur fights wars against both the Romans and the Anglo-Saxons. This makes no sense. Arthur's Saxon wars would have taken place in the 6th century, and by then the Roman Empire, at least as far as Britain was concerned, was little more than a memory. For Arthur to have fought both the Romans and Anglo-Saxons in the way described by Geoffrey, he would have needed to have lived for well over 100 years.

As we have seen, one answer to this conundrum is the possibility that there was not just one but two 'King Arthurs', their separate careers having later been merged into one. Wilson and Blackett, my co-authors of *The Holy Kingdom*, identified the first Arthur as a Romano-British general who the Romans called Andragathius. He, they suggested, was the same person as someone called '*Annun ddu*', who is listed as a son of Magnus Maximus (*Macsen Wledig*) in the genealogies contained in the Harleian 3859 MS. This is the same MS that contains Nennius's *Historia Brittonum* and is kept today in the British Library in London. The physical book we have today is much older than Geoffrey of Monmouth's *History of the Kings of Britain*, which was only published in 1135; however, some of the genealogies are older still and go way back in time to long before the Roman conquest. These genealogies are contained in a section called 'The Wedding Lists of Owain the Son of Hywel Dda' and are probably the oldest extant source of their kind. Hywel Dda (Howell the Good) died in AD 950. His core kingdom was South West Wales, but spread to most of the rest of the country. He was also an ancestor of Rhys ap Tewdwr, who, in turn, was ancestral to many later Welsh and Norman-Welsh noblemen. Thus, 'The Wedding Lists of Hywell's Son Owain' is, today, a priceless resource for tracing ancestry.

The usurpation of Magnus Maximus is well documented in history and so, too, is the negative effect it had on the defences of Britain. Most of the men he took with him never returned, many being settled by him in northern Gaul, thereby giving rise to the colony of Brittany or 'Little Britain'. Others died in battle or were taken prisoner by the Romans. These were either enslaved or absorbed into the opposing army. Either way, they did not return home to Britain. The result of this loss of manpower was significant: the walls protecting northern Britain from the Picts and the coastal forts along the southeast coast that protected southern Britain from Anglo-Saxon pirates were left undermanned. In AD 406, this situation was made much worse when another king of Britain, Constantine III, took a fresh army to Gaul. This army also did not return, which meant that when the Romans finally withdrew from Britain completely in AD 410, there were very few men of fighting age left to defend the former province.

Viewed from across the North Sea, Britain, wealthy but weakly defended, was a plum ripe for the picking. This situation was at its most acute in the east of the country, where the Roman influence has been strongest. In Wales (and Cornwall), which had always been more independent and where Roman rule had had much less impact, the people were not as soft and defenceless as in the east.

Accordingly, it seems likely that this first Arthur (perhaps the same individual the Romans called Andragathius) was in reality a ruler over

'Cornwall', the 'horn' of Britain, which in those days included the whole South West Peninsula and not just the modern county of that name. This scenario would certainly explain the presence on the ground of some very long ditch and bank earthworks that appear to date from this period. These defences, in places called Bokerley Dyke and in others Wansdyke, run, with breaks, from the Dorset–Hampshire border to just south of Bath. Cutting across older Roman roads, they appear to be boundary fortifications separating a province or kingdom in the southwest of England from the rest of the island of Britain. However, even if this was the kingdom of 'Arthur I' (Andragathius), there doesn't appear to be any connection between him and the later legends concerning Camelot and the Round Table.

As I looked into this mystery further, it became clear to me that the story of the second King Arthur had been merged with the first. This added to the confusion because details that really applied to Arthur II, and therefore had a Welsh context, had been moved to South West England.

An example of this occurred in the 1960s following a dig at South Cadbury Castle in Somerset. This 'castle' is actually an Iron Age hillfort rather than the sort of stone building we normally associate with the name. Its relative proximity to Glastonbury and the village of Queen Camel – it is about 11 miles from the former and much closer to the latter – caused John Leland, in his *Itinerary* of 1542, to claim that it was the site of King Arthur's Camelot. This identification subsequently became fixed in the minds of scholars, thereby leading them further astray. Between 1966 and 1970, Professor Leslie Alcock of Cardiff University carried out a dig on South Cadbury, proudly producing evidence that, although it dated back to the 1st millennium BC, it had been reused by the Britons during the Arthurian period. On this slender base, Geoffrey Ashe, a history writer who lived in Glastonbury and had been involved with the dig, promoted the idea that far from being a king, Arthur was simply the leader of a small war-band. His 'Camelot', far from being the glittering city of Arthurian romance, was in reality the collection of Arthurian period wooden huts that archaeology had identified on this hilltop. Of course, there was no real evidence for any of this other than the simple fact that the hilltop had been reused as a fortification during the 5th and 6th centuries. It did, however, dovetail nicely with the assumption that Glastonbury was the real Avalon, where Arthur had been taken for burial after the Battle of Camlann. What few people realized, then or later, was that Glastonbury's own claims were highly suspect.

The process of transforming the reputation of Glastonbury from a muddy fen to the most important religious institution in Britain seems to have started at the time of St Dunstan and King Edgar (mid 10th century). It was pretty much complete when, in 1136, Geoffrey of Monmouth published his translation of the Welsh annals as *The History of the Kings of Britain*. Fortunately, Geoffrey's book is not our only source for the story of Arthur or even the first. However, these earlier sources all suffer from the same weakness: in the form that we have them, none is contemporary with Arthur. Even when the content is old in composition, we are not in possession of the original documents, only of medieval copies.

The very earliest source to mention Arthur by name is Nennius's *Historia Brittonum*. This is contained in the Harleian 3859 collection, a small, leather-bound book that is kept today in the British Library. I have examined this book, which, being written on vellum (sheep's skin), is notable for its repulsive smell. Yet even this book, old as it is, is only a copy. It dates from around 1100, while the original text is thought to have been put together roughly AD 825. Like Geoffrey's work, it is therefore open to accusations of medieval forgery and wishful thinking. However, even if we had the original manuscript of Nennius to hand, it would still have been written nearly two centuries after Arthur was fighting his battles.

The location of Arthur's capital of Camelot has been identified in many other places besides South Cadbury Castle: from Camelford (in Cornwall), to Camelodunum (Colchester in Essex), to Carlisle (in the very north of England on the borders of Scotland). However, one clue to its true location is that according to the legends, Arthur's wife Guinevere was the daughter of 'King Leodegrance', and his capital city, or so we are also told, was called

Carmelide/Cameliard. Now 'Leodegrance' is clearly a corruption of the French *Leo-de-Grand*, meaning 'Leo the Great'. Since lion is *leon* in Welsh, Caerleon, which is often translated as 'Castle of the Legions', can also mean 'Castle of the Lion' – that is, Castle of Leo. Therefore, it seems likely that Camelot/Carmelide/Cameliard are really one and the same place: Caerleon.

According to Geoffrey of Monmouth, this is where Arthur was crowned and where he held his plenary court. It is also where, shortly before his coronation, he fell in love with and married Guinevere. For a wedding present, and as part of her dowry, her father, King Leodegrance, gave Arthur the Round Table.

This got me thinking. Given that Arthur was crowned at Caerleon and this town had a connection with Leodegrance, it seemed logical that the Round Table would be similarly connected. Anxious to ascertain what this might be, I decided to go back to Wales to follow up on this clue.

CHAPTER 8

King Arthur's Round Table

Having taken a train from London to Newport, I took a bus to Caerleon. To enter the town itself, I first had to cross the bridge over the River Usk. In Roman times, and for a long time after, this was the major artery leading into the heartlands of Gwent. Given the strength of its currents and extreme range of tides, navigating it could not have been easy. Little wonder therefore that the Normans built New Port instead, close to the confluence of the Usk and Severn Estuary.

The town of Caerleon – really not much more than a village nowadays – was small but quaint. To say that it was atmospheric is an understatement: it positively reeked of undiscovered mystery. The commercial infrastructure, such as it was, consisted of a few craft shops (mostly in the aptly named *ffwrwm*, ie 'forum', centre), a couple of tearooms and a handful of pubs. There was none of the glitzy Arthuriana and New Age tat that characterizes modern-day Glastonbury or Tintagel. It was all very quiet and sedate. At the heart of the village was the Roman Baths Museum, a splendid building covering what, in Roman times, would have been a major amenity: the public baths. Next to this was the National Roman Legion Museum, an impressive stone and glass building with a columned portico. Inside this were numerous relics, including inscribed stones that dated back to when Caerleon was the home of the Legio II Augusta (from AD 75 to c.AD 290), one of the four legions originally sent to Britain by the Emperor Claudius. The Roman presence in Caerleon, which later reverted to native British occupation, ended after another usurping emperor, Carausius (AD 286–293), moved the 2nd Legion to Kent. Here, it was stationed at Richborough and rebranded the Legio II Britannica.

The ruins of Roman Caerlon, not all of which have been excavated, are extensive. Indeed, recent excavations have revealed that, by the standards of the day, this small town was once a large city. I left the museum and, after walking about half a mile over fields we now know cover extensive, unexcavated archaeology, came to an enormous, circular structure. It turned out to be an amphitheatre, a miniature version of the Colosseum in Rome. A sign informed visitors that during the Roman period this was used for gladiatorial combats, military training, theatrical events and maybe even circuses. Large enough to seat 6,000 spectators, it could accommodate an entire legion. Seeing this, my mind turned back to the story of Leodegrance and his gift to Arthur of the Round Table. Geoffrey tells us that this too was very big, certainly large enough to sit 150 knights at once. Such a table, if it ever really existed, would have been no ordinary piece of furniture: it would have been huge. Of course, Geoffrey (or his source) could have been exaggerating, but if we assume that each knight needed two and half feet of sitting space (30 inches), then the diameter of the round table would have needed to be roughly 120 feet, or 36 metres. Looking at the great, grassy space in the middle of the amphitheatre, I could imagine a huge table, shaped like a doughnut or ring, with knights seated round it.

Then I remembered something else that Geoffrey says. He tells us that when he returned from fighting, Arthur held his plenary court at Caerleon. Now this too is interesting, for a plenary court means one that is attended by everyone who is a member of that court. At such a court, all the members of the Round Table would be required to be present. This would be perfectly possible in the space provided by the amphitheatre. In fact, there would have been enough room there for all the knights and their entire entourages and families to attend. Logically, they would have sat where the legionnaires used to sit – on the banked terraces surrounding the central area. To me, the evidence was overwhelming that it was here, in the Amphitheatre of Caerleon, that Arthur held his plenary court, which in modern parlance we would call a parliament. For his banquet they would not have needed a dining table as such, for the Roman custom was to eat while sitting or lying on the ground. The 'Round Table' that Arthur was given as a wedding gift by Leodegrance was probably the amphitheatre itself.

Leaving the amphitheatre, I walked onward to the river, where some remnants of the town's Roman walls are still standing. Seeing these framed against willow trees growing on the riverbank, I was reminded of Alfred Lord Tennyson's poem *The Lady of Shallot*. This poem, which I had had to learn at school, was the inspiration for J W Waterhouse's painting of the same name that today hangs in the Tate Britain art gallery in London. Verse two goes:

> *Willows whiten, aspens quiver,*
> *Little breezes dusk and shiver*
> *Through the wave that runs for ever*
> *By the island in the river*
> *Flowing down to Camelot.*
> *Four grey walls, and four grey towers,*
> *Overlook a space of flowers,*
> *And the silent isle imbowers*
> *The Lady of Shallot.*

In 1856, Tennyson lodged at the Hanbury Arms, which stands next to a round tower that, in Norman times, was part of Caerleon Castle. Here, in a window seat overlooking the river, he wrote his epic cycle of Arthurian poems, *Idylls of the King*. Walking now myself along the river bank, towards this pub, and with a view of the window, it seemed likely that though it predated *Idylls of the King* by some 23 years, Tennyson had Caerleon in mind when writing *The Lady of Shallot*. Looking out over the river, I could almost see her floating in her funeral barge downstream, past the willows and aspens that grow so thickly here on the banks of the River Usk. The implication was clear: in Tennyson's mind at least, Caerleon was the mythic city of Camelot.

Further evidence for making such a deduction was all around me. In Arthurian times, Caerleon still had its walls intact as well as various amenities such as public baths, barrack blocks, relatively good housing for the local aristocracy and a bustling market place, and for centuries it had been a major centre of Christianity. According to various Welsh Annals, it was the original seat of the archbishopric that in the 6th century was moved first to Llandaff (Cardiff) and then later to Menevia (St David's).

Caerleon's religious eminence was not without reason. Within its precincts were churches dedicated to the two earliest recorded British martyrs, St Julius and St Aaron, and as a port it had extremely good communications. Ships from Caerleon could easily sail up the River Severn to the old Roman city of Gloucester or downstream to Devon and Cornwall and, beyond them, to Gaul, Spain and the Mediterranean. Meanwhile, looming over the town and dominating the entire area, was a truly massive Iron Age hill fort. Lookouts posted here could see for miles in all directions. They would spot any attackers, whether they came by land or sea, long before they arrived. Then, using a system of beacon hills that probably went back to long before Roman times, they could alert not just the local population but the whole region of Glamorgan/Gwent. The conclusion was obvious: Caerleon had to be 'Camelot' – King Arthur's capital.

Fortunately, if you know where to look, there are contemporary documents to hand that proved beyond doubt that he and his dynasty existed. On my next trip to Wales I was to be shown some of these, which would result in my quest taking a new direction altogether.

CHAPTER 9

Old Stones and a Forgotten Dynasty

When I first came across the newspaper report of the discoveries by Wilson and Blackett in Wales, my initial response was scepticism. After all, didn't everybody know that Arthur came from Cornwall and was buried at Glastonbury? However, when I thought about it more deeply, I could see the logic of what they were saying. If 'he' – and I use the singular because, for reasons that will become clearer later, I am less sure about the relevance of an earlier 'Arthur son of Magnus Maximus' – had ever truly existed, he would have spoken Welsh, not English, for that was then the native language of the island of Britain. It also made perfect sense for him to have been a king in South Wales. Wales has, after all, retained its language and identity long after the Anglo-Saxon invasions of the 5th and 6th centuries. Indeed, the very existence of Wales as an entity separate from England can be regarded as the real legacy of King Arthur's struggles. By contrast, South West England, including Somerset and Glastonbury, was conquered by the Anglo-Saxons relatively early on. The details of this conquest are contained in the *Anglo-Saxon Chronicle*, which makes no mention at all of any King Arthur. Wales, by contrast, remained independent of England right up until the Norman period. Was it really so illogical, then, that the real King Arthur should have been a Welsh king who was buried in Glamorgan rather than Somerset? I was beginning to think not.

Recalling memories of this article, I was quite excited as well as surprised when, out of the blue a few months later, Alan Wilson phoned me. Intrigued, I went to his house in Cardiff and there had the opportunity to see for myself the memorial stone with its inscription. To my untrained eyes, it looked genuine enough. I hazarded a guess that it was most likely a recycled Roman coffin lid, which had been reused as a makeshift tomb-marker by someone in too much of a hurry to quarry a fresh piece of stone. That fitted rather well with the legend surrounding the death of King Arthur. If chaos had followed his death, then his burial would have been a necessarily hurried affair. Under these circumstances, his remaining followers may well have made use of an old coffin lid that was lying around and scratched on it an inscription in less than perfect Latin. Such an explanation fitted the facts, but I was keen to see the church for myself.

The next time I went to Wales, Alan accompanied me to the church and showed me exactly where he and Baram believed it had once been located at the time the church was in use. This was close by the spot where, for various reasons, they trusted that Arthur still lies buried. Alan regretted greatly that for safety reasons he was not able to dig deeply enough to find his remains, but, fortunately, this church was not the only physical evidence linking this part of Wales with the Arthurian epic and he promised to show me more.

Some weeks later, I took him up on his word and he took me to see the ruins of the old abbey of Margam, which lie close to the Port Talbot Steelworks. This was belching out smoke and filling the air with an acrid stench. In front of us was a small brick building whose original purpose was not clear – a barn, stable or something else. Whatever it had been, it was now functioning as a museum; filled almost to the brim with an assortment of ancient memorial stones gathered from all around the local area.

Alan led the way in, introducing me to various large, inscribed stones that for him were like old friends. Mostly they were what are called 'wheel crosses', ie they terminated not in a conventional cross, as might a grave stone today, but rather in what looks more like a cartwheel. Indeed, it seems likely that this similarity was deliberate, the 'wheel of life' being a common symbol both for the repetition of time and for the inevitability of fate. The captions by these stones said they were all 9th century or later, but once more Alan begged to differ. 'The theory goes that wheel crosses were invented around AD 650 in Northumbria, a petty kingdom, which at one time extended all the way from York to as far north as Edinburgh. Then, between AD 700 and 800, the idea of sculpting a cross to look like a wheel was taken from England to Ireland. In the 9th or 10th century, or so the experts tell us, this style of cross was brought back from Ireland to Wales. However, I have to tell you that this whole sequence of events is entirely wrong in almost every respect,' he said. 'In actuality it was the other way round. The idea of wheel crosses, along with Christianity itself, was taken from Wales to Ireland and Scotland. It was transferred from there to Northumbria. In other words, the journey of ideas was in reverse. After all, think about it! St Patrick himself was Welsh. Our histories say that he was born in Cowbridge, which, as the crow flies, is only a little over ten miles from where we now are standing. It stands to reason that these crosses are much older than people think; in his youth, St Patrick himself would have seen some of them. That would be before he was captured by pirates and was taken to Ireland. Very likely he took the wheel cross idea with him.'

'Well, if that's the case,' I replied, 'how come the archaeologists have got it so wrong? Surely they would know if they were that much older?'

'That's just the thing,' Alan replied, 'they don't know. They don't know the truth about these stones because they don't know our Welsh history; they only know English history. Because they have the colossal advantage of total ignorance, they feel free to invent nonsense.' He went on to explain how it was not really their fault that they didn't know since real Welsh history from before the Norman Conquest is not generally taught even in Welsh schools. Educationally speaking, the period from the 5th to the very end of the 11th centuries really is a Dark Age. Yet there is no reason why this should be. The history of Britain, especially Wales, is among the best-documented in Europe for this period. There are, he said, huge numbers of texts, many of them genealogies of the royal houses and nobility, that give us a complete 'who's who' for the 5th, 6th, 7th and later centuries. They tell us people's names, family relations, titles, where they lived and much else besides. 'The trouble is,' he continued, 'if you don't know the history, then you can't see the evidence that supports that history.'

As an example of this, he took me over to a very large memorial stone that stood about eight feet high, topped by a giant, lopsided wheel. The carving was somewhat crude, but at the foot of the stone you could still discern figures, probably representing the Virgin Mary and John the Baptist. A label near it informed us that it was '10th century' and that it originally stood near the church in Margam Village. Written in Latin on the stone, with a few gaps where letters had worn away, was an inscription. Reconstructed it read: CUNOBELIN P[O]SUIT HANC CRUCM P[RO] [A]NIMA RI …, which translates as 'Conbelin raised this cross for the soul of Ri …'

Alan was put out by the statement that the stone was 10th century. He pointed out that not just anyone raised a stone cross such as this in ancient times. He explained: 'This stone actually tells us that it was raised by someone called Cunobelin, which is the Latinized form of the Welsh name Cynfelyn. It would have cost a lot of money to have this cross carved, and not just anyone would have been allowed the privilege of raising it. Yet there is no record of any king, nobleman or important churchman going by the name Conbelin or Cynfelyn living in Glamorgan during the 10th century. If there is, then I haven't seen it. However, if we go back in time, to the 5th or 6th centuries, then there are several potential candidates. One of them was a brother or uncle of King Maurice, the father of King Arthur. You look it up.'

Leaving the Cross of Cunobelin, he beckoned me over to a smaller stone, shaped like a pillar and about four feet in height. It had evidently once stood on top of Margam Mountain and must at one time have had an upper part, probably also shaped as a wheel. All that was left now was the memorial's shaft, but this too carried an inscription. Because it was deeply carved, it was as legible as if it had been written yesterday. It read: BODVOC – HIC IACIT – FILIUS CATOTIGIRNI PRONEPUS ETERNALI VEDOMAU.

This translates as: *Here lies Bodvoc, the son of Catotigern, the great grandson of the eternal [G]uedo the great.* 'This Stone', said Alan, 'almost certainly dates back to the 5th or 6th century.' He explained how Catotigirn, or *Catigern* as he is more usually called in Welsh genealogies, was the second son of Vortigern, the King who, in AD 449, invited Hengest, his brother Horsa and their retinue of Saxon warriors to settle in Kent in return for their help in fighting the Picts. This, as far as the ancient Britons were concerned, was to have disastrous consequences. For once the Saxons had dealt with the Picts, they rebelled against their hosts. Along with his brother Vortimer, Catigern resisted this first Saxon invasion. However, to the sorrow of the Britons, he fell in the Battle of Aylesford in AD 455 while fighting hand-to-hand with Horsa, who also died. This means that the Bodvoc Stone was probably raised as a memorial at some time in the late 5th or early 6th centuries and not the 10th. It was from the era of King Arthur.

Over the following year, I came back to Wales on numerous occasions, and Wilson and Blackett showed me more sites. By this time we had agreed to co-author a book that would bring together their myriad of researches into the lost history of Britain and, specifically, the real story of King Arthur. This book was eventually published in 1998 and called *The Holy Kingdom*.

I researched the names on the Bodvoc stone further and discovered the identity of his great-grandfather: 'Vedo the Great'. It turned out that Vortigern's father was called Guitaul or Gwidawl depending on source. Vedo was clearly another variant form of this name, the 'V' being pronounced then as a 'U' or 'W' today with the same sound as if it had a 'G' as a prefix. A comparison would be the French name 'Guillaume' which became 'William' in English. Given these circumstances and that this Guitaul was of royal descent from a family who ruled over the Gloucester area (near where Vortigern came from), there could be little doubt that he was the great-grandfather listed on the stone. The absence of any mention of Vortigern, Bodvoc's grandfather, could be explained by the simple fact that, as the reviled traitor who invited the Anglo-Saxons to settle in Britain, he was an ancestor you didn't want to brag about.

Looking at this stone, I felt a rush of excitement, for it is not often you see the evidence of the Arthurian epoch written on stone. However, as I was about to discover, this was just the start: the Bodvoc Stone was not the end of my journey but the beginning.

CHAPTER 10

Origins of the Rosy-cross

As well as showing me the memorial stones in the Margam Museum, Alan also accompanied me to several churches with old stones of their own. Foremost among these was the church of St Illtyd, after which the Vale of Glamorgan town of Llantwit Major is named. Prior to the Norman invasion, of which much more will be said later, this was a major church and college. Because of its eminence, it is in possession of some very fine memorial stones of its own, comparable with those I had seen earlier at Margam. Some of these stones were again shafts of former crosses that had lost their 'wheels'. What was special about them was that they carried quite long inscriptions, two of them mentioning 'Illtutus' (St Illtyd) by name. St Illtyd, Alan informed me, is recorded in the genealogies of Wales as a cousin of King Arthur son of Maurice. In addition to St Illtyd, one of these stones also mentioned that it had been raised by St Samson, who again was a cousin of this King Arthur. The biographical 'Life' of St Samson records that he later moved to Brittany, where he became the Bishop of Dol. All this was interesting because the mention of Samson's name on these stones was a further clue to their antiquity. As Bishop of Dol he is recorded as having signed papers at the Church Council of Paris, which took place in AD 556; he died in AD 570. Thus, the stones he raised at Llantwit must certainly date from before AD 556. They also cannot be from the 10th century.

Leaving these stones, which stand near the door, I walked on down the north aisle. Here, my attention was immediately caught by several large flagstones which, intriguingly, were unmarked with names or any other kind of writing. What made them interesting was that they were decorated with foliated crosses, sometimes contained within a halo. They were of a style which, had they been from the 17th century, I would have called 'Rosicrucian'. By this term I mean a style of cross that is based on the symbol of a crucified rose rather than a wheel.

This symbol, which I was now beginning to think could be of great antiquity in Wales, became famous after 1614. In that year, the first of a number of controversial pamphlets was published in Germany – the *Fama Fraternitatis Roseae Crucis*, or 'The Rumour of the Brotherhood of the Rosicross' – in the German language. It was soon available in other languages, including French, Italian and English, causing a Europe-wide furore. It announced the existence of a secret order that called itself the Brotherhood of the Rosy-cross.

This brotherhood was, allegedly, founded in Germany on the return of a pilgrim there who called himself Christian Rozencreutz. It was claimed that while travelling in the East, he had met and been instructed by certain adepts. They had taught him a great deal about healing and other esoteric matters, and on his return to Europe, he set up an esoteric school of his own in order to pass on this arcane knowledge. All this had happened way back in the 15th century, for CRC, as he is referred to in the pamphlet, died over 110 years before their writing and, therefore, around 1500.

There were several, different versions of the 'crucified rose', the prime symbol of the movement. The first was a simple calvary cross, with a rose at its crossing and a halo of light radiating from it.

Another was a budded or floriated cross of gold. Such a cross was evidently to be worn as a pendant. In its most advanced form, it features a figure representing the risen Jesus Christ, a rose growing from his aura. On the cross bar is written 'Immanuel' and below this a quote from the Bible: 'I am a flower of Sharon, and a Rose in the Valley.' (Figure 3)

Figure 2: Calvary cross   Figure 3: Foliated cross of gold

The basic symbol – a crucified rose on a calvary cross – was not much different from those on the flagstones I was looking at. Could there be a connection between the 17th-century Rosicrucian Brotherhood and those who designed the flagstones? For now, I had no answer to this, but I felt sure that if I looked hard enough, I would discover there was a connection.

The connection with tombstones evidently goes right back to the beginning of the Rosicrucian movement, for the publication of the *Fama* (and later another pamphlet called the *Confessio*) had evidently been triggered by the rediscovery of CRC's own tomb. According to the pamphlets, it was only after this event that the brothers decided it was time they went public. Yet despite their promises made in the pamphlets, they continued to keep their identities secret.

After a few years had gone by and the brothers had still failed to come forward and make themselves known, the general consensus was that the whole thing had been a hoax: there was no Brotherhood of the Rosy-cross. Even so, there was still a lingering suspicion that even if a Brotherhood of the sort described in the pamphlets did not actually exist, the 'hoax' could be a cover story for something else: a secret society with a different name, perhaps, but nevertheless an agenda similar to that described in the pamphlets. If such a society did indeed exist, then it could be inferred from their contents that its members were well educated. As for their motive in publishing the pamphlets, might this have been to test public opinion? Did they simply want to see what sort of a response the pamphlets generated before revealing their real identities and agenda? These would presumably have been linked to the esoteric understanding of the primary Rosicrucian symbol: the crucified rose.

In the event, the pamphlets caused such an uproar (including death threats) that the 'brothers' deemed it wise to keep their heads down. The location of CRC's tomb and the identities of the pamphlet writers remained a secret, although a German pastor called Johann Valentin Andreae admitted writing a third pamphlet called 'The Chemical Wedding of Christian Rozencreutz'. He didn't admit to having penned the first two, and so their authorship has never been established.

The Rosicrucian affair had long fascinated me, so I was on the lookout for clues that might reveal more about it. It seemed strange, at first, that South Wales could have any connection with such a pan-European movement. But then I noticed that lying near to the Samson stone was a sculpted funerary effigy of a lady. With her expensive-looking dress and fashionable 'ruff' around her neck, she was clearly aristocratic and from the Elizabethan period (1558–1603). It is true that ruffs went out of fashion towards the end of the 16th century, but this was still only a couple of decades before the publication of the Rosicrucian manifestos. Thus, the evidence in stone was that there were at least some people in Wales of a class and fashion-ability to act as potential links between the culture that gave rise to the earlier, floriated cross on stones and the 17th-century movement we call Rosicrucianism. The congruency of symbols used by the Rosicrucians of the 17th century and the medieval Welsh stonemasons who had fashioned the flagstones in Llantwit hinted at linkage between the two. Accordingly, I decided to examine what those links might be and whether this might point the way towards a connection with some deeper mystery. This mystery, though, was a deep secret. Indeed, it was buried so deeply that only these scattered symbols gave any hint that it was even there.

Given the location of the stones, it seemed likely that this secret was in some way concerning King Arthur. However, this was only speculation. Without more information and more data, I could not be sure that I was even looking in the right direction. I soon realized that to even begin to understand what the connection might be between the flagstones of Llantwit and a 17th-century German sect society that called itself the Rosicrucian Brotherhood, I would need to make a much deeper examination of the medieval history of the British Isles. The obvious place to begin such a study was the Norman Conquest of England in 1066, but this is really only a stepping stone. Of greater interest was the history of Wales, which is not taught at all in schools and is therefore a complete mystery to all but a very few people, even those living in the Principality itself. Therefore, I make no apology for digressing from the immediate quest and exploring in some detail Wales' medieval history, for without this basic understanding, it is not possible to grasp what follows and its extraordinary implications for our own times.

CHAPTER 11

Normans in the Pays de Galles

E ngland's medieval history effectively begins in 1066 – the year
that William, Duke of Normandy (later known as 'William the
Conqueror') defeated King Harold II of England at the Battle of Hastings.
William was subsequently crowned King William I. The coronation took
place in Westminster Abbey, in front of the tomb of King Edward the
Confessor, whose death the same year had triggered the invasion. The
reason William selected Westminster Abbey was that he wanted to remind
everyone, friends and foes alike, that Edward had promised him that he
should succeed to the throne. By holding the ceremony in front of the
Confessor's tomb, he was symbolically invoking the spirit of the deceased
as his witness. He did this because his blood claim was very weak. Edward
was the son of William's aunt Emma, who was not of English royal blood,
although she had been married to two kings of England. William's real justification for taking the throne was conquest, but by invoking Edward as his
'Confessor' or witness, he was able to give his usurpation some legitimacy in
law. This had far-reaching consequences, for as a result, a new tradition was
established. From that time onward, English monarchs have nearly always
been crowned at Westminster in front of Edward the Confessor's tomb.

The extension of William's rule throughout the rest of England was also
relatively quick and easy. The only serious resistance came from the North,

and this he subjugated with great ferocity. Thus it was that England, quite a large country by European standards, became a vassal state of the much smaller Dukedom of Normandy.

As a reward for their support, William shared out the proceeds of the conquest – in the form of earldoms, baronetcies and bishoprics – with his followers. By contrast, the people of England, until then free men, were reduced to serfdom, with even the nobility, for the most part, stripped of their lands and titles. The Norman conquest of England was quick, revolutionary in its impact and long lasting. Indeed, in its formation of a class system that is more rigid in England than in almost any other European country, its effects are still with us today. Little wonder, then, that the most important date in English history is 1066; the impact of William's conquest was so great that nothing before – at least in the intervening years since the Roman withdrawal from Britain in AD 410 – remotely compares.

Having taken control of England, William prepared the way for a future campaign to subjugate Wales, at that time a quite separate country. His immediate requirement, however, was to simply contain the Welsh; he needed to make sure that they did not interfere with his plans for the Normanization of England. To accomplish this aim, his strategy was the establishment of 'Marcher Lordships' on the England-Wales border. The Marcher Lords, or Marquises as they came to be called, enjoyed special privileges over and above those of ordinary earls and barons. These included the right to hold courts, build castles, raise armies and even wage war without first seeking the permission of the king. Furthermore, through a policy of encroachment, they soon began to hold land in Wales, too. Since these land holdings were not under the jurisdiction of the English Crown, with regard to these properties, the Marcher Lords had the Palatine powers of minor kings. This put them on a par with the leading nobles of Wales who were themselves often styled as princes or even kings.

On looking into the matter further, I soon discovered that Wales differed from England in other ways, too. Although it occupied quite a small part of the Island of Britain, it had nearly always been divided up into even smaller, competing principalities. To a large extent, this was a direct result of geography. Most of Wales is very mountainous so that its fertile plains and valleys are separated from each other. Even so, at times when a particularly strong leader emerged (such as Rhodri the Great, c.AD 820–878), he might establish himself as overlord of most of the country. This, however, was rare. More commonly the country was divided. There was stiff competition between the different princes ruling the separate parts, with each anxious to extend the boundaries of his petty kingdom at the others' expense. This was in stark contrast to England, which had been unified as a single kingdom for more than a century. The small kingdoms of the early Anglo-Saxons – Wessex, Kent, Northumbria, Mercia and the rest – had gradually been joined together to form a single entity. Thus, although there were regional differences, England was already a single political entity ruled over by just one king.

The two countries also had different religious traditions. The Welsh, or rather one should say British, Church was much older than the English. It looked back to apostolic times for its foundation and had a whole pantheon of local saints to its credit. Much less hierarchical than the English, it regarded itself as at least equal to Rome. The English Church, by contrast, was only founded in AD 597 as a result of the mission of St Augustine. He was sent to England by Pope Gregory I, and as a consequence, the English Church was subordinate to the Church of Rome in a way that the Welsh/British Church was not. Furthermore, because the English Church, in emulation of the Roman, was hierarchical, it was easy for the Normans to take control of it. All William had to do was replace its senior churchmen with men of his own choosing.

To further strengthen their grip on the religious loyalties of the people, the Normans instigated a huge rebuilding programme. Nearly all the old Anglo-Saxon churches and abbeys, including Canterbury Cathedral, were demolished. In their place they built far grander structures. The message was clear: the Normans were not only in control of the secular world in this life but also the gateways leading to heaven.

An equivalent show of force, heavenly and temporal, should have been enough to awe the Welsh into submission. The fact that it wasn't was further evidence of hidden strength. The source of this, I was soon to discover, was a much clearer picture of King Arthur and all that he stood for. As I later discovered, his story was much more than an empty legend: it was accepted history and so too was the legend of Camelot. Before I could get to this, though, I had to first investigate what really happened when the Normans invaded Wales and what effect this had on them.

CHAPTER 12

The Roll of the Round Table

B y 1090, the Normans had fully cemented their grip over England, and they were ready to turn their attention in earnest towards the conquest of Wales. A golden opportunity to begin this arrived around 1092 (the exact date is uncertain) when war sprang up between two rival Welsh rulers: Iestyn ap Gwrgan (Justin son of George), the King of Glamorgan and Gwent, and Rhys ap Tewdwr (Rees the son of Tudor), the King of Deheubarth, whose lands included the counties of Pembrokeshire, Cardiganshire and Carmarthenshire. (Map 2: Major Kingdoms of Wales)

The exact cause of the conflict between these two kings is a matter of debate. A border dispute was clearly an issue, but it seems there was also an argument over the ownership of a parchment scroll; simmering tension over this seems to have escalated into outright warfare.

The scroll in question was called the 'Roll of the Round Table'; it was said to date back to the times of none other than King Arthur himself. The story goes that after spending centuries in Brittany, it was brought back to Wales by Rhys. He proposed that a full *Gorsedd*, a gathering, of the Bards (something we will describe more fully in a later chapter) should be held in its honour at the abbey of Llancarvan in Glamorgan. Although outside his own jurisdiction, he chose this location because Llancarvon Abbey was even then a very old foundation; it went back to even before Arthurian

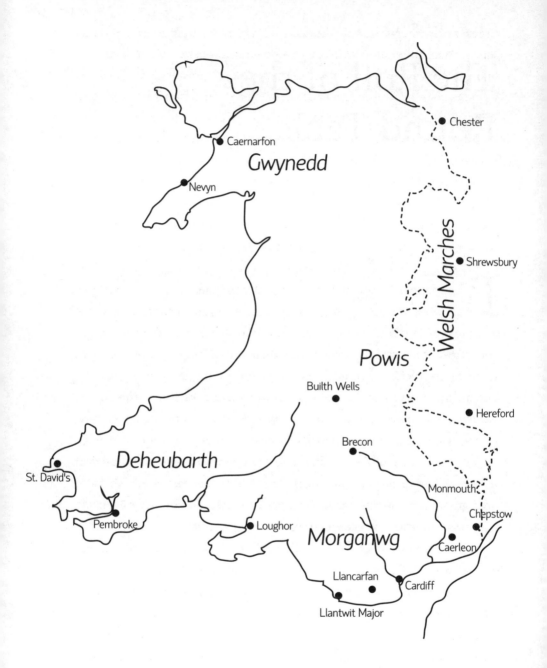

Map 2: Major Kingdoms of Wales, *c.*1092

times and was closely associated with a number of eminent Dark Age saints. Also, although it was in Glamorgan, there was a tradition that no one was allowed to bear arms in this parish. This meant that the Abbey was effectively neutral territory, where even political opponents could relax somewhat in each other's company.

The *Gorsedd* festival was held and both kings attended, but then Iestyn left early without saying goodbye to his guest, Rhys ap Tewdwr. His pretext for such rude behaviour, or so it is written in some accounts, was that Rhys had made improper advances towards his wife, a lady who was much younger than either of them. According to another account, Iestyn stole the Roll of the Round Table and took it back to Cardiff Castle, his own home. His justification for doing so was that in Arthur's time Caerleon had been the capital of his kingdom. Although the capital of Glamorgan was Cardiff, Caerleon was in his kingdom, too. As King of Glamorgan–Gwent and therefore Arthur's successor in both blood and title, in his opinion, the Roll had to stay under his protection.

Whatever the truth is of these allegations, war broke out between the two kings, with Rhys ap Tewdwr initially in command of stronger forces. Recognizing his weak position, Iestyn accepted an offer of help from Einion ap Collwyn, Lord of Ceredigion (Cardiganshire), who was a disaffected vassal of Rhys and who had a sizeable retinue at his disposal. In return for his help, Iestyn promised Einion the hand of his youngest daughter, Nest, with whom the young nobleman was smitten. In addition, Iestyn turned for further military assistance to his neighbour in the east – the Earl of Gloucester. This earl, Sir Robert Fitzhammon, was a Norman and a cousin of King William Rufus, a son of William the Conqueror. Sir Robert was only too willing to oblige, bringing 12 knights with him and a sizeable army of perhaps a thousand retainers. In the ensuing battle, which took place to the west of Cardiff, he made sure that Einion and Iestyn's men were at the front and therefore taking most of the casualties. Rhys ap Tewdwr was killed, but although Iestyn was victorious, it was a pyrrhic victory for him. The Welsh of both sides were left much weakened and the real winner was Sir Robert.

Quite naturally, Iestyn's other ally, Einion, now expected him to uphold his side of the bargain and to allow him to marry his daughter Nest. However, Iestyn was not a man whose word could be trusted. Having obtained victory over Rhys and guessing that Einion was now too weak to do anything about it, he went back on his promise; the young nobleman was left wifeless. This angered Einion enormously and he now turned to Sir Robert Fitzhammon for redress.*

This split in the Welsh ranks suited the Normans perfectly. Having now seen with his own eyes how rich the Vale of Glamorgan was and how weakly it was defended, Sir Robert had plans of his own. He made a bargain with Einion that in return for helping the Normans to overthrow Iestyn, he would enable him to marry Nest. As part of this plan, Sir Robert ordered his men to board their ships and pretend to leave for home. They then waited for a few days, out of sight of the coast, until such time as Iestyn had stood down his army, which consisted of conscript labourers rather than professionals. Then, before Iestyn could do anything about it, the Normans returned in force; with lightning speed they seized the Vale of Glamorgan, with all its castles, including the strategically important Cardiff Castle.

The bulk of these castles, along with their associated manors, he shared out among his trusted retainers. The knights, the ancestors of some of the most important Anglo-Welsh families of the Medieval period, were thereafter known as the 'Twelve Knights of Despoilation'. Fitzhammon kept the best parts of the Vale for himself, including Cardiff, Llantwit Major, Cowbridge and Kenfig. As for King Iestyn ap Gwrgan, he was killed in the fighting according to some accounts, but others say that he retired to Keynsham Abbey (near Bristol) where, already a very old man of over 100, he lived out his remaining days.** (Map 3)

Not all of Glamorgan was lost to the Welsh. Iestyn's sons retained a number of Lordships in the more mountainous parts of the county to the north of the Vale and also most of Gwent. Also, unlike the treacher-

---

* See Chart 3: The First Norman Lords of Glamorgan p.226
** See Chart 4: The Children of Iestyn ap Gwrgan, Last King of Glamorgan p.227

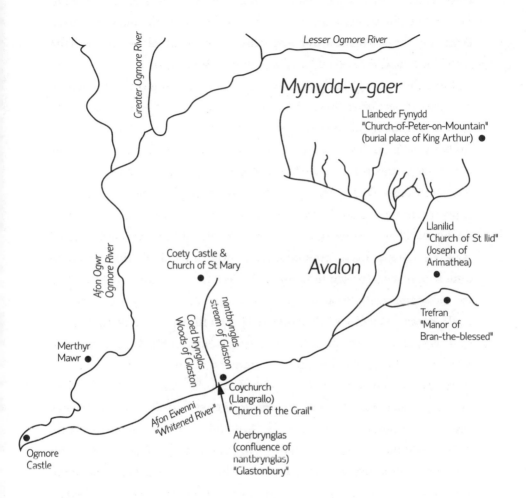

**Map 3: Royal lands retained by Welsh princes after the
initial Norman Conquest**

ous former King of Glamorgan, Fitzhammon kept his promise to Einion. He allowed the young man to marry Nest, her dowry being Senghenydd district to the north of Cardiff near which, in later centuries, the 'Red Earl', Sir Gilbert de Clare, would build Caerfilly Castle.

From these small beginnings, the Norman barons gradually spread their rule to include most of South, West and East Wales. By the 13th century, the only region still maintaining its independence from England was Gwynedd or North Wales. Here, for a mixture of reasons, partly geographic but also to do with strong leadership, a Welsh dynasty held out against over-whelming odds. During the reigns of two of England's weakest kings, firstly John (r.1199–1216) and then his son Henry III (r.1217–1272), the Prince of Gwyneth, Llewellyn ap Iorwerth (better known as 'Llewellyn the Great') was able to assert his independence. He adopted the title 'Prince of Wales' and, with respect to their fiefdoms in Wales, claimed seniority of title over the Norman barons. Because this was a time of major rebellions in England itself, it was possible for him to get away with this and even prosper.*

This situation was not to last. Henry III's son, Edward I, was made of sterner stuff than either his father or grandfather. He was determined both to put the barons in their place and to finish the conquest of Wales once and for all. Accordingly, in 1277, he invaded Gwynedd and forced Llewllyn the Great's grandson, Llewellyn ap Gruffydd, to submit to English rule. This turned out not to be enough, so, in 1282, he invaded again. This time Llewellyn was killed in an ambush, while his brother David was captured soon after. The latter was hanged, drawn and quartered for treason, and both his and Llewellyn's heads were displayed on spikes on London Bridge.

After this, all of Wales was nominally under English rule, but what came to me as a great surprise was the discovery that even then there were still a couple of tiny, independent Welsh Lordships (notably Caerleon or 'Camelot') hanging on. By the time Edward I died, in 1307, only one remained. This was the Lordship of Coity, which survived for a very special reason that we will explore in another chapter.

---

* See Chart 5: The Dark Age Dynasty of North Wales, page 228

What was of immediate interest to me, though, was that this tiny lordship, a sort of medieval Monaco, once owned the church where Wilson and Blackett found their Arthurian relics. This seemed too strange to be a coincidence. There had to be a reason why it alone had survived intact for so long, and this, or so I reasoned, was probably something to do with its Arthurian connections. Was this because the Lords of Coity were protected for some reason, I asked myself? Could it be that they alone were privy to some secret, and if so, what might this have been? These were fascinating questions that would, in time, lead to further, exciting discoveries. First, though, I decided to look into the connections between Wales and the extraordinary Arthurian literature that flooded France in the late 12th century, especially the story of the Holy Grail.

CHAPTER 13

The House of Anjou

Following his conquest of the Vale of Glamorgan, Sir Robert Fitzhammon took over Cardiff Castle and used it as one of his principle residences. He was close friends with Prince Henry, who, in 1100, following the death of his elder brother, William II ('Rufus'), was crowned King of England as Henry I. Some ten years earlier Henry had formed a relationship with Nest, the daughter of the late Rhys ap Tewdwr, Prince of Dyfed. With her father dead and her family dispossessed of their lands, it was perhaps out of necessity that she became his mistress. Later, with Henry's blessing, she married Gerald of Windsor, the Sheriff of Pembroke Castle. She bore him three sons and a daughter, the latter being the mother of the author and monk Gerald of Wales.

By all accounts stunningly beautiful, Nest had other lovers and gave birth to quite a number of illegitimate children, including Henry's eldest son, Robert Fitzroy. Otherwise known as 'Robert the Consul', he was born soon after the conquest of Glamorgan and was subsequently raised by Sir Robert Fitzhammon. In due course and according to plan, he married his stepfather's only daughter, Mabel; after Fitzhammon's death (in 1107) he inherited, in right of his wife, the titles Earl of Gloucester and Lord of Glamorgan.

Robert the Consul is important to our investigation, as he was the principle dedicatee of Geoffrey of Monmouth's book *The History of the Kings of Britain*. Geoffrey awarded him this honour for a very good reason: through his mother he was partly of royal Welsh blood. Thus, by making him the chief dedicatee of his book about the ancient kings of Britain, Geoffrey was reminding him that even if he was illegitimate, these were his ancestors and, therefore, his own blood counted for something. Also, as Lord of Glamorgan, he had near absolute power in the parts of Wales that he controlled. Furthermore, as the dead King's eldest son and a powerful baron in his own right, he was in a perfect position to usurp the throne, taking it by force if necessary.

If Geoffrey had hoped that Robert Fitzroy would make a play for the crown himself, he was to be disappointed. In the Civil War that followed Henry's death, he opted instead for the role of kingmaker. Fiercely loyal, he preferred to support the claims of the Empress Mathilde, the legitimate daughter of Henry I and therefore his own half-sister. Nevertheless, there was a sudden explosion of interest in all things Arthurian that took place after the publication of Geoffrey's book, and this was partly due to Robert the Consul taking an interest in his maternal ancestry.

Within a few weeks of Henry's death on 1 December 1135, Stephen of Boulogne succeeded in getting himself crowned at Westminster. Stephen was a popular figure at court and, tall and handsome, he had been Henry's favourite nephew.

But Mathilde was not about to accept his *fait accompli* without a fight, for she too was powerful and had a much better claim. Now married to Geoffrey, Count of Anjou (a province of Northern France), her first husband had been the Emperor of Germany and she was used to getting her own way. She believed passionately that the throne of England was rightfully hers and was not afraid to fight for it. As a result, the country was plunged into a bloody civil war that raged, off and on, for nearly 20 years. During this conflict, Robert the Consul was staunchly supportive of his sister's cause. For as long as he lived, she had a good chance of gaining the throne and, indeed, very nearly did. His death in 1147 took away that opportunity and, reluctantly, she returned to France.

The ambitions of the House of Anjou now lay with Mathilde's own son, Henry of Le Mans. Eventually it was agreed that Stephen should remain king for as long as he lived, but that he should be succeeded by Mathilde's son. Therefore, in 1154, one of England's greatest if not always most popular ruler was crowned as King Henry II. Now, I found this piece of history interesting because it implied an unexpected link between South Wales and the writing in French of the first Arthurian romances.

In 1152, not yet King but having already succeeded to the title Duke of Normandy, Henry II had married Eleanor of Aquitaine. She was one of the most extraordinary ladies of the Middle Ages and every bit his equal. Ten years older than him – she was 30, while he was only 20 when they got married – she had a somewhat chequered past. At age 15, upon the death of her father, she had inherited the Duchy of Acquitaine and County of Poitiers, two very wealthy territories in the southwest of France. As this made her an extremely eligible heiress, there was no surprise that she was quickly married off to Prince Louis, the Dauphin of France. This marriage took place on 25 July 1137, but was overshadowed almost immediately by the death of Louis' father on 1 August. On Christmas Day, the Dauphin was crowned as Louis VII and Eleanor of Acquitaine found herself Queen of France.

At first, although their temperaments were completely different, the marriage seems to have been amicable enough. Eleanor might have scandalized the stuffy clergymen of Northern France with her frivolity, but she bore the King a daughter and there was every expectation that, in due course, there would be a son. Then, in 1145, Louis announced that he was going on a crusade. Always keen on adventure, Eleanor decided to accompany him. She brought with her a contingent of soldiers and ladies from the Duchy of Acquitaine with the expectation that they would recapture the city of Edessa that had fallen to the Turks. The crusade, however, was a disaster both militarily and for their marriage. As they crossed through Anatolia, their forces were cut to pieces by the waiting Turks, and they themselves were lucky to survive.

They eventually made it to Antioch, but here Eleanor's reputation suffered irreparable damage. The Prince of Antioch was her uncle, Raymond of

Poitiers. She wanted to accompany him in an attempt at recapturing the city of Edessa, but Louis was hell-bent on going quickly to the Holy Land itself. The situation was further complicated by rumours of an affair between Eleanor and Raymond, which would have been incest as well as adultery. Against her will, Louis dragged her away to Jerusalem, from where an abortive campaign was launched against Damascus. Disheartened by their failure, the King and Queen, now separated and barely on speaking terms, departed for home on different ships. They were eventually divorced in 1152, which cleared the way for her second marriage, eight weeks later, to the future king of England.

From her first marriage, Eleanor had two daughters, the elder of whom, Marie, later married the Count of Champagne. A highly cultured woman, she remained close to her mother despite the divorce. She also modelled her court at Troyes on Eleanor's at Angers. Here, she drew to herself a circle of Arthurian enthusiasts, which included the troubadour Chrétien de Troyes. He was to write a series of French Arthurian romances. The first of these, *Erec and Enide*, was published in about 1170, while the last, *Perceval, the Story of the Grail*, was left unfinished when Chrétien died in 1190.

During nearly all of this period, Henry II, who as a boy had been close to his uncle Robert the Consul, was the King of England and Eleanor was its Queen. Marie, meanwhile, was very fond of her half-brothers, especially Richard – who, later, was to achieve universal fame and admiration as Richard the Lionheart. As we can see, there is a clear connection between the Welsh bards at the court of Robert the Consul and the troubadours at the court of Marie, Countess of Champagne, that runs via Anjou.

Further confirmation of the importance of Anjou in the development of the Continental Grail tradition is contained in the works of the pre-eminent German writer on the subject, Wolfram von Eschenbach. In his book *Parzifal*, which completes the unfinished work of Chrétien de Troyes (*Perceval, the Story of the Grail*), he informs us that he was told the full story of the grail by a singer called Kyot. He, he says, found the details of Parzifal's family tree while searching among archives in Anjou. This 'Kyot' has been identified as Guiot, a poet and singer of the period in question who did come from Northern France, from the wealthy town of Provins. It is generally recognized, however, that Wolfram's main source was Chrétien. Where his story differs from the earlier version, it is more likely to have been because he changed it himself, not because he was told of a better version by Kyot. Nevertheless, it is worth noting the connection with the House of Anjou. It was, of course, the family possession of Henry II, the second husband of Marie de Champagne's mother. If Kyot had gone there searching for confirmation of the Grail legend, then the place to look would have been Henry and Eleanor's library in Angers. Here, he may well have found ancient genealogies that came originally from Robert the Consul.

What Kyot would certainly have found there (if he didn't have one already) is a copy of Geoffrey of Monmouth's *History of the Kings of Britain*. This gives a pretty full account of the story of King Arthur and also mentions Peredur (ie Percival) as being present at the plenary court he held in Caerleon. In those pre-Saxon days, Caerleon was one of three Archdioceses in Britain (the other two being London and York). It was also the capital city of Siluria, which included parts of what is now England, as well as the whole of South East Wales. Given these details, Wolfram (via Kyot) could not have been ignorant of the Welsh connection to the Grail legend. The question then is: exactly what was this connection and how did it come about? Once I began to investigate this, it became clear that the sanitization of our history books, mostly done by clerics of the 18th and 19th centuries, has cost us a great deal. The traditional story of the Arthurian kingdom is intricately bound with the coming to Britain of the Holy Grail. This event, as I was to discover, was linked to the invasion of Britain by the Romans in AD 43 and, more specifically, to their impact on the Glamorgan Dynasty.

CHAPTER 14

The Coming of the Grail

The genealogies of the Glamorgan kings indicate that 'Arthur son of Maurice' – usually called *Athrwys* in Welsh documents, but also sometimes *Athwyr* or *adras* – was directly descended from King Caractacus ('Caradoc'). We know from the Roman historian Tacitus that he was the King of the Silures, the British tribe who occupied Siluria. This territory was rather larger than present-day Glamorgan, stretching roughly from Carmarthen in the West to the River Severn in the East and taking in Breconshire, parts of Gloucestershire, Herefordshire and Worcestershire. Tacitus tells us that Caractacus and the Silures proved to be a major obstacle to the Romans, resisting their invasion for nine long years. He was a Pendragon, which is to say commander of a confederacy of many tribes, and he won many battles. Eventually, though, superior Roman equipment meant that his luck ran out. He lost his final battle and was subsequently betrayed into Roman hands. He and his family were taken back to Rome in chains with every expectation of a grisly death. Caractacus, however, was made of sterner stuff and did not give way to fear. Instead, he made an impassioned speech to the Senate, which had a surprising result. He was unexpectedly pardoned by the Emperor Claudius and, provided he stayed in Rome and never again bore arms against the Romans, was allowed to go free.

This much is documented in Roman history. For what happened next we have to rely on more local traditions. These tell us that at least some, maybe all, of his family converted to the then new religion of Christianity. Their house on the Esquilline Hill in Rome, known as the Palatium Brittanicum, became a centre for Christian worship. There were then two Christian congregations in Rome: one founded by the Apostle Peter and a one resulting from the missionary efforts of Paul and others among non-Jews. It seems that one of Caradoc's sons, Linus, became the first bishop of this gentile church. Meanwhile, one of Caractacus' daughters, Claudia (*Gwladys*), married a Roman senator called Rufus Pudens. He, like his wife Claudia, was a Christian convert, and they are mentioned in the letters of Paul, their son Timothy being the recipient of two of them. Claudia was also eulogized by the Roman poet Martial, who seems to have been very taken with her red hair:

> '*Red-haired Claudia who came over, veiled foreign woman*
> *of Pudens ...*
> *The food having meaning of worshipping the god through art ...*
> *Such high degrees of beauty are rarely joined together, confusing*
> *endearments and sweet powers of perception.*'

At the start of another poem, Martial makes it clear that she is indeed British when he writes: 'Veiled Claudia with eagerness red-haired Briton.'

Most of Caradoc's family seem to have stayed on in Rome, but some of them at least were later allowed to return back home to Britain. Welsh records remember in particular the return of his father, Bran Fendigaid – 'Bran the Blessed' – and another of Caradoc's daughters, Eurgain or 'Eugenie'. These two, we are told, brought with them a venerable confessor called St Ilid. He was evidently an Israelite and, in Welsh texts, is generally identified with Joseph of Arimathea.

Exactly why Joseph should also be called Ilid is not explained. However, he is credited with organizing a Christian college – the first of its kind – on behalf of his patroness, St Eurgain. According to the Welsh records, this college was not at Glastonbury but on the other side of the Bristol Channel in Glamorgan, at what later developed into the town of Llantwit Major.

Taking this evidence into account, I was convinced that the original 'Island of Avalon', if it existed at all, must have been somewhere in the vicinity of this church and not at Glastonbury in Somerset. The church of St Illtyd (a later saint and not to be confused with Ilid) in Llantwit Major was, of course, where I had seen the curious tombstones with their 'Rosicrucian' designs that first compelled me to make the current investigation. I was not too surprised, therefore, when further research revealed intense rivalry between Llantwit Major in Glamorgan and Glastonbury in Somerset. This concerned the theft of a bell by none other than King Edgar in about AD 940.

The story goes that St Illtyd, who lived in the mid 6th century, had a falling-out with a local king and went to live in a cave. One day, a man riding an ox cart came by, and Illtyd had a conversation with him. It transpired that he was on his way to take a newly cast bell to St David. Illtyd asked him if he could see and hear the bell, which turned out to have such an exceptionally sweet sound that he was entranced. The man left and in due course delivered the bell to St David. However, when an attempt was made to ring it, it made no sound at all. David questioned the man and, on learning how it had played a beautiful note for Illtyd, understood that it was God's will that he should have it. He sent the bell back to Illtyd, who hung it in his church.

In a corollary to this story, we are told that the late 10th-century King Edgar of Wessex invaded Glamorgan with his army, looting churches as well as houses. Visiting Llantwit Major, he stole the bell of St Illtyd and tied it around the neck of his favourite horse, no doubt intending to give it to his favoured monastery of Glastonbury. That night, he had a dream that the horse died from a spear thrust into its chest. When he awoke, he realized that he had done wrong in plundering the churches and ordered that goods which had been taken should be returned. Of his horse, however, there was no trace, and Edgar died a few days later without returning the bell. However, the horse was not really lost and made its own way back to the River Severn. The bell around its neck rang so sweetly that every horse that heard it followed. Eventually, a great herd of horses swam over the river and found their way to St Iltyd's church. On arrival, the King's horse died and the bell fell from its neck. Rejoicing at its miraculous return, the monks placed it back in the church and then shared out the other horses amongst themselves.

Now while this story, which was written down only in the 12th century, is clearly apocryphal, it does tell us something about the rivalry between Llantwit Major and Glastonbury: both churches were claiming an apostolic foundation from St Joseph of Arimathea. The implication is that St Illtyd has precedence over both St David (for whom the bell is silent) and King Edgar. By inference, Llantwit Major is also superior to Glastonbury, Edgar's favourite church and the place where he was subsequently buried.

I found this an interesting story, and it prompted me to take another look at Llantwit Major's subsequent history following the Norman conquest. This was to take my quest in an entirely different direction.

CHAPTER 15

The Despoilation of the *Clasau*

The story of Illtyd and his bell may be fictional, but what certainly isn't is the profound effect that Sir Robert Fitzhammon's invasion of Glamorgan had upon the spread of Arthurian traditions among the Norman and French nobilities. Sir Robert divided up the manors and castles among his chief retainers, but he also redistributed the wealth of the churches. Up until the Norman takeover, the organizational structure of the Church in Wales was entirely different from the one in England. Churches were very much associated with their founding 'saints' who, like Illtyd (a first cousin of King Arthur), were usually members of the ruling families. In general, the saints were married men with children, and consequently the churches they founded remained family possessions. They were called *clasau* and were run as family businesses that were more or less independent of the church hierarchy. A *clas* was, in fact, more like a college than what we would term a church. It functioned both as a seminary for priests and as an educational establishment where the children of the nobility could be taught how to read and write. Some of these, such as Llancarvan (founded by St Garvan, but closely associated with St Cadoc), were major institutions with considerable reputations. Others were much smaller. The major ones would have satellites in other parts of Wales. These churches would look to their own mother church, the chief *clas* of their founder, for inspiration and leadership rather than to the local cathedral. For centuries, these churches continued to belong to the family of the founder, for when he died their ownership passed to his heirs. In Wales, unlike in England, where it was the tradition that the eldest, living male heir inherited everything, legacies were spread evenly among all the sons. Thus, after a generation or two, a church could have a majority of lay owners: the sons, grandsons, etcetera, of the saint who had originally founded it.

In his book of 1598, *The Story of the Burrowes of Merthyr Mawr*, John Stradling, a local antiquarian, explains all this:

'*The divergence from Continental practice was particularly marked in Wales. Here the Church was subordinate to the state in political matters and, even after the various churches had one by one come to accept the leadership of Rome, during the three centuries preceding the Norman conquest, little advance was made towards the establishment of diocesan or parochial control and the Church in Wales remained essentially local in character and tribal in outlook ...*

There was no exclusive ecclesiastical authority over a special region or "diocese" and the sphere of a particular church was not determined by the boundaries of a parish. Each monastery [ie clas], with its subordinate churches, formed a separate group with an independent organization acknowledging no superior ecclesiastical control. The monasteries had for the most part been established during the sixth and seventh centuries by religious men or "saints", pious founders who gave their names to the monastic house with which they were associated. Many of them were members of the families of regional dynasties who, assuming the religious habit, made the family territories the centre of their missionary enterprise, thus establishing a family right to the church of their founding. They were men of great religion, zeal and devotion to learning, exercising their influence less by accident of birth than by their own personal character.'

In addition to the church itself, most *clasau* owned other properties that had, over the years, been given to it as bequests. The most famous example of this was the church of Llandaff (now Llandaff Cathedral), which tradition says was founded by King Lucius but which was rebuilt by St Teilo at the time of King Meurig (early 6th century). Many bequests were made to this church, often by the Kings of Glamorgan, but sometimes by other individuals, too. The standard procedure with these bequests was to write the details about them – what land had been donated, its location and how it was delineated – into the margins of the church's chartulary or principal bible. Every church had a chartulary; by writing such contracts into the pages of the bible, they became oaths in perpetuity. They were also signed off by witnesses to the gift, generally the king and his family and various members of the clergy (the local bishop, perhaps an abbott, plus one or two younger priests or monks).

All this changed when the Normans invaded, as they had scant regard for Welsh law. Sir Robert Fitzhammon, in particular, had no scruples about taking over the *clas* churches in the places that he controlled. In most cases he gave them over to continental religious orders that were encouraged to start new monasteries and priories. Thus, the famous *clas* church of Llancarvan (where the *Gorsedd* for the Roll of the Round Table had been held) was reduced to the status of a parish church. It was transferred, with its revenues, to the jurisdiction of the Benedictine abbey of St Peter's Gloucester (now Gloucester Cathedral). Meanwhile, Llantwit Major and Llandough, the two other great *clasau* of the Vale of Glamorgan, were given over to the newly founded Benedictine abbey of Tewkesbury. Stripped of their monks (many were transferred to Tewkesbury and Sherborne abbeys) and the revenues from their extensive lands, they became mere shadows of their former selves. New French-style monasteries were founded in their place. At Margam, where the Kings of Glamorgan had once lived, a Cistercian abbey was built that was soon to become the largest monastery in South Wales. Not far away, in the Vale itself, a second house was founded called Ewenny Priory. This too was run by the Cistercians, a more extreme

version of the Benedictines. In Cardiff itself, the Lords of Glamorgan established yet another Benedictine abbey, this one dedicated to the Virgin Mary.

These changes caused consternation in Wales, especially with the church
of Llandaff. This church, originally founded by King Lucius (Lleirwg) and
rebuilt at the time of King Mauricius (Meurig), found itself in dire straits
because of the theft of its lands. Accordingly, the local bishop made a direct
appeal to the Pope for restitution. Under the circumstances, given that the
Lords of Glamorgan had Palatine – effectively dictatorial – status, this was
the only authority to which they were subject.

To back his claim, the Bishop had a book compiled, composed of tran-
scripts of all the land donations contained in the church's chartulary. Copies
were made of this book, and these have survived to the present day. This is
very important, since although the chartulary itself has long since disappeared, it means that we still have a record of the land charters that were
recorded centuries earlier. These charters were each signed off by members
of the royal family and the local clergy of their times. As they tell us who
these people were, and often their relationships to one another, we are able
to use them to build a family tree of the ruling dynasty. This confirms the
information we know from other sources that King Arthur (called here
Athrwys) was the son of Maurice (Meurig) and grandson of Theoderic
(Tewdrig), all three of them Kings of Glamorgan in the period of the 5th
to 6th centuries.

As we have seen, the church of St Illtyd at Llantwit Major was also a
very important *clas* church. It claimed to be a refounding of the earlier
college of Eurgain, the daughter of King Caractacus, after she returned to
Britain from Rome in about AD 60. It seemed significant, therefore, that
following the Norman Conquest, both this church and Llandaff were given
by Fitzhammon to his new priory church of St Mary Tewkesbury. Could
it be, I wondered, that along with various treasures, books and clergymen,
something else had also been transferred? Perhaps even a bardic school
with Welsh links? Anxious to see if this might be the case, I decided to
investigate further.

CHAPTER 16

The Noble Sanctuary
of the West

I t was midday when I arrived in Tewkesbury, driving up from the Forest of Dean. My first port of call was the abbey, which, these days, is actually not a monastery at all but rather the local parish church. It turned out to be an exceptionally beautiful building, not least because it survived the Reformation relatively intact. The reason for this was all around me: royal connections. Clearly, it was also not without reason that it is known as the Westminster of the West of England; the church was filled with the tombs of earls and dukes, some of whom were of royal blood. As we have seen, the original monastery was founded by Sir Robert Fitzhammon, the same Earl of Gloucester, who, in 1092, seized the Vale of Glamorgan. However, the church building we see today was only begun by him. It was mostly constructed by his successor, Robert the Consul, who, in 1107, became Lord of Glamorgan and Earl of Gloucester by right of his marriage to Fitzhammon's daughter Mabel. In 1121, however, he was awarded the Gloucester title in his own right. This was done by order of Henry I, who was, of course, his natural father.

During the course of the next 400 years, Tewkesbury Abbey was added to and further beautified by a succession of Earls, Countesses and Dukes of Gloucester. Among their number were four Earls of Clare and several members of the family, including Lady Isabella Despencer, who, uniquely

Map 4: The Severn and Avon rivers

one suspects, married two earls with the same name. The first of these was Richard Beauchamp, Earl of Worcester, while the second was Richard Beauchamp, Earl of Warwick, also his cousin.* (Map 4)

All this building work ended abruptly with the Dissolution of the Monasteries in 1536. Then, had the local people of Tewkesbury not stepped in, the abbey, like so many others, would have been destroyed. However, they insisted that it was their parish church as well as being a home for monks. Accordingly, for the price of its lead roof and its bells, they were allowed to buy it back. Thus it was that this magnificent, medieval church was able to survive, more or less intact, until the present time.

As I walked around, my attention was drawn to a tomb surmounted by an elaborate canopy. A caption attached to it informed me that it commemorated a certain Sir Guy de Brien, the second husband of Elizabeth Montacute, Countess of Gloucester. She had died in 1359 and was buried with her first husband, Sir Hugh le Despencer (the son of the more famous Hugh le Despencer the younger, who was executed in Hereford in 1326). Sir Guy de Brien died in 1390, and his tomb was placed opposite theirs on the other side of an aisle. My guidebook informs me that he was one of the earliest Knights of the Garter; in fact, he is listed as number 57 in that august order, being invited to join by the founder himself, Edward III. This was hardly surprising, as Sir Guy had shown great valour at the Battle of Crécy, where he acted as Standard Bearer to the King himself.

Sir Guy's tomb was certainly special, but what drew my attention was the coat of arms depicted on his shield: or, *three piles azure conjoined at the point*. When I saw these arms, my heart nearly missed a beat, for they clearly represented something I was very familiar with: the symbol of Awen, which is drawn either as \|/ or /|\ and is associated in Wales with 'Bardism', a pre-Christian, poetic philosophy that is closely connected to what is generally referred to as Druidism. The Awen symbol represents one of the deepest secrets of ancient British mysticism, going back to long before the Roman

---

* See Chart 6: The Despencer Lords of Glamorgan, page 229

invasions. A dictionary translation of the Welsh word *Awen* is 'poesy' or 'the muse'; however, this is a superficial rendering. Actually, *Awen* or 'Ave' is the name of the ancient British goddess of inspiration, the equivalent of the Greeks' Athena or the Romans' Minerva.

According to the teachings of Bardism, the symbol of Awen derives from three shadows cast by a standing stone: one at dawn, one at midday and the last at sunset. In Medieval times (and probably long before), a '*Gorsedd*' – that is, a formal gathering of the bards – could only be held during the hours of daylight. This was because the ancient Britons, like the ancient Egyptians, believed that the sun was the 'eye of God'. It followed, therefore, that if the sun was not visible in the sky, then God was not watching and any proceedings were invalid. In practice, the *Gorsedd* had to be held between the times of the first and last shadows cast by the 'Station Stone', ie the period represented by the Awen symbol.

It struck me as interesting that on the arms of Sir Guy, the 'piles' (flat-pointed wedges) were blue, while the background to the shield was yellow. This suggested that they were intended to represent the three shadows cast by a pillar on a sunny day: the blue piles symbolizing the shadows, while the yellow background represented sunlight. This being so, it suggested that Sir Guy must also have had some knowledge of bardic traditions.

Later, I decided to investigate this, and quickly discovered that the de Brien family (also called Bryan or Brionne) had large land holdings throughout the southwest of England, including Hazelbury Bryan in Dorset. However, Sir Guy himself had been Lord of Laugharne, a district in what is now Carmarthenshire in South Wales. This was interesting from an esoteric point of view, for I now suspected that his adoption of the Awen symbol on his arms could have come about following contact with the remnants of an earlier tradition of Welsh Bardism. This raised a further question, though: what was so special about Laugharne? Why should secret, bardic knowledge have been preserved there?

I found the answer in an old book entitled *Iolo Manuscripts*. This was first published in 1848 and gets its name from 'Iolo Morganwg' (pronounced

Yolo Morganoog), the bardic name of an old stonemason and antiquarian called Edward Williams. When not plying his trade, he spent much of his time walking round Wales, searching the libraries of gentlefolk for old manuscripts in the Welsh language. These, with the owner's permission, he would then copy into his notebooks, his intention being to publish them at some future date. Unfortunately, as this work had not been completed when Iolo died (in 1826), it was left to his son, Taliesin Williams, and some friends from the 'Honourable Society of Cymmrodarion' (a London-based group of Welsh antiquarians) to publish the work. They did so in 1848, providing copies of the original Welsh texts along with their English translations and copious notes. It was this book that I now consulted.

On seeing the arms of Sir Guy de Brien and noting the connection with Laugharne Castle, I remembered a text that I had read in one of the *Iolo Manuscripts*: that Laugharne – known anciently as Aberllychwr – had links with the most famous bard of the Dark Ages, Taliesin. I checked the book and found the following:

> '*Taliesin, the son of Henwg [viz pronounced Henoog], was taken by the wild Irish, who unjustly occupied Gower, but while onboard ship, on his way to Ireland, he saw a skin coracle, quite empty, on the surface of the sea, and it came closely to the side of the ship; whereupon Taliesin, taking a skin-covered spar in his hand, leapt into it, and rowed towards land, until he stuck on a pole in the weir of Gwyddno Garanhir; when a young chieftain, named Elphin, seeing him so entangled, delivered him from his peril. This Elphin was taken for the son of Gwyddno; although, in reality, he was the son of Elviri, his daughter, but by whom was then quite unknown: it was, however, afterwards discovered that Urien Rheged, King of Gower and Aberllychwr, was the father, who introduced him to the court of Arthur, at Caerlleon upon Usk; where his [Taliesin's] feats, learning and endowment, were found to be so superior, that he was created a golden-tongued Knight of the Round Table. After the death of*

*Arthur, Taliesin became chief Bard to Urien Rheged, at Aberllychwr
in Rheged.'*

This passage contains a number of interesting things. Firstly, it confirms
that Caerleon-upon-Usk was the site of Arthur's court. This should come
as no surprise, for we have already identified this town as the most likely
candidate for being the Camelot of legend. Taliesin is a well-known and
indeed famous bard of the late 6th century. Many of his poems have
survived, and some of these are even dedicated to Urien Rheged. That after
Arthur's death he should go to the court of Urien makes sense in the light of
several other notices in the Iolo Manuscripts. According to these, the story
of Urien is that he was originally the ruler of a district called Rheged, more
or less contiguous with today's county of Cumbria in the north of England.
Perhaps it was for this reason that the same name, Rheged, was also applied
to this territory he is said to have conquered between the rivers Tawy and
Towey in South Wales. How it came into Urien's possession is explained in
another of the *Iolo Mss* documents:

> *'Gylmore Rechdyr, King of Ireland, came to Wales in the time of
> Constantine the Blessed [c.AD 420-30], and unjustly seized that
> part of Glamorgan which is bounded by the Tawy and Towey,
> including the Cantred of Gower [a peninsular near Swansea] and
> Loughor, and the three Commots, namely, Kidwely, Carnwyllion
> and Iscennen [three 'hundreds' or municipal divisions of southern
> Carmarthenshire]; which country he arbitrarily subdued, and it
> continued under usurpation to the time of King Arthur [6th century],
> who sent a redoubtable prince of the Round Table, being a person
> of astonishing prowess, called Urien, the son of Cynvarch, the son of
> Meirchion Gul, the son of Ceneu, the son of Coel Godebog, and with
> him ten thousand men of daring onset and stout hearts, to recover
> these districts from the usurping chieftain, Gilmore the Irishman.
> Urien put him and his forces to flight, killing them unsparingly ...
> After Urien had reconquered Gower and the Three Commots, he was
> anointed King of that country, which was thereupon called Rheged.'*

Loughor or Aberllychwr is the place we now know as Laugharne, which, coincidentally, was also the birthplace of that modern bard Dylan Thomas. Taliesin would have known all about the Awen symbol, so I reasoned that the fact that, in his day, Loughor/Laugharne was associated with a bardic chair could well be the reason that Sir Guy adopted the Awen symbol for his arms. By doing so, he was identifying his house with the ancient legends and traditions associated with Urien Rheged.

Sir Guy's effigy lay between the aisle and a small chapel dedicated to St Margaret. This chapel too was interesting from an esoteric point of view. Attached to one wall was a relatively large sculpture of a pelican feeding its young with its own blood. This is, of course, a Christian symbol of self-sacrifice – on one level it represents Jesus Christ shedding his blood in order to feed those who follow him. However, there are other, more esoteric, meanings to this symbol. By chance, I was accompanied on my visit to Tewkesbury by a friend who is a Freemason. He informed me that the pelican is a prominent Masonic symbol relating to the degree of Rose Croix or 'Rosy-cross'. He also told me that Tewkesbury Abbey itself has strong Masonic connections: indeed, it is used for provincial Masonic services and gatherings of 'Mark Masons'.

On returning home, I looked up Rose Croix on the Internet. I discovered that it is the 18th degree of 'Scottish Rite', which claims to be the oldest form of Freemasonry. This degree, it seemed, was one of the most important of the 33 degrees that make up the Scottish Rite. Those who hold it are termed 'Prince Knight of the Rose Cross', and such gentlemen are permitted to wear a particular type of jewel of which I found example pictures. These featured a pelican feeding its young on one side, with an eagle on the other. Above the pelican is a cross and, rising from this, a rose.

I told another Masonic friend of mine about this, and he referred me to two pictures of Queen Elizabeth I, the Phoenix and the Pelican Portraits, which he thought I might find interesting, too. These portraits, both attributed to Nicholas Hilliard, are thought to have been painted by him in 1575, when Elizabeth was 42 and had already reigned as Queen for 16 years. Today, the Pelican Portrait is in the National Gallery in London, while the Phoenix Portrait is not far away, in the Tate Britain Gallery. The two portraits, which appear to be mirror images of one another, get their names from the pendant jewels the Queen is wearing: in one a phoenix and in the other a pelican.

There is much interesting symbolism in these pictures, but what struck me was the way that their being mirror images of one another seems a curious echo of the Masonic jewel showing a pelican on one side and a phoenix on the other. Substitute eagle for phoenix (as is commonly done) and there seems to be a congruency of images. This is not to suggest, of course, that Elizabeth was a Freemason or had attained the Rose Croix degree of Scottish Rite; however, it does imply that there might be some sort of a connection between the symbolism of this degree and some secret 'Rosicrucian' knowledge of which the Queen herself was an initiate. A possible further connection could be read into the fact that, in the Phoenix Portrait, she delicately holds a red rose in her right hand, while, in the Pelican Portrait, the design of her blouse or dress top, possibly made from fine silk, is decorated with meandering rose branches and flowers. This implied connection between Queen Elizabeth I and some secret group or doctrine connected with rose symbolism was something I would follow up later.

In addition to its remarkable collection of effigy-topped tombs, Tewkesbury Abbey also boasts one of the best collections of stained-glass windows in England, many of these too going back to the Middle Ages. As well as scenes taken from the Bible, they depicted imaginary likenesses of such Earls of Gloucester as Sir Robert Fitzhammon, Hugh (the younger) le Despencer and the four Earls of Clare, who were also Earls of Gloucester.

I was familiar with the names and arms of these lords from studying a book that was probably written in about 1525, *The Founders' and Benefectors' Book of Tewkesbury Abbey*. This attractive book, written in Latin, is illustrated throughout with pictures of the various earls and their wives along with their arms. The last benefactor listed is George, Duke of Clarence, the younger brother of Edward IV and Richard III. He was murdered in the Tower of London in 1478, and legend has it that he was drowned in a butt of Malmsey wine. More likely, his body was simply immersed in a barrel of wine to keep it in a good state of preservation while being transported from London to Tewkesbury for burial. The book was unfinished, leaving out the fact that, following his death, the Dukedom of Clarence passed to the crown. No mention is made either of Richard III, who was Duke of Gloucester before he became King. He was not buried at Tewkesbury and, unlike George, doesn't seem to have been a significant benefactor of the abbey. This suggests that the book was probably commissioned by the Duke of Clarence and abandoned after his death. Interestingly, at that time the Clarenceux King of Arms, today one of the most senior heralds based at the Royal College of Arms in London, would have been Clarence's family herald. It is very likely, then, that the book was put together under the guidance of Duke George's chief herald who would have had access to all the archives of Tewkesbury Abbey.

The Abbey church, however, was not just a mausoleum for the rich and famous. Sitting as it does at the confluence of two major rivers, the Warwickshire Avon and the River Severn, it was strategically placed and consequently played an important role in that epic struggle of the 15th century known to history as the Wars of the Roses. Indeed, in 1471, one of the last battles of that bloody war was fought just outside Twekesbury Abbey. As a result of this battle, the Yorkists achieved total victory for a time and peace returned to England until 1483. In my quest for the real meaning of Rosicrucianism, it was this epic struggle, symbolized by red and white roses, that I would investigate next.

CHAPTER 17

Origins of the
Wars of the Roses

My investigations into the secret traditions of Wales had already come a long way. I was now convinced that the legends about 'King Arthur' were mostly based on the life and career of King Arthur son of Maurice, a 6th-century ruler who was crowned at Caerleon (Camelot) and used this as his capital city. I had also been shown ancient stones that clearly dated from his time, thereby proving the veracity of the traditional history of the area. Meanwhile, I became aware that the wheel crosses of this era, many of which are preserved in the museum at Margam Abbey, were later replaced stylistically by 'Rosicrucian' crosses. Quite why this happened, I wasn't sure, but most of these seem to date from around the time of the Wars of the Roses (late 15th century). Accordingly, I decided to investigate this period and, in particular, their impact on Wales.

The Wars of the Roses came about as the result of rival claims to the throne of England by different branches of the royal family descended from Edward III. He himself, a grandson of Edward I, was a relatively successful and popular king. This was especially so in the earlier part of his reign when England was living through what, in retrospect, would be regarded as a golden age. His victory in 1346 in the Battle of Crécy, at the start of the Hundred Years War with France, made him a hero. However, this was overshadowed by the calamity of the Black Death (1348–50), which killed over a third of the population of England. It left a bitter aftertaste and brought widespread disillusionment with religion. After all, if the good were just as susceptible to the disease as the wicked and their prayers went unheard, what was the point in worshipping God? Strange as it may seem, this disaster was to set England, until then an unquestioningly devout, Catholic country, on the path to Reformation and eventually the scientific Enlightenment.

Edward III had five legitimate sons who came to manhood. This was unusual, but under normal circumstances should have caused little problem. Unfortunately, his eldest son, Edward, 'the Black Prince', died in 1376 before he could inherit the crown. Instead, his son Richard II, who was only a boy of nine, was crowned the following year. He proved to be a weak, sensitive king at a time when strength was needed. Meanwhile, Edward's second son, Lionel, didn't have any sons, while his third son, John of Gaunt, Duke of Lancaster, was father to Henry Bolingbroke. In 1399, the latter successfully deposed his cousin Richard II and had himself crowned in his place as Henry IV. Richard died a year later in suspicious circumstances that were suggestive of murder. As he had no children, this left Henry in a very strong position and the House of Lancaster as the ruling dynasty.* Henry IV died in 1413, to be succeeded by his son Henry V. Famous for his military prowess at the Battle of Agincourt (October 1415), he is generally regarded as a hero. He would likely have been one of England's greatest kings had he not died from dysentery in 1422. He was still only 34 years old at the time, younger than even Alexander the Great. He was succeeded by his son, Henry VI, then only a baby of one. This would have been a recipe for disaster in any age, but it was especially so in the febrile atmosphere of the 15th century – a time when protracted warfare with France had created a generation of hardened fighting men with few other talents. Furthermore, although Henry VI was able to hang on to his throne into manhood – itself a major achievement – his position was not unchallenged. For although Edward III's second son, Lionel, Duke of Clarence, had no son to succeed him, he

---

* See Chart 7: The Lineage of the House of Lancaster, page 230

was father to a daughter, Philippa. She had married Edmund Mortimer, 3rd Earl of March. Their son, Roger, the 4th Earl of March, also had a daughter, Anne, who married Richard, Earl of Cambridge, the son of Edmund of Langley, Edward III's fourth son. This meant that their son, Richard Duke of York, had not one but two claims on the throne.*

The first – the weaker – was through the line of his father Richard. More important was the second: the descent through his mother, Anne Mortimer, from Lionel's grandson Roger Mortimer 4th Earl of March. For, in 1385, and therefore prior to his deposition, Richard II had publicly proclaimed that Roger Mortimer and his heirs should inherit the throne after him. The deposition of Richard by Henry Bolingbroke made this declaration of Richard's redundant, even though it had been given in Parliament. However, the situation had now turned full circle. The Yorkists, fortified by the legitimacy of their claim, set about deposing Bolingbroke's grandson, Henry VI.

The Wars of the Roses broke out in 1455 with the first Battle of St Albans. Richard, Duke of York, was killed in 1460 at the Battle of Wakefield, but his mantle was picked up by his eldest son Edward, the next Duke of York. In 1461, he took revenge for the death of his father by inflicting two crushing defeats on the Lancastrians: the Battles of Mortimer's Cross and Towton. The Battle of Tewkesbury, in 1471, was particularly important as it not only put Edward IV in an unassailable position, but cleared the way for Henry Tudor to take over as the principal Lancastrian claimant.

This is because during the battle, which the Lancastrians lost, Prince Edward, the son of Henry VI and his heir apparent, was killed. According to some accounts, on seeing that the battle was lost, he fled for sanctuary into the Abbey church itself. Despite it being against all the rules of war, he was pursued inside by the victorious Yorkists and butchered. Because of this sacrilege, before it could be used again for services, the church had to be thoroughly cleaned and reconsecrated. A year later, Prince Edward's

---

* See Chart 8. The Lineage of the House of York, page 231

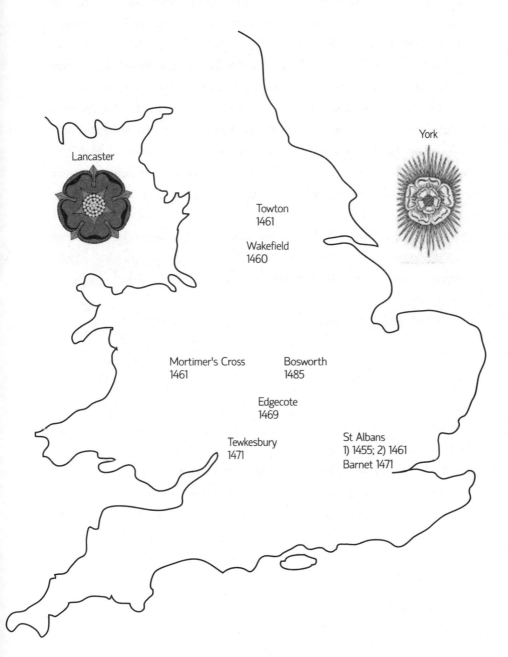

Lancaster

York

Towton
1461

Wakefield
1460

Mortimer's Cross
1461

Bosworth
1485

Edgecote
1469

Tewkesbury
1471

St Albans
1) 1455; 2) 1461
Barnet 1471

Map 5: Major battles in the Wars of the Roses

father, Henry VI, who was already a prisoner in the Tower of London, also died. This left Henry Tudor, Duke of Richmond, as the last remaining Lancastrian claimant to the throne.

This, in a nutshell, is what the Wars of the Roses were all about. However, it was clear to me that the use of roses as symbols for the two rival houses of Lancaster (red rose) and York (white rose) was important from an esoteric point of view. Quite what they symbolized and why the two rival dynasties had chosen these flowers as their emblems was, at first, not clear. Even so, I was sure that if I dug deeply enough, I would find the answer and, curiously enough, once more it was Wales that held the key.

CHAPTER 18

The Rambling Briar-rose of England

I found the first clue to the mystery of the rose in Shakespeare's play *King Henry VI Part 1*. He sets one of his early scenes in the play in the gardens of the Temple in London. The Temple, which today houses the offices of many law firms, had originally been the English headquarters of the Order of the Knights Templar. After the Templars were disbanded in 1306, the Temple's lands were confiscated and given to the Knights Hospitallers. During the Middle Ages, the Temple Gardens were used for jousting, but, no doubt, there were also areas reserved for growing roses.

In the scene, a group of nobles pluck roses from a rambling brier. Richard Plantagenet – later to inherit his uncle's title of Duke of York – and the Earl of Warwick pluck white roses; their rivals, the Earls of Somerset and Suffolk (supporters of Henry VI), pick red ones. These roses then become the badges of the opposing factions: white for York and red for Lancaster.

The white Rose of York, the 'Rose of the Field', is actually *Rosa alba*, the common briar rose. These unspectacular, single roses are native and grow wild throughout most of Britain in the hedgerows surrounding fields, where they produce a rich harvest of hips. The deep, red Rose of Lancaster is *Rosa gallica officinalis*. This is a cultivar that was very popular in the Middle Ages both because of its rich colouring and strong perfume, which is retained by the petals even when dried. As the name suggests, *Rosa gallica* was widely grown in Gaul (Gallica). However, while the device of picking roses in the Temple Gardens works well in the play as a means of defining early on which nobles are taking which side, it has no factual basis. In actuality, the symbolism of the roses is much more complex than this, and the wearing of white and red roses as badges came rather later than this scene would suppose and for different reasons.

So what is the truth about the roses? Well, Shakespeare's choice of the Temple Gardens was no accident. The growing of ornamental roses in England was almost certainly introduced at the time of the crusades. At the time, the experts at rose-growing were the Arabs, particularly those from Damascus, where the so-called Damascene roses originate from. The Arabs used to grow roses not just for ornament, but also to extract the wonderful perfume known throughout the East as 'attar of roses'. This is still used to this day in the manufacturing of Turkish Delight, a jelly-like sweetmeat that probably has its origins in Persia. The crusader states were not always at war with their neighbours, and for quite a long time the Kingdom of Jerusalem was at peace with Damascus. It was probably during this period that the Damascenes taught the Franks techniques of rose growing that would be familiar to gardeners today. In particular, they showed them how to graft the buds of tender varieties of roses onto more vigorous, wild briars.

What does all this rose cultivation have to do with the story of the Wars of the Roses? Well, I found the answer to this (and much more besides) when studying a highly illustrated and very beautiful scroll dating from the time of the Yorkist king Edward IV. This scroll, which was probably published for his accession in 1461, is now housed in the Free Library of Philadelphia in the USA. Very generously, the curators of the Museum have placed images, plus a full explanation of the scroll on the Internet. It can be viewed on their website at: http://www.freelibrary.org/medieval/edward.htm

The scroll's purpose was essentially royal propaganda: an open display of ancestry that would trump the claims of Edward's Lancastrian rival, Henry VI, whose grandfather, Henry IV, had deposed his cousin, Richard II, in 1399 and usurped the throne of England for himself. As we have seen, both

Richard II and Henry IV were grandsons of Edward III, but the former was descended from his eldest son, Edward, known as the Black Prince, while the latter was the son of Edward III's third, surviving son, John of Gaunt, Duke of Lancaster.

As Richard had no children and died in 1400, things might have sorted themselves out were it not that Edward III's second son, Lionel, Duke of Clarence, had a daughter, Philippa. She married Edmund Mortimer, Earl of March, and their granddaughter, Anne, married into the Yorkist line. This mattered because, not only were the descendants of Lionel, Duke of Clarence, the theoretical heirs of Richard II, but he himself had declared them as such in Parliament. As is to be expected, the scroll shows clearly how Edward IV and his Yorkist line descended from Lionel of Antwerp. The Philadelphia scroll (and others like it) was therefore a major weapon in the propaganda war that was waged parallel to the blood-and-guts war to decide who was the legitimate King of England.

Needless to say, rose symbolism comes into all this complex genealogy. The rambling rose from the Temple Gardens, with all its suckers and its myriad branches is, of course, a symbol for the family tree of the royal house of Britain. The *rosa gallica*, the beautiful red rose that was adopted by the House of Lancaster, represents the 'grafting' of the Norman-French line to the stock of the ancient House of Anglo-Saxon England. This grafting began when the Throne of England was seized by William the Conqueror and King Harold II Godwinson was killed in the Battle of Hastings. The grafting proper was fully implemented by the marriage of William's third son, Henry I, to Princess Mathilda of Scotland. Through her mother, she was herself descended from Alfred the Great and was, therefore, connected directly to the briar stock of England.

As Edward IV, like Henry VI, was a descendant of Henry I and also of the later French House of Plantagenet, in theory he could also have adopted the red *Rosa gallica* as his badge. He didn't do this for a very good reason. He had a further trump up his sleeve: one that he plays with daring force in the Philadelphia Roll.

Ann Mortimer, who was Edward's grandmother (the mother of his father, Richard Duke of York), was the granddaughter of Roger Mortimer and Philippa Plantagenet. The Mortimers were an extremely powerful family and at times close to the Royal Family. Titled Earls of March, their seat was Wigmore Castle. It lies in the northeast of the county of Hereford and is therefore on the border or 'Marches' of Wales. It was near here, at Mortimer's Cross, that on 2nd of February 1461 Prince Edward of York (soon to become Edward IV) won his first great victory over the Lancastrians. Legend has it that at dawn, just before the commencement of battle, a sun dog appeared in the sky. This is a rare phenomenon, giving the appearance of three suns in a row, the two outer 'suns' being refractive images of the central one. Edward took the appearance of three suns as a good omen, believing that it implied the Holy Trinity was on his side. After the battle he adopted the radiant sun as a personal emblem, and consequently, this symbol, as well as the white rose of York, is to be seen in many places on the Philadelphia Roll. This is why Shakespeare's play *Richard III* begins with the sentence:

'*Now is the winter of our discontent*
Made glorious summer by this sun of York [ie Edward IV];
And all the clouds that lour'd upon our house [York]
In the deep bosom of the ocean buried.'

Edward's and Richard's maternal ancestors, the Mortimers, had been next-door neighbours of Llewellyn the Great, Prince of Wales. He was a remarkable man who not only established himself as the paramount chief in Wales, but was also deeply involved in English politics. Indeed, as an ally of Simon de Montfort, he was present at the Battle of Lewes (1264), which established the principle of elective Parliaments in England. Llewellyn's relationship with the Mortimers was volatile, but, in 1230, he made an alliance with Ralph de Mortimer who thereupon married Llewellyn's daughter Gwladys dda (Claudia the good). This meant that since Llewellyn claimed to be descended from the original kings of Britain, ie the Brutus lineage, the subsequent Mortimers, descended from this marriage, could claim the same thing. Consequently, Edward IV was able to further legitimize himself as the true King of Britain by virtue of pre-Saxon royal blood that descended from time immemorial.

This is also shown on the Philadelphia Roll, where the Brutus lineage is highlighted. In addition, Edward is depicted on horseback, with his horse decked out in a marvellous surcoat. This coat bears his arms, but at the centre of these is placed the attributed shield of Brutus himself: three gold crowns on a blue background. Clearly, the Brutus lineage was central to Edward's claim on the throne.

It was for this reason, or so I believe, that Edward IV chose the briar, 'rose-of-the-field', as his other main emblem. As any gardener knows, cultivated roses have a tendency to send out suckers from the root stock. The white rose of York therefore symbolizes a flower from the old root stock of Britain: the authentic line of British royalty onto which not only the Plantagenet Dynasty but also the earlier Saxon line of Alfred the Great was grafted. For, according to Geoffrey of Monmouth (and a plethora of other historical documents), the Brutus dynasty predated even the invasion of the Romans.

Descent from Llewellyn was Edward's trump card, but the Welsh themselves also featured prominently in the Wars of the Roses. Edward IV's chief opponents at the Battle of Mortimer's Cross were Owen Tudor (grandfather of the later Henry VII) and his younger son Jasper Tudor, Earl of Pembroke. The latter escaped, but his father, who as the husband of Henry V's widow, Catherine of France, was stepfather to Edward's rival, Henry VI, was captured. In retaliation to the butchery of his own father, Richard Duke of York, following his defeat at the earlier Battle of Barnet, had Owen Tudor beheaded. His head was placed on a spike in the marketplace at Hereford, and it is said that a madwoman combed his hair, washed his face and set candles round it.

Not all the Welsh were on the side of the Lancastrians – the Yorkists too had their supporters. Prominent among these were two brothers, Sir

William and Sir Richard Herbert, whose family home was Raglan Castle (near Monmouth), with prominent members of the family buried at St Mary's church in Abergavenny. Suspecting that I might find further clues to my quest for the real secret of the Welsh rosy-crosses, I decided it was time I paid this church a visit.

Henry Tudor and the Prophecies of Merlin

The details of the many other battles in the Wars of the Roses need not concern us here. What is important is that both sides had what were, in their eyes at least, legitimate claims to the throne of England. It was a struggle that would not be finally resolved until 1485 when Henry Tudor, the last Lancastrian claimant, defeated Richard III and had himself crowned as Henry VII. To cement his victory, he married the heiress to the Yorkist claim, Edward IV's daughter Elizabeth. The symbol of this union was the Tudor Rose, half red and half white, which was to become the most important badge of the subsequent Tudor Dynasty.

Henry's primary claim was through his mother, Margaret Beaufort – a great-granddaughter of John of Gaunt by his second wife, Catherine Swinford – rather than his father Edmund Tudor, who was the son of Catherine of France, the widow of Henry V, by her second husband, Owen Tudor.

As his personal banner, Henry Tudor adopted the red dragon on a green-and-white background that we today associate with Wales. He did this because, as part of his private propaganda, he wanted to present himself as the fulfilment of certain prophecies contained in Geoffrey of Monmouth's *History of the Kings of Britain*. For as well as Geoffrey's flowery translation of the Welsh Annals, this book also contained a translation of another book, *The Prophecies of Merlin*. Rather like the Book of Revelation, which closes the Bible, Merlin's prophecies use very obscure imagery. They begin with the story of how, as a boy, Merlin was brought to the court of King Vortigern.

As the King of the Britons credited with having invited in the Anglo-Saxons, Vortigern gets a bad press. His stupidity led to their colonizing of England and the marginalization of the native Britons to the mountainous region of Wales, Cornwall and parts of Scotland. For this reason, Vortigern is called *mandubrad*, meaning 'traitor', in the Welsh triads. In fact, he is regarded as one of three great traitors of the Cymry (Welsh), the other two being Avarwy, son of Lud (the 'Mandubracius' of Julius Caesar), who made a pact with the Romans, and the other Medrawd (Mordred), who betrayed King Arthur and brought about the collapse of his revived kingdom.

The Merlin of the *Prophecies* is a somewhat different figure from his Hollywood caricature. Said to have been born in Carmarthen, he is more of a psychic than a magician. His story begins when, as a boy, he is taken to Dinas Emrys. Here, Vortigern is having a castle built, which he intends to be a refuge of last resort. To the King's annoyance, the builders are having problems for, every night, what they have built the day before falls down. Vortigern asks his magicians for guidance and is told that to make the building secure, they must first sacrifice a boy with no father and sprinkle his blood on the foundations. Merlin is such a boy, which is why he is brought to the castle. When Merlin discovers that he is to be offered as a human sacrifice, he is outraged. Nevertheless, he keeps his head cool and engages the King in conversation. Bit by bit he exposes the ignorance of the so-called magicians, revealing that, in reality, they know nothing of consequence. He explains that the problem with building the castle is that beneath it there is an underground pool. After excavation reveals this to be the case, he challenges the magicians to tell the King what lies at the bottom of the pool. They don't know, of course, but he explains that there are two stones: one containing a red dragon and the other a white. The King then orders that the pool be drained, and after this is, indeed, revealed to be the case, the dragons emerge from their stones and begin fighting.

All this is a prelude to the subsequent prophecies, which concern the destinies of these two dragons. The red one, Merlin explains, symbolizes the native British, ie the Welsh, while the white symbolizes the Anglo-Saxons. Emerging from their stones, they start fighting. Initially, the white dragon is victorious and the red is forced to retreat. However, Merlin prophesies that the red will eventually defeat the white:

> '*Cadwallader [the last Welsh king of Britain, who died in Rome in AD 689] shall summon Conanus [the first king of Brittany at the time of Magnus Maximus] and shall make an alliance with Albany [Scotland]. The foreigners [Anlo-Saxons] shall be slaughtered and the rivers will run with blood.*
>
> *The mountains of Armorica [Brittany] shall erupt and Armorica shall be crowned with Brutus' diadem [the crown of Britain]. Kambria [Wales] shall be filled with joy and the Cornish oaks shall flourish. The island shall be called by the name of Brutus [ie Brittania] and the name given to it by the foreigners [ie England] shall be done away with.*'

The full meaning of this prophecy, like most of the rest of the book, is necessarily vague, but it could, at a stretch, be interpreted by Henry's supporters as applying to him. Henry crossed over to Wales from Brittany, bringing some Bretons with him. His army was largely composed of Welshmen, although there were also Scots fighting under his banner. He himself, of course, claimed descent from the legendary Brutus, the eponymous 'father' and founder of the British nation. He could, therefore, be said to be wearing Brutus' diadem.

There is also an obvious parallel between the red and white dragons of Merlin's prophecy and the red and white roses. York was a prominent city in Anglo-Saxon times and, in many respects, the epitome of the new state of England. It was certainly one of the first Anglo-Saxon kingdoms and more purely Angle or English by blood than counties on the western side of Britain. Lancaster, by contrast, and more especially Lancashire as a whole, was joined to Wales as part of Cymry for a very long time. Indeed, just to the north of it lies the county of Cumberland, whose name retains the heritage of being part of Cambria. For these reasons, the red rose of Lancaster can be thought of as a surrogate for the red dragon of Wales. It is, therefore, not unreasonable to interpret the Wars of the Roses as a continuation of the much earlier conflict between the Britto-Welsh (red dragon) and the Anglo-Saxon invaders (white dragon), although, as I was to discover later, this is an oversimplification.

To summarize, my trip to Tewkesbury, which was now coming to an end, posed as many questions as answers. I had come there searching for clues that perhaps the esoteric schools of South Wales, which were once based at *clas* churches such as Llantwit and Llancarvan, had been transferred to Tewkesbury following the Norman invasion. I had not found direct evidence of this, but even so there were some intriguing signs of other links with Wales. The tomb and arms of Sir Guy de Brien indicated a connection with bardism that fitted with his taking over of Loughor Castle, a site previously connected with Urien Rheged and the 6th-century bard Taliesin. Tewkesbury had also featured prominently in the Wars of the Roses and these, I was discovering, were linked to Merlin's dragon prophecies. The conflict between the red and white dragons in Merlin's prophecies seemed to be prescient of the actual wars of the red and white Roses in the 15th century. Furthermore, the accession of a Welshman, Henry Tudor, as King of England could be interpreted as the fulfilment of Merlin's most important prophecy: the restoration of Brutus' diadem.

All of this was certainly food for thought. However, there was something else that this investigation had drawn my attention to, and this was the connection between the Tudor Dynasty (notably Queen Elizabeth I) and Rosicrucianism. The two paintings of her, with their reflected images, hinted at this. Even though she herself was not a Freemason, the fact that she was wearing jewels signifying the Masonic degree of Rosecroix in the paintings seemed too much of a coincidence to have no meaning. The implication was that this Masonic degree and her own private 'Way' were drawing inspiration from the same source, one which may be connected with the mystery of the Welsh tombstones and which, for want of a better name, we could call Rosicrucianism. Inexorably, it seemed, I was being drawn back to a secret connection between the 5th- and 6th-century Welsh memorial stones and the chief emblem of the 17th-century Brotherhood of the Rosy-cross. Investigating this mystery further was my next task.

CHAPTER 20

Old Stones and the Rosy-cross

This phase of my quest had begun in Wales after I saw what seemed to be 'Rosy-cross' symbols on certain memorial stones. Yet these stones, we know, were carved long before the 17th century when, as we have seen, the so-called Rosicrucian Brotherhood announced its existence. To recap, that announcement involved the publication, initially in German, of several short pamphlets. The first of these, the *Fama Rosicrucitatis*, or 'Fame of the Rosicrucians', was first published in 1614, but appears to have been written in about 1610. Together with a sequel called the *Confessio*, it claimed that there existed a hitherto secret brotherhood of Christian initiates whose intention was to bring about a spiritual and scientific revolution. The symbol of the Brotherhood was a crucified rose, emblematic of both Jesus Christ and of the alleged founder of their order, who enigmatically styled himself Christian Rosencreutz, which is German for 'Christian Rosy-cross'.

The publication of these pamphlets, which were soon translated and printed in all the major languages of Europe, caused an uproar. Some people, mostly intellectuals from the Protestant north of Europe, hailed the secretive brothers as Masters of Wisdom. These supporters not only wanted to hear more about CRC's proposed programme of reform, but were keen to be initiated into the Brotherhood themselves. At the same time, on the other side of the religious divide, the rulers of France, Spain and other

Catholic countries denounced the movement as subversive; they ordered that loyal subjects should seek out these 'brothers' and turn them in to the established authorities. As heretics, they would then be subjected to the full rigours of the Inquisition.

That may have been their desire, but, as it turned out, the brothers proved to be as elusive as the Loch Ness monster. For although there were some relatively well-known authors such as Robert Fludd and Michael Maier, who claimed to be Rosicrucians, in reality this was an aspiration rather than the truth. In any case, as these authors lived in England or some other Protestant state, they were out of reach of the Catholic authorities. Eventually, on both sides of the argument, the consensus became that the Rosicrucian furore was no more than an elaborate hoax.

As I have written extensively about all this in my earlier work *London: A New Jerusalem*, I won't say much more here. However, one relevant point of interest that can be extrapolated from the pamphlets themselves is that Christian Rosencreutz, if he actually existed, was born in 1378 and died at the age of 110 in 1488. Of course, there is nothing to link this legendary – perhaps non-existent – German philosopher and teacher with Britain. He would have been 21 in 1399 when King Richard II of England was deposed, and would then have lived right through the entire period of turmoil we call the Wars of the Roses. This means he would have witnessed the reigns of the Lancastrian Kings (Henry IV, V and VI) and also those of the Yorkists, Edward IV and V, and Richard III. Finally, as a very old man, he would have still been alive in 1485 when Henry Tudor defeated Richard III, married Elizabeth of York (the daughter of Edward IV) and thereby united the red rose of Lancaster and the white rose of York to give a hybrid – the Tudor rose.

All this is not to say that there is a direct connection between the genesis of the German Rosicrucian movement and the English Wars of the Roses; however, there could be an indirect one. Whoever wrote the Rosicrucian pamphlets must have known about the Wars of the Roses and how the red and white roses symbolized different, royal houses. The question is:

was he (or were they) in possession of other information concerning rose symbolism? If so, what was the crucified rose truly meant to symbolize? The Crucifixion? The Masonic degree of the Rose Croix? Or maybe something even more esoteric? To find answers to these questions, I went back to Wales and started looking for other clues, beginning with what had once housed the greatest library of Welsh literature anywhere in the country – Raglan Castle.

CHAPTER 21

Raglan Castle and the Welsh Renaissance

Anxious to see if I could get a better understanding of what was really going on with the Wars of the Roses and, if possible, to discover if there was a connection between what I was starting to refer to as the 'Welsh Renaissance' and the use of Rosicrucian symbolism on tombstones, I decided that it was time I visited Raglan myself. I had read about its importance some years earlier while studying the *Iolo Manuscripts*. Here, it is recorded that during the 15th century, under the protection of the Earl of Pembroke, regular meetings of the bards were held at Raglan. The *Iolo MSS* also mentions that, at that time, Raglan's library was the best in Wales. With all this in mind, I decided to pay a visit to both Raglan and the nearby town of Abergavenny.

It was early spring when I eventually found myself driving up to the castle itself. As I parked the car and turned to face it for the first time, it looked absolutely magnificent. With its enormous gatehouse flanked by imposing towers and largely intact curtain wall, it looked everything that a castle should: impregnable. This turned out to be an illusion! In reality, the castle I was looking at was but an empty shell. For like so many others in England and Wales, the inside was in a state of near total ruin. This was the result of a terrible act of vandalism for which Oliver Cromwell must take the blame. In 1646, following a long siege, he ordered that the castle be 'slighted', ie turned into an uninhabitable ruin. I looked in vain for its famous library, but this too had been deliberately torched. Had it lasted another 150 years or so, it would certainly have been visited by old Iolo, and he would undoubtedly have copied many of its precious manuscripts for posterity. As it is, we cannot be sure of exactly what it is we have lost or even if, by some good fortune, certain volumes were stolen rather than burned. If so, they may still be languishing unrecognized on a bookshelf somewhere. This is a slim hope; however much we may wish differently, it seems unlikely that any of the books have survived. Nevertheless, the sheer bulk of the castle and the elegant style of the surviving walls and towers were proof enough of the wealth and power of its former owners, the Herbert family. During the Wars of the Roses, one of these, Sir William Herbert, the Earl of Pembroke, who had held bardic festivals, had been a veritable Prince of the Welsh in all but name. How this all came about made an interesting story that turned out to be crucial to understanding the importance of Wales in the development of the Rosicrucian mystery.

The Wars of the Roses, which took place on and off between 1455 and 1485, mark even more of a watershed in Welsh history than English history. Before them, the Welsh, although politically subjects of the Crown, were treated with a great deal of suspicion, an attitude that went back to long before the Norman invasions. To make rebellion harder, Wales itself was covered with castles, mostly owned by Marcher Lords. Although in some parts of the country, especially in the South, there were quite large colonies of English immigrants, the ordinary people were not allowed to intermarry or mix with the Welsh. Conversely, except by special act of Parliament, any Welshman living in England was not allowed to buy either land or a house. Meanwhile, the native Welsh aristocracy, even those with royal pedigrees, were denied noble titles and very few were given the honour of knighthood.

The spread of Welsh literature, especially of a patriotic nature that might lead to rebellion, was also closely controlled. Printing presses were banned and, for a time, so were even pen and paper. Despite being the first book to be printed in Welsh, Sir John Price's *Yn Y Lhyvr Hwnn* (literally 'In This

Book'), appeared in 1546 and was printed in London. It was not until 1718 that a permanent printing press was established in Wales. This was nearly three centuries after Johannes Gutenberg had invented it. With the *clasau* closed down, all education was in the hands of monks, friars and nuns belonging to recognized orders. Until the founding (in 1822) of St David's College, Lampeter, there were no universities at all in Wales. Before then, if a Welshman wanted higher education, he had to get it in England, which usually meant going to Jesus College, Oxford.

As we have seen, in 1399 Henry Bolingbroke – afterwards King Henry IV – deposed his cousin Richard II in a coup, the latter dying in suspicious circumstances the following year. This sudden change in dynasty had a profound effect in Wales. Henry's usurpation caused enormous instability, and all the resentment that had been building up for centuries boiled over.

An early casualty of these times was Sir Thomas le Despencer, Earl of Gloucester and Lord of Glamorgan. He was the son of Sir Edward le Despencer, who had been a great benefactor to Tewkesbury Abbey. He was also the father of Isabel le Despencer, the benefactress of the same church who married two husbands, both called Richard Beauchamp. Sir Thomas, extremely unpopular in England as well as Wales, was beheaded by a Bristol mob in 1400. However, this was only the beginning; much worse trouble was to follow.

CHAPTER 22

The Glendower Rebellion and its Aftermath

O n 16 September 1400, Owen Glendower (*Owain Glyndwr*), who claimed to be descended from the old Kings of Powys, was proclaimed Prince of Wales by a small group of followers. Despite attempts to douse the flames of revolt before they got out of control, the Glendower rebellion spread quickly and grew in strength. In 1404, he was crowned at Machynlleth, while shortly afterwards, at Harlech Castle, he called the first Welsh Parliament. This body declared that from then onward, Wales was to be independent from England and it was to have its own laws. These would be based on the laws of Howell Dda (*c.*AD 880–950), the 9th-century King of Dyfed, whose son Owen's genealogies are preserved in the Harleian 3859 Manuscript. The old British Church, too, was to be restored, with the Norman monasteries closed and their clergy expelled.

Glendower may have been a Welsh Nationalist, but he had English allies. Principal among these were Edmund Mortimer, Earl of March, and Henry Percy, Earl of Northumberland. Had these allies coordinated better and not overreached themselves, Glendower might have succeeded in obtaining a certain degree of independence, perhaps as a restored Prince of Powys.

As it was, the three hatched a radical plan that would never have been accepted by the ordinary English peasants, let alone the majority of barons. They proposed in secret that once they had defeated the King (Henry IV), they would partition England between them. Glendower would rule over the whole of Wales as well as the English Marcher counties of Cheshire, Shropshire, Herefordshire and part of Gloucestershire; the north of England would go to Henry Percy; and Edmund Mortimer would take over what was left of England south of the River Trent. It was a bold plan and even they, when sober, must have had doubts as to whether they could make it happen; yet in 1403 it did look as if they might be successful. Aided by the French and with a promise of further help from the Scots, Glendower caught Henry on the back foot.

This dire situation for the English monarch turned around when he defeated the army sent from Northumbria before it could have a chance of linking up with Glandower's forces. Harry 'Hotspur', the son of the Duke of Northumberland, was killed and the rebel alliance shattered. Glendower, however, was still making advances in Wales, and it was left to 'Prince Hal', then the official Prince of Wales, but better known as as Henry V, to sort out the problem.

Hal realized that trying to engage Glendower in battle was pointless. All that was necessary was to deprive him of a power base. Therefore, he set about the reconquest of Wales, bit by bit, castle by castle. Eventually, in 1409, Glendower's last stronghold of Harlech Castle fell to the English. His family was captured and sent to the Tower of London and imprisonment from which they would never emerge alive. Glendower himself was never actually captured, but he was a broken man. A fugitive for the rest of his life, he was rumoured to have died from natural causes around 1415.

The Glendower rebellion, although it failed in its objectives, had important consequences for both sides. Not all of the Welsh had flocked to Hal's banner, with many, particularly in the South, regarding him as a destructive nuisance. Indeed, Prince Hal had much support among Wales's yeoman archers, many of whom had fathers and grandfathers who had fought for England at the battles of Crécy and Poitiers. This loyalty to the official Prince of Wales was reinforced as he earned a reputation as a good soldier who led his men personally into battle. It was noted with satisfaction that he was willing to risk his own life as well as theirs.

A formidable opponent of Glendower's and staunch supporter of Prince Hal was a Welsh captain called Dafydd ap Llywelyn ap Hywel Fychan ap Hywel ap Einion Sais, better known simply as 'Davy Gam'. His family had long been retainers of Prince Hal's mother's family, the de Bohun Earls of Hereford, who were also Lords of Brecon. His local knowledge and support proved very important in putting down the rebellion. Indeed, Prince Hal knew him personally and had paid a large ransom for his freedom when, at one point, he was captured by Glendower's men. Consequently, when Hal, as Henry V, took the English army to France in 1415, Davy Gam went with him in command of a retinue of Welsh archers.

The principle event of this campaign was the Battle of Agincourt, when Henry's small army of 6,000 men, mostly archers, routed a French force that was at least three times as large. During the end stages of this battle, which was mostly fought on foot, the King went to the aid of his brother Humphrey Duke of Gloucester, who had been wounded. A surge of French knights closed in around them, and the King himself was put in grave danger of being either captured or killed. Fortunately for him, Davy Gam saw what was happening and, along with his son-in-law, Roger Vaughan, and two other Welsh squires, Gruffyd Vaughan and William ap Thomas, he came to the King's rescue. The fighting was fierce and, in the ensuing melée, both Davy Gam and Roger Vaughan were mortally wounded. The King, however, was saved and went on to win the day. In gratitude to his rescuers, he knighted all four of them on the spot, though Davy Gam and Roger Vaughan may have been already dead by then. Sir William ap Thomas, however, was very much alive and was made a 'Knight Banneret'. This title, which could only be awarded by a king on a battlefield, was senior to an ordinary knighthood. It meant that Sir William, known on account of the colour of his armour as the 'Blue Knight of Gwent', now had the right to raise a retinue in his own name. He and his men fought again at many battles, doing so under his own arms, which would be displayed on a rectangular banner rather than a lance pennant.

Retuning to Wales, Sir William married Gwladys, the daughter of Davy Gam and the widow of Roger Vaughan. She was by all accounts a great beauty, as well as rich, and was known as the 'Star of Abergavenny'. A widower himself, who had previously been married to another widow, Isabel Bloet, William ap Thomas lived at Raglan Castle. Initially, this belonged to his stepson by his previous marriage, but William used some of Gwladys' money to buy it outright. In this way, what was to become the ancestral home of one of Britain's most powerful families was established.*

Sir William ap Thomas died in 1445 and was succeeded by his eldest son, William Herbert. A staunch supporter of the Yorkist cause, he was to be a prominent figure in the Wars of the Roses; he fought at both the Battles of Mortimer's Cross (February 1461) and Towton (March 1461) which put Edward IV on the throne. In 1468, he successfully took Harlech Castle by siege and was created Earl of Pembroke the same year as a reward. This made him the first full-blooded Welshman to receive a peerage since the Norman Conquest of England in 1066. Unfortunately, he was not able to enjoy his title for very long as, the following year, he and his brother Richard, after losing the Battle of Edgecote, were both beheaded on the orders of their former ally, the 'kingmaker' Earl of Warwick.

Despite this setback, the Herbert family continued to grow in importance. William, Herbert's eldest legitimate son (another William), later exchanged the Pembroke title for that of Earl of Huntingdon. Upon his death in 1491, Raglan castle – though not his title – passed to his daughter. This might have been the end of their aristocratic pretensions had not the 1st Earl of Pembroke also had an illegitimate son, Sir Richard Herbert of Ewyas. A friend and contemporary of Henry VII and the eventual victor of the Wars of the Roses, he set about rebuilding the family's fortunes.

---

* See Chart 9: The Herbert Earls of Pembroke and the Sidney Family, page 232

After my visit to Raglan Castle, I carried on driving to nearby Abergavenny. I parked the car and then made my way by foot to the parish church of St Mary, which, in the 14th century, was a Benedictine priory. A moderately large structure, it seemed to be in pristine condition in stark contrast to the castle; indeed, it had been refurbished in the not too distant past. Entering through the west door, I proceeded along the southern aisle and presently found myself among a collection of old tombs, each surmounted by one or more effigies. During the late Middle Ages, the Herberts of Raglan had been the principal patrons of this church, and so it is here that many of them and their wives lie buried.

This association began with Sir William ap Thomas, the 'Blue Knight of Gwent', whose effigy, along with that of his wife Gwladys, still lies on top of an elaborate tomb of alabaster. Next to this monument was an even finer memorial, this one surmounted by effigies of Sir Richard Herbert of Coldbrook (who along with his brother, the 1st Earl of Pembroke, was beheaded after the Battle of Edgecote) and his wife Margaret. Cut into the wall opposite these two tombs was a third, this one in memory of Sir Richard Herbert of Ewyas. These tombs were on a par with many I had previously seen in Tewkesbury Abbey and, in fact, the entire collection – there are other tombs in the church besides those belonging to the Herbert family – is the finest in Wales. It all spoke of their high status.

On the floor, near these tombs, were a couple of large flagstones. Although unnamed, they were clearly funerary monuments themselves, presumably originally intended to mark the position of graves beneath the church floor. These stones, although not exactly 'Rosicrucian' in the normally accepted sense of the word, nevertheless featured floriated crosses of a type I had seen elsewhere in Wales. I wondered, could this be the evidence I was looking for? Were these further connecting links between the older wheel crosses that were on display in Margam and the later 12th-century crucified-rose symbol of the Rosicrucians? In short, were they a transitional style? This, however, was only a taster of what was to come. I was to find something even more interesting on the other side of the church.

CHAPTER 23

The Tree of Jesse

A t this point I had no answer to the Rosicrucian question, so I took a few pictures of the tombs and slabs, and then, leaving the Herberts to their eternal slumbers, I crossed over to the north side of the church. Here, there were one or two more tombs, but there was also something else that I later discovered is unique to this church. For lying on one side, his hand around the stump of a tree, was an enormous, wood-carved statue of Jesse, the Father of the biblical King David. The stump was a reference to the way that the family tree of Jesse had been hacked down at the time of the Babylonian conquest of Jerusalem in 586 BC. The Bible tells us how the Babylonians beheaded the sons of Zedekiah, the last King of Judah, who was then blinded and taken in chains to Babylon. This was, or so it was assumed at the time, the end of the Royal House of David, the 'stump' of Jesse representing his felled family tree.*

The statue itself was about eight feet long and it was carved out of one large log. From the church guidebook, I learned that it would originally have had a tree-like stem rising from the side of the stump, and that this would have had other, smaller statues in its branches. These statues would have represented the ancestors of Jesus Christ, the reason for this being a prophecy contained in the Book of Isaiah:

---

* See Chart 10: The Tree of Jesse to Jesus, page 233

'There shall come forth a shoot from the stump of Jesse, and a branch shall grow out of his roots.

And the Spirit of the Lord shall rest upon him, the spirit of wisdom and understanding, the spirit of counsel and might, the spirit of knowledge and the fear of the Lord ...

In that day the root of Jesse shall stand as an ensign to the peoples; him shall the nations seek and his dwellings shall be glorious ...

He will raise an ensign for the nations and will assemble the outcasts of Israel, and gather the dispersed of Judah from the four corners of the earth.

The jealousy of Ephraim shall depart, and those who harass Judah shall be cut off ...

Ephraim shall not be jealous of Judah and Judah shall not harass Ephraim.'

(Isa 11:1-2,10,12-13)

In this context, 'Ephraim' is a reference to the Northern Kingdom of Israel which separated from Judah, the Southern Kingdom, shortly after the death of David's son Solomon in about 931 BC. The biblical reference concerns an expected messiah, a descendant of Jesse, who will reunite the two parts of David's kingdom, Ephraim and Judah. Therefore, it refers to some future king: one who will bring together the dispersed people of Israel as a whole.

I found the presence of this curious sculpture in a Welsh church puzzling. When complete, with its 'shoot' growing from the stump and bearing ancillary statues of Jesus' ancestors, it would have been a very large construction, perhaps even reaching as high as the roof. This statue would also have been expensive to commission and someone would have had to pay for it. The question is: who? Since the sculpture has been dated to the 15th century, it seems certain that it was commissioned by one of the Herberts: perhaps either Sir William ap Thomas or Sir William Herbert, 1st Earl of Pembroke, both of whom were buried in the church. However, this still left the question of why had it been commissioned at all unanswered.

On returning home, I looked into the matter further. I discovered that, although this sculpture of Jesse was unique, the 'Jesse Tree' was a relatively common theme for church windows. A Jesse window would normally portray the lineage of Jesus Christ, whose descent from Jesse is given in the New Testament. However, during the Middle Ages, before the advent of English translations, the most common version of the Bible used by the church was the Latin Vulgate. This contains the following words for the Isaiah quote: '*et egredietur virga de radice Iesse et flos de radice eius ascendet.*' This translates as '... a rod out of the root of Jesse, and a flower shall rise up ...'

There are several interesting things to say about this quotation. Firstly, the word *virga* (rod) is almost the same as *virgo*, meaning the Virgin (Mary). Secondly, the idea of a flower growing on the rod of Jesse can be understood as a hidden reference to the primary symbol of the Rosicrucians, the crucified rose, and also the many tombstones I had seen with floriated patterns of flowering rods. The implication was clear: the flowering rod was a reference to the family of Jesse and therefore of King David.

Just why this symbol should have so excited the Herberts of Abergavenny I could not tell for the moment. At first I could think of no better explanation than that the statue, with its messianic rod, had been commissioned as an act of piety. But then two things occurred to me. First of all, the rod or 'sucker' that grew out of the side of the stump could be the hidden meaning of the floriated cross symbols that I had seen in this church and in several others. These were not traditional calvary crosses, but always had arms that terminated in either buds or leaves. In other words, they symbolized a tree: the messianic, regrown tree of Jesse.

The second idea that occurred was a possible reason for the Jesse statue's placement in this particular church. As we know, Sir William Herbert, 1st Earl of Pembroke and son of Sir William ap Thomas by Gwladys, the daughter of Davy Gam, was beheaded. It is true that he had a son and heir, but he didn't amount to much and lost the Earldom of Pembroke. Thus, the beheading of the 1st Earl was effectively the cutting down of the hopes and expectations of his family. Yet despite this disaster, all was not lost. He also had an illegitimate son, Sir Richard Herbert of Ewyas, whose family tree grew like a sucker from the root stock of the felled tree. Through him, the Herberts found their way back into power, eventually regaining their lost title of Earl of Pembroke. In other words, the destiny of the Herbert family was, in a sense, analogous to that of the biblical Jesse. Of course, this couldn't be said openly and in so many words, but the symbolism of the Jesse tree spoke for itself: Jesse was a surrogate for the 1st Earl of Pembroke whose line seemed finished until it was restored by its offshoot: the rod of his illegitimate son Richard.

This much was clear, but already I could see that this was only a small part of what was a much bigger story concerning the old Welsh aristocracy. Also, Sir William Herbert was not the only Yorkist in Wales. I had to move my attention from Abergavenny to Llandaff Cathedral in Cardiff.

CHAPTER 24

The Keepers of the Skull of Teilo

Having found so much of interest in Abergavenny, I decided that it was time I paid another visit to Llandaff Cathedral and, in particular, to the Mathew Chapel. I wanted to see if I could find any further evidence here of a connection between the symbolic Jesse Tree and the primary emblem of the Rosicrucians: the crucified rose. Thus, a few days after visiting Abergavenny, I found myself once more going through the doors of Cardiff's Cathedral.

This former *clas* church – one of the oldest Christian foundations in Britain – lies on the River Taff, just a couple of miles west of Cardiff Castle. Legend has it that it was originally built by order of King Lleirwg (Lucius). If so, then it would have been in the early 2nd century AD when Britain was visited by Saints Dyvan and Fagan. It is most likely true that these saints were indeed active in the Cardiff area, as it was here they also founded churches of their own. St Fagans, now home to the National History Museum, lies to the west of Cardiff, while Merthyr Dyvan is slightly south of this, near Barry. Therefore, we can be sure that these saints were active in the Cardiff area, and it is only reasonable to assume that they did help their patron, King Lucius, found a church of his own at Llandaff. What is more certain is that, following extensive damage incurred during the 5th century, Llandaff (church on the Taff) was rebuilt by St Teilo. This was in the early

6th century, at the time when Meurig (Mauricius) was King. After that, the church again fell into ruins and was rebuilt on several other occasions. The present church, which includes 20th-century work, was largely rebuilt by the Victorians.

Entering through the west door, I walked up the northern aisle. Unlike most, if not all, cathedral churches in England, Llandaff is not cruciform in plan: there is no crossing in the middle of the church and so there are no transepts. Instead, the north and south aisles terminate in chapels on either side of the chancel or main altar area.

Proceeding up the northern aisle of the church, I came to a large tomb that sat awkwardly among the stalls. Its inscription said that it belonged to Sir William Mathew and his wife Jeanette Stradling. Later research revealed that he was the younger brother of David Mathew (whose effigy I would shortly inspect) and that he was knighted after the Battle of Bosworth by King Henry VII. However, of immediate interest was that his tomb, which was early Tudor and bore effigies of both himself and his wife Jeanette, was also decorated with a number of shields. These were mostly repetitions of the arms of the Mathew family; a lion rampant, though confusingly painted with the wrong tinctures for the Radyr branch of the family. What was more interesting to me, though, was a shield on the head of the tomb. This was painted with the arms of Cardiff: gules, three chevrons argent. This is one of the variants of the arms of Iestyn ap Gwrgan, last King of Glamorgan, the other variant being its reverse: argent, three chevrons gules. The presence of Iestyn's arms on this tomb indicated that the Mathew family (sometimes spelt Matthew or Matthews) regarded themselves as descendants of the Kings of Glamorgan. This, as we shall see later, is important. It also explains their close association with Llandaff Cathedral.

My primary interest at this time was the north or 'Mathew' chapel, which I knew contained more medieval tombs and effigies, as well as early 20th-century stained-glass windows representing the Welsh King Arthur and his grandfather, King Tewdrig. The Mathew family, like the Herberts of Raglan, attained fame and fortune through their involvement in the

Wars of the Roses. The patriarch was Sir David Mathew of Radyr, whose effigy, though not now his tomb, lies on the floor by the High Altar. He was another supporter of Edward IV and, just as Sir William ap Thomas was the progenitor of the later Herbert Earls of Pembroke, Sir David was the ancestor of the Mathews. Reading about this, I decided to investigate him further, and what I discovered was quite extraordinary.* Sir David Mathew, who was born in 1400, was the father of Sir William Mathew of Radyr, whose tomb I had seen in the aisle. Already an old man of 61 at the time, he took part in the Battle of Towton – the Yorkist victory that established Edward IV's supremacy over the Lancastrians for eight years. This battle was fought on Palm Sunday, 14 March 1461, just seven weeks after Edward's first victory at Mortimer's Cross. Towton took place in Yorkshire and is said to have been the largest and most bloody battle ever fought on British soil. More than 50,000 men were involved, and by the end of it, only 22,000 were still alive: a casualty rate of nearly 60 percent. During the battle, in a replay of what happened to Henry V, Edward's life was saved by David Mathew, who, like Davy Gam at Agincourt, was only a captain at the time. His effigy, which shows him dressed in full armour, is a full six feet seven inches in length. Clearly he would have been an exceptionally tall man even by today's standards, but in those days he must have seemed a positive Goliath. One can only imagine Edward's relief when he saw this huge man leading his company as they hacked his way through the enemy and came to his rescue. In gratitude, after the battle was over, Edward immediately awarded him the title of 'Knight Banneret' and appointed him Grand Standard Bearer of England. This was an unheard-of honour for a Welshman, and, once more, it underlines how, through military service to the Crown, certain families were able to undo centuries of prejudice and climb the social ladder.

This, however, was not to be Sir David Mathew's only or most important claim to fame. Around 1404, there had been a raid on Llandaff Cathedral, which caused a great deal of damage. Accounts differ, some blaming the

---

* See Chart 11: The Mathew family of Llandaff and the relic of Teilo, page 234

raid on Glendower's men, others on pirates from Bristol. In any event, a mob smashed open the tomb of St Teilo, the church's primary patron, and scattered his bones. The tomb remained damaged until, many years later, Sir David paid for its repair. In 1480, in recognition of this laudable act, Bishop Marshall presented him with the skull of Teilo and appointed him its guardian.

Sir David's wife was Gwenllian Herbert, who was first cousin to Sir William ap Thomas, the 'Blue Knight of Gwent'. In the 15th century, therefore, the Mathews were close relatives of the Herberts. This may partly explain Sir David's allegiance to the cause of the White Rose of York at a time when most other Welshmen of rank, including, later, his own younger son Sir William Matthew of Radyr, were drawn to the Red Rose of Lancaster.

Sir David Mathew died in 1484, but the skull of Teilo, to which healing powers were attributed, remained in the family for centuries. Eventually, in 1658, a certain William Mathew died without issue in the small village of Llandeilo Llwydiarth in Pembrokeshire and passed it on to another family: the Melchiors. It was kept by them for many years, used as a cup for drawing water from a local holy well with links to Teilo. However, because the Mathew family had neglected their duty as guardians, it was prophesied that bad luck would befall them for 200 years. This certainly came to pass, but then, in 1927, it was purchased back from the Melchiors by a descendant of Sir David Mathew; eventually, in 1996, it was returned to Llandaff Cathedral. Today, supported by the wings of silver angels, the skull cup sits like the Holy Grail in a reliquary that is kept locked away from the prying eyes of would-be thieves or hooligans.

All this drama, of course, lay in the future. During his own lifetime, Sir David could only lay the foundations for his family's later eminence when his descendants became Sheriffs of Glamorgan and eventually Earls of Llandaff. Much of this success was attributed to the blessing of St Teilo, but there were other saints associated with Llandaff, one whose tomb I then went to investigate.

CHAPTER 25

The Arms of Joseph of Arimathea

Teilo's tomb, which is on the other side of the high altar from the Mathew Chapel, is not the only one in the church belonging to a saint. Perhaps the most important tomb inside the chapel itself is that of St Dyfrig or Dubricius. He was the successor of St Teilo in the role of bishop and, as we have seen, is credited with crowning King Arthur at Caerleon. His tomb and effigy, however, are medieval, his remains having been moved to Llandaff in 1120.

Like the tomb of Sir Richard Herbert of Coldbrook at St Mary's Abergavenny, Dyfrig's is sunken into the wall. Lying on it, fully robed and holding a bishop's crosier, is an effigy of the saint dressed as a bishop. However, what interested me more was that, set into the wall above it, was a small replica shield. This did not display any heraldic arms, real or imagined. Instead, there was a representation of the aftermath of the Crucifixion. This consisted of a calvary cross with a ladder leaning against it. Also shown were other implements mentioned in the Gospels as being used either prior, during or after the Crucifixion of Jesus: the Spear of Longinus, the whipping post and flail, the three nails and hammer used to drive them in, the reed with the vinegary sponge, etcetera. I studied this shield intently and then suddenly something struck me. On the shield, hanging over the cross itself, was a wreath representing the crown of thorns. This, however,

Figure 4: Tomb of Bishop John Marshall in Llandaff Cathedral.

was positioned in the precise position that a single rose would be in the normal Rosicrucian emblem. Could it be, I wondered, that this was an early version of the Rosy-cross emblem? After all, roses are notoriously thorny and, therefore, it is only a small step to make the assumption that the crown of thorns was, in fact, made from the stems of roses.

This threw a whole new light on the matter, although it would be some time before the full significance of this shield would sink in. Then, turning round, I received another shock: right opposite the tomb of Saint Dyfrig was that of John Marshall, the bishop who gave Sir David Mathew custody of the skull of St Teilo in 1480. This, as befitting his status, was quite a large affair, with his effigy lying on top. What immediately caught my attention was another plaque attached to the end of it. This one was square rather than shield-shaped, but it depicted the same scene of the aftermath of the Crucifixion. Again, there was the cross with its crown of thorns, the ladder, the whipping post, the nails, the spear and the reed with sponge. The main difference was that, this time, there was a haloed figure standing at the foot of the cross, presumably Jesus Christ himself, although it could have been meant to represent some other saint.

I was amazed when I saw this plaque. For a start, it meant that the image depicted on the Dyfrig shield was not unique, and this implied that the cross with its crown of thorns was not an accidental design. Also, this was clearly an emblem associated not so much with the Crucifixion itself as its aftermath. The tableau was of Calvary *after* the Crucifixion when the body of Jesus Christ had already been removed. Yet the removal from of Jesus' body from the cross didn't just happen. The Bible tells us that it was brought down by Joseph of Arimathea, who subsequently laid it in his own tomb. The ladder would have been his and so too would a pair of pincers, shown on the Marshall plaque, which would have been required to remove the nails. This seems important given that Joseph of Arimathea, or 'St Ilid' as he is called in Wales, was the apostle who first brought Christianity to Britain according to the legends and many lists of saints. Also important is that one of these plaques was attached to the tomb of Bishop Marshall. He would have been alive during the Wars of the Roses and knew Sir David Mathew, to whom he entrusted the skull of Teilo. This implies that the symbol of the cross with the crown of thorns hanging from it was also known in Wales at that time. Sir David Mathew died in 1484 and Bishop Marshall in 1496. Given that the later Rosicrucian documents imply that Christian Rozencreutz, the legendary founder of the Rosicrucian Brotherhood, died in 1488, this all seemed significant.

While there is no suggestion of a direct connection, the fact remains that the cross with the crown of thorns was a potent symbol in Wales at the time. It could be argued, therefore, that a type of 'Rosicrucianism' (whatever we really mean by that term) had its origins in Wales at the time of the Wars of the Roses. Quite how this may have morphed into the later Rosicrucianism of the 17th century was something that I now wanted to look into. I didn't have to look very far.

CHAPTER 26

The Rise of the House of Tudor

S o far, we have looked at what I now call the Welsh Renaissance through the eyes of two important families, both of whom were Yorkists. This, however, gives a rather distorted view, for during the Wars of the Roses, the majority of the Welsh were on the side of the Lancastrians. The reasons for this are manifold, but at the core they boil down to the simple fact that Wales then had its own cadet branch of the Royal family, the Tudors, and they were Lancastrians. How this came about and how Henry Tudor, Earl of Richmond, eventually took the throne of England, is one of the most extraordinary yet underexplored stories in the whole history of Britain. For in doing so, he not only brought the brutal Wars of the Roses to an end, but, perhaps unwittingly, laid the foundations for the English Reformation and the birth of a Protestant England. This, as I have written in my book *London: A New Jerusalem*, was the unnoticed legacy of the real Rosicrucians.

The full story of the Tudors begins many generations before Henry with the rise of Llewellyn the Great (1172–1240) as 'Prince of Wales'. Among his supporters was a powerful warrior named Ednyfed Fychan (1170–1246). He came to Llewellyn's notice after a battle fought against the forces of the Earl of Chester. Ednyfed personally defeated and killed three knights, cutting off their heads and bringing them back to Llewellyn. After this,

Llewellyn ordered that his family's arms be changed to reflect this victory; accordingly, Ednyfed's shield became gules (red), a chevron of ermin, three helmeted heads argent, two above and one below.

Llywellyn also appointed Ednyfed as his Seneschal or chief Steward – effectively his right-hand man. In part, this was due to his proven prowess on the battlefield, but it was also a reflection of something else: the royal blood of his wife. Ednyfed's own pedigree seems a bit vague, but he married twice, and his second wife was Gwenllian, the daughter of the Lord Rhys of Dyved. The latter was a grandson of Rhys ap Tewdwr, the King of Dyfed, who died at the time of the invasion of Glamorgan by Sir Robert Fitzhammon. Through Rhys ap Tudor, the Lord Rhys was able to trace his ancestry back to Hywel Dda (AD 880–950), King of Deheubarth (southwest Wales) and grandson of Rodri the Great. As we have seen, to mark the occasion of Howell's son Owen getting married, he published 32 pedigree lists celebrating the family's ancestry. Included in the lists, which can today be read in the Harley 3859 MS in the British Library, are Roman Emperors, Kings of Britain and numerous saints. Thus, because she was descended from Howell and Owen, Gwenllian, the wife of Ednyfed, was able to claim this blue blood as her own. This claim then extended to all their proven offspring.*

A sixth-generation descendant of theirs was another Owen – Owen Tudor (c.1400–61). Born the year that Richard II died, he was too young to take part in the Glendower rebellion. However, because older members of his family were closely involved in this insurrection, much of the Tudors' land was confiscated by the Crown. Consequently, Owen's father, Meredith Tudor, found it necessary to leave Wales and seek a new life in London. To help his son progress, the boy was put under the guardianship of a second cousin, Lord Rees. As a result of this connection, young Owen found himself enrolled as a pageboy at the court of Henry V and, in 1415, went with the English army to France. Still only 15 at the Battle of Agincourt, he seems to have acquitted himself well. As a result, he was promoted

---

* See Chart 12: The Welsh descent of King Henry VII, page 235

from page to squire and was given the right to bear his family's arms in England (the three helmeted heads of Ednyfed Fychan).

What happened after that is not at all clear. In 1420, Henry V married Catherine de Valois, the daughter of the King of France, with the understanding that on her father's death, Henry would succeed him. In the event, in 1422, Henry predeceased his father-in-law. Queen Catherine was left on her own with a baby boy, the young Henry VI. By this time, Squire Owen Tudor was around 22 years of age, handsome and available. How and when it happened we cannot say for sure, but the young widow of Henry V fell hopelessly in love with the Welsh squire and they became lovers. This was one of the greatest romances of the late Middle Ages, for although no documentation survives to prove it, they claimed they were married in secret in 1429. If it actually happened, this was in contravention of an Act of Parliament of 1428, which made it illegal for the widow of a king to marry without the permission of the king's regents. This was done because the King himself, her son Henry VI, was only six years old at the time.

Between then and her death in 1437, Catherine and Owen had at least six children, including four boys. Two of these became monks, but the other two, Edmund Tudor (b.1430) and his younger brother Jasper (b.1431), were to be important figures in the Wars of the Roses. Both were, of course, half-brothers of Henry VI, who, far from disowning them gave Edmund the title of Earl of Richmond and Jasper the title of Earl of Pembroke, thereby silencing all dissent about their legitimacy. He also arranged for Edmund to marry Lady Margaret Beaufort. She was the daughter of John Beaufort, 1st Duke of Somerset, and therefore, like Kings Henry IV, V and VI, was descended from John of Gaunt, Duke of Lancaster.

It was natural that such an important heiress, with the royal blood of Edward III in her veins, should be married off to someone important. Her family, however, were barred from the Royal succession because they were from Gaunt's second wife who was not married to him at the time his children by her were born. The assumption, therefore, was that the Tudors and Beauforts, as cadet branches of the Royal family, would buttress the main line of the Lancastrian Plantagenets, but have no personal claim to the throne. Needless to say, when the Wars of the Roses did break out, the Tudors supported Henry VI and remained loyal to the Lancastrian cause throughout.

CHAPTER 27

Pembroke Castle and the Tudor Rose

Anxious to understand the influence of Wales on this period in history better, I took my family on holiday to Tenby and used this as a springboard for investigating the rest of Pembrokeshire. While there, we visited Pembroke Castle. A huge complex of buildings, it still dominates the surrounding town as it has done ever since the Norman invasion of *c.*1092. A guide showed us the room where Henry VII was born. It was a sad story, for in November 1456, his father, Edmund Tudor, died in captivity leaving his wife, Margaret Beaufort, heavily pregnant. The following January, she gave birth to their only son, Henry. To help visitors visualize the scene, the local tourist board had thoughtfully provided a tableau of wax models in period dress. They looked authentic enough, but what these mannequins couldn't convey was the fear that must have gripped Henry's mother who was then herself only 14 years old. Because of her age and small size it was, by all accounts, a difficult birth that nearly killed both mother and child. It must have been cold, too. For although there was a fireplace in the room, it was the middle of January, and in those days there was no central heating. For poor Henry it was an inauspicious start to what would one day prove to be a most remarkable life.

In 1461, Owen Tudor, was at the head of a largely Welsh army with his younger son Jasper by his side. Their aim was to join up with the main body of Lancastrian forces further north. However, before they could link up, they were confronted and defeated at Mortimer's Cross. Jasper escaped back to Wales, but Owen was captured. Then, in revenge for the beheading of the previous Duke of York, he was taken to Hereford by the Yorkists and was himself beheaded.

With Owen's eldest son, Edmund Tudor, already dead, the hopes of the Tudor family lay with the second son, Jasper Tudor, and Edmund's little son, Henry. Jasper Tudor escaped to France, but Henry and his mother Margaret were still lodged at Pembroke Castle when, in 1461, it was captured by Wales' pre-eminent Yorkist, William Herbert. He now became the boy's gaoler, although, in reality, he was more like a stepfather. Being Welsh, the old man understood well the value of the boy's bloodlines and that he was not only descended from the royal houses of both France and England, but, like himself, was also a scion of the ancient Kings of Britain from before the Anglo-Saxon invasions. Cadwallader, the last native King to claim rulership over the entire island of Britain, died in Rome in AD 689. However, because of the Rhys ap Tewdwr lineage, Henry Tudor could legitimately claim descent from him. Through his own mother Gwladys, the 'Star of Abergavenny', Sir William Herbert was also descended from Rhys ap Tewdwr, although without the added bonus of being a scion of the royal houses of England and France, too. Thus, little Henry Tudor was both a distant relative of the Herberts and a very valuable heir. Sir William Herbert intended to capitalize on this.

The young boy was mostly housed at Raglan Castle, where he was schooled according to Welsh traditions. Henry, though still a boy, was central to William Herbert's plans for a Welsh Renaissance. In fact, he was groomed so that one day he would marry one of the Earl's daughters. With access to the great library, Henry was in a position to read many of the books that were later burnt by the Parliamentarians of Cromwell's times. He would also have witnessed Herbert's gatherings of the bards, the poets of Wales who kept old traditions alive. For them, lack of pen and paper was not an imposition but a positive stimulus to hone their traditions of memorizing verses known as triads. It is very likely that Henry was encouraged to learn at least some of the triads, too, many of which were nationalist in character. Thus, although he was a Lancastrian, he grew up like no other. Immersed in Welsh cultural assumptions, he was being prepared to take over from William Herbert to be what was effectively the real Prince of Wales.

In 1469, the rules of the game changed more than anyone at the time could have imagined. Richard Neville, the 'kingmaker' Earl of Warwick, fell out with the Yorkists and changed sides. A major battle was fought at Edgecote, and this time the Lancastrians were victorious. On Warwick's orders, Sir William Herbert (recently awarded the title of Earl of Pembroke) and his brother Richard were both beheaded. Warwick restored Henry VI to the throne; his nephew, Henry Tudor, was returned to the custody of his uncle Jasper, who was given back his lands and his earlier title of Earl of Pembroke.

This Lancastrian restoration did not last long. In March 1470, the Yorkists again defeated the Lancastrians, putting Edward IV back in charge. This time, however, Henry Tudor, now a teenager, was able to escape with his uncle to Brittany. Shortly afterwards, Edward's rival, Henry VI, died in the Tower of London, and, as we have discussed already, in 1471 the latter's only son, Edward Prince of Wales, was slaughtered in the aftermath of the Battle of Tewkesbury. This left Henry Tudor, the Earl of Richmond, as the principal surviving Lancastrian contender for the throne.

In contrast to the weedy, effete and at times even insane Henry VI, Edward IV, tall, handsome and brave in battle, was a popular ruler. Nevertheless, by the end of his reign, he had grown fat and debauched. Few mourned his passing in 1483, expecting that he would be succeeded by his eldest son, Edward V. This was not to be. Still only boys, he and his brother Richard, Duke of York, were taken from their mother's custody and for their 'safety' lodged in the Tower of London. Neither were ever seen again, their uncle, Richard III usurping the crown for himself. This was a disastrous start to what was to prove a very short reign. Few people liked or wanted Richard as King so that when Henry Tudor, now a mature man of 28, landed in Wales, people flocked to his banner. At the subsequent Battle of Bosworth fought on 22 August 1485, Richard was slain, and Henry Tudor, Duke of Richmond, became King Henry VII.

This, as it turned out, was the start of not just a new reign but of an entirely new dynasty. Prior to Bosworth, Henry had little or no experience of battle, sensibly putting his army under the command of the Earl of Oxford. However, he was highly intelligent and, like Edward IV before him, had a good grasp of how to use symbolism to aid his cause. The banner under which he fought at Bosworth (and which was later brought to St Paul's Cathedral in London) was emblazoned with neither the arms of his ancestor Ednyfed Fychan – the three helmeted heads on a red background – nor the more recent arms of his own father, Edmund Tudor – the arms of England and France quartered inside a bordure of alternating gold fleur-de-lys and martlets on a blue background. Rather, he adopted a banner with a red dragon (*draig goch*) emblazoned over a field of white and green. This banner, now the flag of Wales itself, symbolized how the Tudors were restoring the throne to its earliest line: that of the Brutus. It was an omen of what was to come.

CHAPTER 28

Henry VII and the Restoration of the Brutus Lineage

In taking the throne of England, Henry presented himself as fulfilling ancient Welsh prophecies that one day the line of Cadwallader, the last truly British King, would be restored to the throne. The traditional history of Wales and even England at that time stated clearly that, long before the Roman invasions of the island, the Cymry, led by Brutus, came from Troy. Brutus became Britain's first King, and after his death his line carried on ruling over the entire island. Even during Roman times, the royal line of Brutus, in theory if not always in practice, still ruled over much of Britain. After the Romans left Britain for good, the old line reasserted itself, although King Arthur's unfortunate death at the Battle of Camlan left the Britons in disarray. Disunity meant that bit by bit the Anglo-Saxons gradually took over the bulk of the island, eventually replacing the diadem of Brutus with a sovereign crown of their own.

According to Geoffrey of Monmouth's *History of the Kings of Britain*, Uther Pendragon, symbolically if not actually the father of King Arthur, adopted a golden Dragon as his personal emblem. If this story is true, then this 'dragon', which was carried into battle, was very likely a *carnyx*, a type of animal-headed, bronze trumpet of a kind that the pre-Roman British had used in battle. Arranged in groups, these instruments gave out a frightening roar that was intended to unsettle the enemy even before the start of any actual fighting. Aware of the potency of this dragon symbol and its connections with Merlin's prophecies that one day the Britto-Welsh would regain the sovereignty of the island, Henry used the *draig goch* banner as a recruiting sergeant on his long march through Wales from Haverford West en route to London.

Henry was not the only one to fight under a symbolic banner representative of a *carnyx*. His opponent Richard III used the symbol of the White Boar both as a personal badge and on his banner. The reasons for his choosing a boar are obscure, and it has been suggested that a pun on the word 'Ebor' – short for *Eboracum*, the Latin name for York – was intended. There is, however, another possible explanation. We now know from the archaeological discovery of several Dark Age helmets that the boar was a prominent symbol used by the Anglo-Saxons. Not only that, but, although they could be dragon-like, the bell of a typical *carnyx* was more usually made to look like a boar's head. Indeed, I have seen one such instrument on display in Edinburgh in the National Museum of Scotland. Thus, the Red Dragon banner of Henry Tudor and the White Boar banner of Richard III can be understood as both symbolizing *carnices* or battle-horns. As such, they are stand-ins for Geoffrey's conflicting red (Welsh) and white (English) 'dragons' whose ongoing struggle was prophesied by Merlin.

There was, of course, a calculated risk in Henry's strategy of linking his cause with the Red Dragon symbol. For although the *draig goch* banner was highly attractive to the Welsh, it would do nothing to draw the English to his cause, and may well have had the opposite effect. In fact, at the start of battle Henry's army numbered only about 5,000, of which about half were Welsh, with most of the others either Scottish, French or Breton. It should, therefore, have been relatively easy for Richard, who on paper at least could command forces well in excess of these numbers and who was a far more experienced soldier to put down the

Tudor rebellion. In the event, his deep unpopularity with the country at large counted against him. Of the major Lords who promised and were obliged to give support, only the Duke of Norfolk showed up in time. Meanwhile, Lord Stanley, whose intervention on Richard's side would have decided the day in his favour, kept his men out of the fight until near the end. When he did intervene, it was to rescue Henry and ensure Richard's defeat.

One good reason for Stanley changing sides was that he was married to Henry's mother Margaret, but an equal one was that Richard was holding his eldest son hostage and had threatened to kill him if the father did not fight for him. Stanley's response to being blackmailed in this way was to reply that he had other sons. Nevertheless, the threat was enough to ensure that Stanley's men killed Richard. Stanley then took pleasure in placing Richard's circlet – a lightweight crown – on his stepson's head. Henry rewarded his stepfather with the title of Earl of Derby.

To cement his hold on power, Henry VII married Edward IV's daughter Elizabeth, thereby bringing together the two rival houses of Lancaster and York. To symbolize this union, the family adopted the 'Tudor' rose (double blooms with five red petals on the outside and five white within) to be their badge. This, of course, was a symbolic reference to the connection between the red and white roses and the rambling briar that is the royal house of Britain. However, this was only part of the story. The accession of the Tudors was not just a change of dynasty but also of national consciousness. In his attitudes Henry was still profoundly Welsh, which is to say ancient British, and this carried over to his children and grandchildren.

One result of Henry's victory at Bosworth was that the ancient prejudice that had disbarred the Welsh nobility from holding high office in England was reduced, if not entirely removed. He also remembered with affection how his erstwhile gaoler, Sir William Herbert, had more or less fostered him when he was a small boy. He was deeply upset that the old Earl had been beheaded by Warwick, but as the latter was dead by this time, there was no way of taking revenge. Accordingly, soon after his marriage, Henry took his new wife to Abergavenny. There, they attended Mass in St Mary's Abbey, and he was able to pay his respects to the surviving family.

This was to be the start of a renewed relationship between the Royal family and the Herberts: one that would endure for centuries. They, of course, also had family ties with the new Queen, Elizabeth of York, for Mary Woodville, her maternal aunt, was married to Sir William Herbert's eldest son, William the 2nd Earl of Pembroke. She died in 1481, but their daughter, Elizabeth Herbert, was a first cousin of this Queen Elizabeth. Had her father William come over to Henry's side in 1485, he would have been well rewarded, but after Mary's death he married his second wife, an illegitimate daughter of Richard III.

An ineffectual leader, in 1479 he was forced to give up the Earldom of Pembroke in exchange for the far less lucrative Earldom of Huntingdon. If he had been expecting Henry VII to give him back the Pembroke title, he was disappointed as this went back to the latter's uncle Jasper. Instead, William Herbert II found himself left on the fringes of the new court and still relatively poor.

However, not all was lost to the Herberts; although like Jesse's tree the beheading in 1469 of the 1st Earl of Pembroke had left but a stump, the illegitimate cadet branch growing out of its side was fruitful. Without any of the benefits of his half-brother, Sir William Herbert of Ewyas now set about restoring the family fortunes. He accepted the postion of gentleman usher to Henry VII and, in 1509, was appointed Constable and Porter of Abergavenny Castle. He then made two relatively good marriages, the first of these bringing Castleston Castle into the possession of the family. This created a launching platform for his eldest son, another William Herbert, of whom more will be said later.

Henry VII's identification with Uther Pendragon went further than placing a dragon on his banner: just as Uther had called his firstborn son Arthur, so did Henry. The unspoken narrative was that, having restored the true line of Brutus to the throne of England, his son would then build on the firm foundations he had established and create a new golden age. In the event, Prince Arthur predeceased his father so that when Henry VII died in 1509, he was succeeded by his second son, Henry VIII. This was to have profound consequences for both Wales and England.

CHAPTER 29

The Tudor Restoration of the Old British Church

Henry VIII made much use of the Tudor Rose symbol of which he was, of course, a living embodiment. He had the Round Table in Winchester Castle (reputed to be that of King Arthur himself, although now carbon-dated to the late 13th century) repainted in the Tudor colours of green and white. At its centre was a large Tudor Rose, perhaps emblematic of himself as the prime flower brought about by the union of the two houses – York and Lancaster. In the same vein, he changed the collar of the Order of the Garter, the oldest and most esteemed order of chivalry in Europe. From then onward, the collar, somewhat similar to a mayor's chain of office, was to be composed of a necklace of jewels. Each jewel – and there were 26 of them in all, each one representing a living member of the order – was an enamelled Tudor Rose of gold. These were joined together by a gold chain composed of 26 carefully crafted knots. This collar was a new innovation and its symbolism was plain for all to see. The Knights of the Garter were not just an order of chivalry but servants of the Tudor Rose. As such, they were expected to act like a brotherhood, the knots holding their order together as eternal as those between brothers of the flesh.

When young, Henry VIII was a tall, charismatic man who loved hunting and jousting. Had it not been for a suppurating lance wound in his thigh that healed and caused him great pain, he might have turned out to be one of our better kings. Depending on your point of view of him as an ogre or a misunderstood modernizer, we are all familiar, anyway, with the story of his six wives. What is less well remembered is the way in which he envisioned a new kind of Britain: one that would be strong, united, independent of foreign dominance and above all 'Arthurian'. The Acts of Parliament that he passed, making himself Head of the Church of England (in place of the Pope) and dissolving the abbeys, can be understood as stemming from his desire to return to the values and organization of the British Church prior to the mission of St Augustine. He and, later on, his daughter Elizabeth resolutely believed that, having been founded by Joseph of Arimathea, the British Church preceded that of Rome. Seen from this perspective, the Roman Church, with its wealthy order of monks, dissolute Popes and pretensions to be able to grant indulgences in exchange for hard cash, was a corrupt, foreign imposition. The closure of the monasteries and the selling of their lands and buildings could be justified as the acts of a pious king, one descended from Brutus who was intent on purging the British church from sin.

In 1535, an Act was passed through Parliament and this was reinforced by a second Act in 1542. The intention of these Acts was to unify Wales and England as a single country. Five new Welsh counties were created, making 13 in all, and the power of the old Marcher Lords was greatly curtailed. In their place Henry established courts of law presided over by Circuit judges instead of local lords. Such judges, being from outside a given area, were much less amenable to bribes than the Lords who had administered justice under the old system. Meanwhile, the Welsh counties were now able to elect and send their own Members of Parliament to Westminster, a privilege they had not previously enjoyed. All this change, however, did not come without a cost. Proceedings in the new Assize Courts were held only in English. Welsh was to be regarded as a second-class language, and anyone in Wales who wanted to prosper needed to learn English. Although this caused some hardship, the benefits of full citizenship and rights in England, as well as Wales, far outweighed any disadvantages for the burgeoning middle class and Welsh gentry.

A major beneficiary of these changes was another William Herbert, the eldest son of Sir Richard Herbert of Ewyas. As a young man, he made his reputation as a soldier and adventurer in the service of the King of France. Soon he came to the attention of Henry VIII, who dubbed him a knight and rewarded his services by giving him the estates of Wilton and Ramsbury in Wiltshire as well as Cardiff Castle.

Sir William Herbert was married to Anne Parr, the sister of Henry's sixth and last wife, Catherine Parr. This royal connection helped him greatly, especially after the King's death (in 1547) when he was appointed guardian of Henry's son, the boy King Edward VI. Honours soon followed; he was made a Knight of the Garter in 1549 and, in 1551, was raised to the peerage as Baron Herbert of Cardiff and the next day given back the Earldom of Pembroke that was once held by his grandfather. With their new land holdings and old earldom, the Herbert family was back in business. Indeed, the branch growing from the 'stump' of the earlier executed Earl of Pembroke was now even mightier than its forebear. By now, I was beginning to suspect that the Herbert family was close to the centre of the Rosicrucian mystery and formed a link between some clandestine, medieval, secret society and the 17th-century Rosicrucian Brotherhood. However, they were not alone in this, and my attention now switched in a different direction to one of the most important families in the later Tudor and early Stuart periods – the Sidneys.

CHAPTER 30

The Rise of the House of Sidney

The Sidney family, of whom the Tudor poet Sir Philip Sidney is the most famous, also made speedy progress under the new dynasty of the Tudors. The first to come to notice was Sir William Sidney, who at the Battle of Flodden (1513) commanded the right wing of the English army. Henry VIII, delighted by this victory over the Scots, knighted him immediately. He was also rewarded with the Lordship of Kingston-upon-Hull and the manor of Myton, previously the property of a leading Yorkist pretender who Henry had executed in 1513. In 1514, Sir William Sidney witnessed the coronation of the King's sister Mary after she married Louis XII, the King of France. As the bridegroom was an old man at the time and died a few months later, she was soon free to marry again. This time, it was to Sir William's cousin Charles Brandon, 1st Earl of Suffolk. As with the Herbert family, these royal connections did Sidney's career no harm at all. In 1517, he became Henry VIII's 'Knight of the Body', and in 1520, he accompanied the King to the 'Field of the Cloth of Gold', an extravagance that nearly bankrupted the Royal Exchequer.

In 1538, after further loyal service, he was appointed Steward and tutor to Henry's son Prince Edward, then one year old. This appointment was to prove especially fortuitous, not just for him personally but for the future of the entire Sidney family. Edward was seven years younger than Sir

William Sidney's own son Henry, but the two became friends and were often together. This again proved advantageous. In 1539, Henry VIII gave William land in Kent and Sussex in exchange for his estates further north. The old King died eight years later in 1547 and was succeeded by his son, who, although still only a boy, was crowned Edward VI in 1552. His *de facto* regent was John Dudley, Duke of Northumberland, who had previously been Chief Minister to Henry VIII. Dudley's eldest daughter, Mary, married Edward's friend, Sir Henry Sidney, in 1551. No doubt guided by Dudley, the boy King rewarded his old tutor, Sir Henry Sidney's father William, by giving him Penshurst Place, a magnificent country house and estate near Tonbridge in Kent.

Perhaps none of the parties involved – the Tudors, the Herberts, the Sidneys and the Dudleys – realized it at the time, but together, in the next generation, they would change the world. Indeed, the scene was now being set for the cult of the Tudor Roses to give birth to what is sometimes referred to as the Rosicrucian Enlightenment.

CHAPTER 31

The Circle of Dr Dee

T he boy King, Edward VI, died on 6 July 1553, and immediately England was plunged into chaos. He declared his half-sisters, Mary and Elizabeth, illegitimate and nominated a cousin, Lady Jane Grey, John Dudley's (the Earl of Northumberland's) daughter-in-law, as his successor. The failure of this plan was a disaster for all involved and even for some who weren't. Northumberland himself, Lady Jane Grey and her husband Guildford Dudley (Northumberland's second youngest son) were all executed for treason. The rest of the Dudley family was stripped of its ranks and titles, his other sons being imprisoned in the Tower of London. Had it not been for the intervention of Queen Mary's husband, Philip II of Spain, they too might have been executed. As it was, they remained in prison until September 1554.

Also held prisoner in the Tower and in fear of her life was Queen Mary's younger sister Elizabeth, who had to hide her Protestant leanings or face execution as a heretic. Her imprisonment in the Tower, however, had other consequences. During their shared captivity, when they both feared for their lives, she became close to Robert Dudley, one of the late Duke's younger sons, and they would meet for walks. She had, of course, known him since she was eight, but this shared adversity drew them together. Whether they later became lovers is still a matter of debate. However, there is no doubting that Robert Dudley was the love of Elizabeth's life, and under different circumstances they would probably have married. But these were not normal times; external circumstances, the scandal over the death of Robert Dudley's first wife and her fear of allowing any man to become king made this an impossibility. She did, however, shower her favourite with gifts, and in 1564, she awarded him the title of Earl of Leicester.

Elizabeth was a highly intelligent and very well educated woman who, like Leicester and his sister Mary Dudley (the wife of Sir Henry Sidney), had studied mathematics under the tutelage of Dr John Dee. A Renaissance 'Magus' of the first order, Dee was a polymath who combined *bona fide* science with what is now labelled as pseudo science: pursuits such as alchemy, astrology and even spiritualism. In 1555, this landed him in hot water when he was accused of using black magic to try to kill Queen Mary. In fact, all he had done was draw up her horoscope and show it to her sister Elizabeth. It is not recorded whether they inferred the date of Mary's death (17 November 1558) from that. What is true is that he subsequently advised Elizabeth on the most astrologically propitious day on which to hold her coronation (15 January 1559). Despite the fact that she was a constant target for assassins throughout her reign, and yet she went on to have one of the longest reigns of any British monarch (she died on 24 March 1603), it could be argued that Dee picked the right day.

In many ways, Dee was ahead of his time. The dissolution of the monasteries had led to the loss of their libraries, an important resource for anyone doing serious research. When he couldn't interest Queen Mary in the project of setting up a new, national library, he developed one of his own. His house in Mortlake (in South West London) became home to the largest collection of books in the kingdom. It was also the centre of an intellectual circle that included Sir Francis Drake, Sir Humphrey Gilbert, his brother Adrian Gilbert and their half-brother Sir Walter Raleigh. Other members of the group were the Earl of Leicester, his sister Mary, her two eldest sons, Philip and Robert Sidney, and her daughter, Mary Sidney.

This informal group, sometimes referred to as the 'Dee circle', made up what amounted to an esoteric school with Dee as their teacher. From him, they learned such arcane pursuits as astrology, alchemy and geometry.

However, his interests went beyond mathematics and even the occult. Although born in London, Dee was of Welsh stock, and he too believed himself to be descended from the ancient kings of Britain. He also knew of a legend that, long before the time of Columbus, a Prince called Madoc had sailed to North America and claimed it for Gwynedd or North Wales. Because Queen Elizabeth was a granddaughter of Henry VII who was descended from the Royal House of Gwynedd, it could be argued that this Welsh claim to North America, which predates Spanish claims by several centuries, now rested with her. On this basis, regardless of objections from the Pope or the King of Spain, she was entitled to issue licences for exploration and settlement in this new world.

In this context, Dee's geometry (he wrote a much-acclaimed foreword to Henry Billingsley's 1570 translation of Euclid's *Elements*) also had a practical purpose. He was a close friend of the Flemish cartographer Geradus Marcator, whose 'projection' is still used in map-making today. A knowledge of geometry was an essential skill in the growing field of navigation using such maps. The geometric skills that Dee taught to such early English explorers as Drake, the Gilberts and Raleigh gave them a necessary tool for the exploration of the coast of North America and, in Drake's case, for circumnavigating the world.

In 1577, Dee wrote a textbook on the subject, *General and Rare Memorials Pertaining to the Perfect Art of Navigation*. This, however, was not a course in navigation as such, but a political treatise. In this, Dee expounded his belief that England needed to build a 'British Empire' in the Americas. The justification for this call for Imperialism – it was the first time anyone had written of a British Empire – was both Elizabeth's 'Arthurian' descent and the fact that, with the abolition of Catholicism, the British Church (according to this view) had been purified. To help with the realization of his vision, Dee introduced potential investors such as the Queen and Northumberland to adventurers daring enough to actually attempt to set up colonies. Although the early attempts by the Gilbert brothers (in Newfoundland) and Walter Raleigh (in Virginia) ended in failure, these 16th-century experimental colonies opened the way for the more successful settlements of the 17th century that ultimately resulted in the USA and Canada.

Having taken over the throne, Elizabeth lost no time in bringing key members of Dee's circle to her court. Robert Dudley was immediately made her Master of the Horse and, in 1559, Knight of the Garter and Privy Councillor. Sir Henry Sidney, who had been a close friend of Edward VI throughout the latter's life – indeed the boy King died in his arms – was appointed Lord Lieutenant of Ireland. He was there before, and probably realized that this was a poisoned chalice for any aspiring courtier. However, he needed a job and this was what was on offer.

Much to the annoyance of the Queen, Sidney's attempts at quashing successive Irish rebellions proved futile. Furthermore, as stationing an army in Ireland was costing her a great deal of money, Elizabeth was always reluctant to pay him what he was owed. As a result, the Sidneys were always short of cash, so much so that Sir Henry was forced to turn down the offer of a baronetcy as he knew he couldn't afford to live up to being a Lord. A more genial task proved to be that of President of the Council of Wales, which he held from 1560 until his death in 1586. As we shall see, this connection with Wales was to have profound consequences not just for him but for the future of his family.

Sir Henry Sidney's wife Mary Dudley, another member of the Dee circle, was a very close confidante of the Queen. She was a highly intelligent woman who spoke Latin, French and Italian fluently; it was undoubtedly she who was responsible for inculcating a love of learning in her children. In 1562, she showed how much she loved and cared for the Queen when she took on the dangerous task of nursing her through smallpox. She carried out her duties without complaint, deeming it an honour to serve her Queen in this way. Elizabeth recovered, but, inevitably, her nurse Mary caught smallpox from her. Although she too recovered, it is said that it left her so disfigured that thereafter she covered her face with a veil.

Leicester, the Queen's favourite, was close to his sister Mary and was a frequent visitor to the Sidney's family home of Penshurst. In due course, he brought Mary's dazzling eldest son Philip to court. To say that Sir Philip Sidney was a celebrity is probably to underestimate his charismatic appeal both in England and throughout Europe. Like his mother, he was a good linguist and this led him, at an early age, to be employed by Sir Francis Walsingham, Elizabeth's Chief of Intelligence. His formal role was that of diplomat, but he was also a spy. In these two capacities he made a number of European trips.

This could be dangerous work, and indeed, Philip went through a baptism of fire when, at the age of 17, he found himself in Paris during the St Barthomew's Day Massacre. The day, 24 August 1572, should have been a cause for celebration. It was hoped that the marriage of a Protestant, Henry of Navarre (later Henry IV of France) to the Catholic sister of the King would heal France's religious divide. In the event, riots broke out and thousands of Protestants, in Paris to celebrate the wedding, were slaughtered by rampaging mobs. Sir Philip Sidney and Sir Francis Walsingham, who was with him, were lucky to escape with their lives. Both were deeply shocked by what they had seen, and it left a lasting impression with them that would influence England's foreign policy.

The Dee circle was not just about navigation, magic and politics. Collectively, its members engineered a revolution in English letters. Sir Philip Sidney is most famous today as one of England's greatest poets, but he was by no means the only one in the family. His sister Mary wrote poetry and so did his younger brother Robert. His own reputation owes as much to Mary as himself; after his death she carefully edited his poems and saw to it that they were published.

Mary Sidney took after her mother, being exceptionally intelligent, well educated and, like her brother Philip, gifted at languages: she is said to have spoken Latin, French, Italian, Greek and Welsh as well as being at least familiar with Spanish and Hebrew. Her childhood was spent between the family seat at Penshurst and Ludlow Castle, in the border county of Shropshire, where her father presided as Chairman of the Council of Wales. In addition to her academic studies, she learnt how to ride with hounds, hunt with a hawk, shoot with a bow, use a tennis racquet and play the popular game of bowls. As a well-bred woman, she was taught poetry and rhetoric from an early age and was expected to learn enough 'Physic' (medicine) as might be needed in due course by the lady of a large household. It went without saying that she learnt how to sing, play the lute and compose melodies of her own. If ever there was a Renaissance woman, it was her!

At age 13, Queen Elizabeth invited Mary to join the court, where she was a maid of honour for a short time. Delicately featured rather than pretty, we can imagine that even at this age she had charisma. This was certainly noticed by Sir Henry Herbert, 2nd Earl of Pembroke and the richest widower in England if not Europe. Therefore, it was only natural for her uncle, Robert Dudley, to negotiate a highly advantageous marriage for her with his old friend. Although Henry Herbert was 23 years older than she, this was not so unusual for the aristocracy of the time. Indeed, they seem to have had a relatively happy marriage, producing four children, three of whom survived to adulthood.

Mary Sidney, now known as the Countess of Pembroke, had been keen on theatre all her life. With her marriage to one of the richest men in the kingdom, she was in a position to become, in the Earl's name, a major patron of the arts. Their home, Wilton House, was at the epicentre of an artistic and linguistic revolution. It was probably at Mary's instigation that the Earl sponsored William Shakespeare's company, which was accordingly known as 'Pembroke's Men'. The connection with Shakespeare continued, and when the first folio of his works was published, in 1623, it was dedicated to the 'incomparable pair', the Countess' sons – William Herbert, 3rd Earl of Pembroke, and his brother Philip, Earl of Montgomery and, later on, 4th Earl of Pembroke. The printing began in February 1621, just weeks after the death of their mother. She, meanwhile, was recently identified in a quite extraordinary book, *Sweet Swan of Avon*, as the real author of Shakespeare's plays. Discussion of the Shakespeare authorship question goes far beyond the present work. However, it is worth noting that the plays themselves imply a combination of high intelligence, advanced knowledge of poetic metre, access to very obscure books (some only available in foreign languages), detailed knowledge of courtly life and a great sympathy for women. The Countess of Pembroke fits the bill on all these counts and more. She also knew the jobbing actor Shakespeare personally and would have had a motive for keeping her identity secret behind his.

Be that as it may, she is best remembered today for editing and publishing the poems of her brother, Sir Philip Sidney, whose untimely death resulted indirectly from the St Bartholomew's Day Massacre, which had a profound effect upon English policy. In 1577, he was sent by Queen Elizabeth to Prague to convey her condolences to Rudolf II, the newly crowned Holy Roman Emperor, on the death of his father. Philip used this trip as an excuse to travel extensively through Germany, then divided into a multiplicity of small principalities. His orders were to sound out the more important of the avowedly Protestant princes to see if they would be willing to join an informal alliance aimed at curtailing the Catholic powers of France, Spain and the Hapsburg Empire. As a further inducement, willing princes were to be offered the enticing possibility of being elected to the Order of the Garter, the most prestigious in Europe. The garter collar was, of course, composed of interlinked Tudor Roses and this has led to a now widespread belief (first put forward by the historian Dame Frances Yates) that the 'Rosicrucian Brotherhood', which was to go public in Germany a generation later, was somehow connected with the Order of the Garter.

Sir Philip found the warmest response to these overtures in Heidelberg, the capital of a small, Rhineland province called the Palatinate. Sir Philip's visit started a friendship between England and the Palatinate that would have profound consequences for all of Europe. He also met up with William of Orange, the leader of the Dutch rebellion against Spain. On his return, he proposed to the Queen that England should back William and help the Protestant Dutch break free from Spanish rule. She had long been sceptical of such involvement, but eventually, in 1585, agreed to send a small army under the command of his uncle, the Earl of Leicester. Unsurprisingly, Sir

Philip Sidney went over to Holland with this expeditionary force, and in due course he was appointed Governor of the city of Flushing, which was then in the frontline of the insurrection. Disaster struck the following year. In the Battle of Zutphen, his thigh was shattered by a musket ball. Ten days later, the unthinkable happened: Sir Philip Sidney died from gangrene.

The whole of Europe mourned his passing as though Lancelot himself had died on that battlefield, but this was only the final chapter in what turned out to be an *annus horribilis* for the Sidney family. In May, his father, Sir Henry Sidney, died, exhausted but little the richer for all his years of service to the Crown. A few weeks later, his wife, Lady Mary, who had never fully recovered her health after the smallpox, also passed over. Now their son and heir had been killed in battle. It was as though the gods themselves had conspired against the Sidneys and were punishing them for some unknown failing.

Following Sir Philip's death, the new head of the family was his brother Robert. He was Sir Henry's second son and had also been present at Zutphen. Two years later, on 4 September 1588 and just weeks after the destruction of the Spanish Armada, Robert Dudley, the Earl of Leicester, also died. His death was sudden and unexpected, but is thought to have been the result of malaria.

For the young Robert Sidney, this last tragedy was also an opportunity. Leicester's only son and one-time heir had predeceased him by several years. Now, even though his lands were to go to an illegitimate son, Robert could confidently expect to inherit his titles. However, as long as the old Queen lived, this did not happen. For whatever reason, Elizabeth, always stingy about giving honours, refused to give him the titles. It was not until James I came onto the throne that he was rewarded with the family titles of Viscount De L'Isle and Earl of Leicester. The reason for this snub was not obvious, but further investigation uncovered the extraordinary fact that it was Sir Robert Sidney and not his brother Philip who was destined to stand at the epicentre of the Rosicrucian mystery.

CHAPTER 32

The Lady of Penshurst

I was intrigued by the paradoxical situation in which the Sidney family now found itself. Having been close to the Crown for generations, it seemed as though Sir Robert Sidney was definitely out of favour with the Queen. It was true that she had had her reservations in the past with regard to Sir Philip Sidney, even banishing him from the court for a while for challenging the Earl of Oxford, his superior, to a duel over the use of a tennis court. However, his brother Robert was a much less flamboyant character, and she must have known him all his life. Why, then, the snub? Was it just that now her favourite, Robert Dudley, was dead she couldn't bear to call another Robert by the title 'Leicester', or was it something else? Sensing that there was indeed a mystery here, I decided to do some investigations of my own, my first port of call being the village of Penshurst.

Little did I realize that this would put me onto a new path and ultimately lead to a new understanding of the Rosy-cross and its connection not just with Wales but with the deepest, most esoteric secret of Christianity itself: the expectation of a new messiah.

It was with some difficulty that I eventually found the entrance to Penshurst Place. What lay before me was an enormous house, with fantastic gardens and echoes of Hampton Court. To call Penshurst impressive would be an understatement.

The connection with Hampton Court was no accident, as Henry VIII, who is most closely associated with that palace, also made use of Penshurst.

Indeed, he stayed there while courting his second wife, Anne Boleyn, the mother of Queen Elizabeth I. Standing in the Great Hall, a wonderful space that has been used as a location in many movies, it was easy to imagine him sitting at table, gorging on venison and throwing the bones to his dogs. Upstairs was also impressive, with its library, billiards room, corridors and drawing rooms. What astounded me most, though, was a dining room, the walls of which were hung with pictures of the family.

Leaving the house, I walked to the village church where generations of Sidneys lie buried. The entrance was on its south side, hidden behind several 12th- or 13th-century cottages. Held together by ancient oak beams, they were, surprisingly, still occupied; indeed, one of them seemed to be in use as a post office, a notice of opening times still attached to an ancient post box. The antiquity of these buildings, which framed an enclosed passageway leading from the main road to the church, added to a sense of the mysterious. They seemed to be designed to distract attention from a church containing such a big secret that nobody even knew it existed.

This feeling was heightened further when, having entered the church itself, I walked over to the bell tower. This was attached to the western end of the church, but what was of interest here was not the bells, hidden from view anyway, but rather two memorial stones attached to the walls. One of these was a version of a 'tree cross' with what should have been a wheel around its upper section, except that the quadrants of its circular design had been transposed to opposite corners. The effect was to give the impression of a secret or reverse wheel cross, a type I had never seen before.

On the opposite wall was an even more remarkable stone, which appeared to be part of the lid of a sarcophagus. It featured a floriated cross with the ends of its limbs trifurcated. Hidden behind the cross was the figure of a woman, her eyes shut and hands joined in an attitude of prayer. Wearing what appeared to be medieval dress – perhaps from the 14th or 15th century, judging by her appearance – she was positioned in such a way that the central crossing of the floriated cross was placed exactly over her heart. This figure, I discovered, is known locally as the 'Lady of Penshurst'.

Figure 5: Lady of Penshurst

What was also interesting was that the design of this elaborate cross had been taken and used as a motif throughout the church. It was featured in a stained-glass window, on the altar cloth, and above all on the portable cross that is carried in procession before the priest at the start of services. From the evidence all around me, it was clear that the design on this coffin lid was considered significant. I couldn't help thinking that this was not just because the Lady of Penshurst stone had artistic merit. I suspected that it symbolized something important, something which only those 'with the eyes to see' would understand.

I left the bell tower and, at the back of the church proper, came upon a baptismal font. Unusually for such an object, it was brightly painted, gaudily so. According to a booklet I picked up, the font dated from the 15th century. If this is true, then it is quite likely that the Sidney brothers, Philip and Robert, and their sister Mary, Countess of Pembroke, were all baptized in it. What struck my attention, though, was that it had four shields carved on it, and one of these was very similar to the plaques in Llandaff Cathedral. Like them, it carried a representation of the implements used at the Crucifixion. Was this a universal motif in England as well as in Wales? As I had not come across it before, I didn't think so. Certainly, it seemed odd to have a design associated with the Crucifixion emblazoned on a baptismal font, an object not associated with Jesus' death but rather his baptism in the Jordan. It seemed very odd, and I began to suspect that this design also concealed a deeper mystery than was obvious to the casual viewer.

Leaving the font, I walked up the central aisle of the church towards the high altar. Here, I found myself at the entrance of a side chapel that, like the Mathew Chapel in Llandaff, had once been the private preserve of the Lords of the Manor. In this case, this meant the Sidney family, and here there were a number of tombs and other monuments belonging to them. Some of these were highly ornate, dating from the 18th century when the family's fortunes were riding high.

My attention, however, was drawn to a much simpler affair, which also appeared to be the oldest of these tombs. It stood against the outside wall of the church, made mostly of white limestone, although with a large, black horizontal slab covering the lower portion. A long inscription indicated that it had originally been set up in honour of Sir Henry Sidney, the founder of the Penshurst dynasty, but it seemed to have served as a family mausoleum for several subsequent generations. Placed on it were various heraldic badges, but my attention was immediately drawn to one of these showing two coats of arms impaled together. The dexter or right-hand side of this shield was emblazoned with the arms of Sidney: azure (blue) background emblazoned with a pheon d'or (golden broad arrow). It was, however, the second coat that startled me, for clear as day, here were depicted the arms of Iestyn ap Gwrgan, *argent three chevrons gules*.

This was not the only place in the chapel where the arms of Iestyn were on display. The ceiling, which looked as though it had been repainted fairly recently (actually during church restorations carried out in 1966), featured what looked like grapevines. However, the fruits of these vines were not bunches of grapes but rather heraldic shields. I recognized several of the arms on these shields as belonging to prominent Welsh families. Again, one bore the arms of Iestyn and another the arms of Sidney.

It was clear that the 'vines' represented the Sidney family tree, the many shields symbolizing the families with which it was related through marriage. Clearly, someone had married a descendant of Iestyn ap Gwrgan. This raised the question: how had a member of the Sidney family, who lived in Kent, come to meet and marry someone who was entitled to make use of the arms of a Welsh king? Who was she and when did this happen?

Actually, it didn't take much research to work this out, but in doing so, I found clues to the origins of the mysterious memorial stones at the back of the church (the inverted wheel cross and the Lady of Penshurst). It also answered another enigma: after Robert Dudley's death in 1588, why had Queen Elizabeth I been so reluctant to pass on his titles to his nephew Robert Sidney? Granted, this nephew was a sister's son and not a brother's, in which case inheritance of the titles would have been automatic. But even so, Robert Sidney was not just Dudley's nephew but the surviving son of Mary Dudley, who, at great cost to her own health, had nursed the Queen through smallpox. Add to this the long military career of her husband, Sir Henry Sidney, who had served the Crown in Ireland as well as in Wales, and it seemed odd behaviour, even for Queen Elizabeth, that she should fail to reward the Sidney family with Leicester's titles. The mystery of the Sidneys was getting deeper by the minute.

CHAPTER 33

Robert Sidney and the Rosicrucian Furore

A little more investigation indicated that the answer to this conundrum probably lay in South Wales. It turned out that, in 1584, Robert Sidney married a lady called Barbara Gamage. She, it seemed, was the heiress of Coity, a tiny but valuable Lordship in Glamorgan. This would not have mattered to the Queen had not the young couple disobeyed express orders from her. Barbara's father had recently died, and she was to be made a ward of court. Her fate (ie who she would marry) was to be decided by both the Queen and her ministers. Letters to this effect were dispatched by Sir Francis Walsingham to her guardian, an older cousin called Sir Edward Stradling, demanding that she be brought to London forthwith. Stradling, however, pretended the letters had not arrived and, instead, acted boldly in what he clearly believed was in her own best interests. Ignoring both Walsingham's threats and the entreaties of other suitors, he quickly arranged for her to be married to Robert Sidney. He did this, or so it would appear, for the very best of reasons: the mutual love of bride and groom.

Attending the wedding, which was held at Stradling's home of St Donat's Castle, also in Glamorgan, was none other than Henry Herbert, the 2nd Earl of Pembroke. He supported the marriage and, indeed, at the behest of Robert's uncle, the Earl of Leicester, may well have arranged it. Fortunately, once Walsingham discovered that the groom was none other than the brother of his own son-in-law (Sir Philip Sidney was by now married to his daughter), he changed his attitude entirely. It is clear from his subsequent letters to Stradling that he, at least, was delighted to have this wealthy heiress joining the family of his daughter's in-laws. Therefore, we can be sure that he did his level best to mollify the Queen for any perceived snub. Nevertheless, she was someone you crossed at your peril and she also had a very long memory. It seems likely, therefore, that this precipitate marriage, done without her permission, was the principal reason that when Leicester died, she refused to pass on his titles to his nephew. Sir Robert Sidney had to wait until the accession of James I before being created Baron Sidney (1603), Viscount De L'Isle (1605) and finally Earl of Leicester (1618).

Now I found all of this very interesting, not least the light it shed on the origins of Rosicrucianism. As we have seen, though not as famous as his brother Philip, Robert Sidney was a member of Dee's circle of former pupils. As the surviving brother of Mary Sidney Herbert, the Countess of Pembroke, he was a frequent visitor to Wilton House and a friend of her husband Henry Herbert, the Earl of Pembroke. This means that he was also directly connected to their Shakespearean circle of 'proto Rosicrucian' poets we discussed in an earlier chapter. However, this was not his only significant involvement with Rosicrucianism and possibly not the most important either.

In an earlier book of mine, *London: A New Jerusalem*, I investigated the influence of Rosicrucian ideas on both the advancement of science in Britain during the mid 17th century and the birth of modern Freemasonry. As far as Rosicrucianism itself is concerned, the core event of the 17th century was the publication of the *Fama* and *Confessio* pamphlets between 1614 and 1616. As discussed, the affair of the Rosicrucian pamphlets turned into a major furore that greatly annoyed some and intrigued others. Robert Sidney did not admit to being directly involved himself. However, he knew some of the people who almost certainly were, and there are good reasons for thinking that he knew a lot more on what Rosicrucianism was really about than he let on.

In 1972, Dame Frances Yates of the Warburg Institute of London University, one of the most eminent historians of her day, published a seminal work on the subject, *The Rosicrucian Enlightenment*. In this book, still the most important on this subject to appear in the English language, she argued that the Rosicrucian pamphlets emanated from the German city of Heidelberg, the capital of the Palatinate. This is interesting, as they could not have been published without the covert if not open blessing of the Elector Palatine, the ruler of this small Protestant state. What concerns us is that the Elector at the time was Frederick V, and he was married to Princess Elizabeth Stuart, the daughter of King James I of Great Britain.

Frederick and Elizabeth's marriage, on St Valentine's Day, 14 February 1613, was more than just the union of two people: it was the culmination of a plan for a pan-Protestant alliance between Great Britain, the Netherlands and some of the statelets of Germany. This had long been proposed by the Walsingham faction at the former court of Queen Elizabeth, and negotiating such an alliance had been the main purpose of Sir Philip Sidney's European journeys of the 1570s. His untimely death and Queen Elizabeth's coolness towards getting England involved in expensive European wars poured cold water on the idea of such an alliance, especially after the defeat of the Spanish Armada (1588) reduced the threat of England's imminent invasion by Spain. However, the assassination in 1610 of Henry IV of France (whose marriage in 1572 precipitated the St Bartholomew's Day Massacre) renewed the threat to Protestant England. Because of this, James I was open to persuasion that England should find allies in Germany to counterbalance the growing power of Catholic France. Accordingly, he favoured the idea of his daughter, Elizabeth, marrying Frederick, even though he was a relatively minor prince and she had been courted earlier by the King of Sweden.

By the time the wedding took place, both Sir Philip Sidney and Robert Dudley, Earl of Leicester, had been dead for over 20 years. However, Sir Robert Sidney, by now holding the deceased Earl of Leicester's junior title of Viscount De L'Isle, was in a key position to influence events. Following his brother Philip's death in 1586, he took over the position as Governor of

Flushing, and his connection with Holland continued unabated until he relinquished the post in 1616. At the time of the wedding he was in far better favour with King James than he had ever been with Queen Elizabeth and so could influence events. Although Flushing lies on the mouth of the River Scheldt, it has relatively easy access to the Rhine. We may assume, therefore, that Sir Robert Sidney was given a role – possibly informal – to keep an eye on James's daughter and to help her should she find herself in trouble.

In 1619, trouble came with a vengeance. Regarding it as his duty but against all good advice, her husband Frederick accepted the poisoned chalice that was the Crown of Bohemia, thereby triggering the war of religion that Elizabeth had feared so greatly. For although he was crowned in Prague, an army was immediately mobilized by the Catholic Holy Roman Emperor. Despite being an Austrian and living in Vienna, he was a Hapsburg, and they regarded the Crown of Bohemia as their own possession. Frederick's forces were no match for the Imperial army, and they were comprehensively defeated in the Battle of the White Mountain. As a result, he and his wife Elizabeth, now Queen of Bohemia, had no choice but to flee Prague, leaving many of their most prized possessions behind. Furthermore, a second army, this time from Spain, invaded the Palatinate and sacked Heidelberg itself. This meant there was no going home for the Royal couple. They were forced to find sanctuary in exile, living in The Hague from now on.

Robert Sidney, like everyone else in England, could only watch with horror as the Protestant rebellion in Germany was crushed. An old man by this time, he could do little, especially as despite his earlier agreements, King James did not mind whether he became involved. However, the Sidneys remained good friends with Queen Elizabeth of Bohemia and her family.

Sidney's eldest son Robert, who, in 1626, became the 2nd Sidney Earl of Leicester, was closer still. By this time, Charles I had taken the throne in England, and he charged the Earl of Leicester with the fruitless task of negotiating a settlement that would allow his sister Elizabeth, her husband Frederick and their family to be restored to their ruling position in the Palatinate. Such a restoration was eventually enacted under the terms of the Treaty of Westphalia (1648), but by this time Charles had lost his own throne and would be executed the following year.

In 1661, the now widowed Elizabeth, who had remained in The Hague even after her eldest son was restored to his patrimony in Heidelberg, returned to England. She came back home to congratulate her nephew Charles II on his own Restoration, but evidence of her continuing close friendship with the Sidney family is shown by the fact that she stayed not at St James's Palace but Leicester House. This was a large mansion that the 2nd Earl had built on the north side of what is now Leicester Square. Today all traces of this house have gone. It has been replaced by cinemas, restaurants and perhaps some rather less salubrious establishments. Yet it was here, on 13 February 1662, that she died, a day short of the 48th anniversary of her wedding to Frederick and just around the corner from where her own portrait now hangs in the National Portrait Gallery.

Taking all the above evidence into consideration, it became clear to me that it was no accident that Penshurst Church contains Rosicrucian symbolism. The question remained, though: who influenced whom? Were Rosicrucian influences imported from Europe in the 17th century or did they ultimately derive from Wales, being transmitted to Europe by the Sidneys and their associates? As there was only one way to answer this question, I decided I would have to visit Coity, the home of Countess Barbara Gamage before she defied Queen Elizabeth's orders and married the young Robert Sidney.

CHAPTER 34

Coity and the Search for the Real Glastonbury

A quick look at a map revealed that Coity Castle, where Lady Barbara grew up, was only a few miles from the church on the hill where Wilson and Blackett unearthed their Arthurian relics in 1991. This again seemed more than coincidental. Could she, I wondered, have brought something more than just a fortune to the Sidney family? Might she have passed on a secret, something known only to members of her own family? Could this secret explain the presence of the Arthurian relics that Wilson and Blackett found at the ruined church? Suspecting that this might be the case, I made my own plans for a visit to Coity and its surrounding area.

The name Coity, Coitty or Coety, as it is variously spelt, is said to come from the Welsh word *Coedydd*, meaning an area of uncleared woodland or forest. Although only vestiges of this forest remain today, the land owned by the Lordship of Coity was once heavily wooded, as proven by many Welsh names that apply to places in the vicinity. A brief glance at an Ordnance Survey map for the area reveals names such as *Cefn Hirgoed* (Long Wood Ridge), *Derwen Goppa* (Oak Tree Hilltop), *Coed Parc Garw* (Roughland Wood), *Pen yr Allt* (Grove Top) and *Pencoed* (Head of the Wood). Nearby, too, was *Coed-y-Mwstwr* (Bustle Wood), the location of a cave I once visited with Alan Wilson. Although I have not explored this cave in depth myself, he told me of a legend that a tunnel runs from it for about a mile underground, leading directly to Coity Castle. I have little idea whether this tunnel is a natural feature or, more likely in my opinion, the remains of an old mine that was abandoned in antiquity. However, the cave itself is clearly ancient and, at the time of King Arthur, may have been used as a hermitage.

Certainly, Alan believed this to be the case. He told me that he was convinced that this was the cave once occupied by St Illtyd at the time he was shown St David's bell. He also believed that it had been used by Illtyd as a temporary burial place for King Arthur prior to his interment at St Peter's-on-the-hill. I didn't know if he was right about any of this, but the fact that the tunnel ran in the direction of Coity Castle seemed significant. For, if true, it implied there might be some sort of connection between Coity and the old church on the hill, and this seemed worthy of further investigation.

Realizing that the marriage of Robert Sidney to Lady Barbara Gamage was a possible link between the Continental Rosicrucianism of the 17th century and Welsh traditions linked to medieval and Dark Age 'Rosy-cross' memorial stones in Glamorgan, I decided it was high time I investigated the history both of this small town, which is now a suburb of Bridgend, and of the surrounding district. To my surprise, I discovered that not only did the Lordship of Coity have a unique history, but it also had a special status as the last Welsh 'kingdom' to have been held independently of the English Crown. In fact, during the Middle Ages it had been a sort of 'Monte Carlo': a tax-free sovereign statelet. In addition, the Lords of Coity had traced their bloodline back to Iestyn ap Gwrgan, the last king of Glamorgan. This explained the presence of Iestyn's arms on the ceiling of the Sidney Chapel at Penshurst impaled with their own arms, the broad arrow, on the family tomb; clearly, the Sidneys were proud of the ancient-British Royal Blood in their veins. However, I was not yet aware of the full and quite extraordinary significance of this. Investigating further, I discovered that at the time of Iestyn, Coity was already a Royal Lordship; indeed, it was probably established as such centuries earlier. Not surprisingly, it changed hands at the time of the Norman invasion of 1092, but it did so in a unique way.

As discussed, Sir Robert Fitzhammon, the Earl of Gloucester, seized the Vale of Glamorgan from Iestyn and rewarded his 'twelve knights of despoliation' with the various manors and castles that were now at his disposal. However, one of these knights, Sir Paine de Turbeville, was left out of this sharing of the spoils. Perhaps for personal reasons – allegedly, he once had a fist fight with Fitzhammon during which he hit the latter so hard that he was left deaf in one ear – Turbeville was given nothing and told to find his own rewards. Accordingly, he did just that by laying siege to Coity Castle.

This castle, which was on the northern fringes of the Vale, was in the possession of a great-grandson of Iestyn called Morgan. A sensible man, he could see that resisting the Normans was likely to lead to unnecessary bloodshed. Accordingly, he came out from his castle, holding his sword in his right hand and his daughter Assar's (Sara's) right hand in his left. He challenged Turbeville to either fight with him for the castle in single combat or to marry Assar and receive it peacefully. In this way, no blood needed to be shed and Sir Paine would have the castle as a dowry. Turbeville was not a fool and realized that, having fallen out with Fitzhammon, he needed new allies. There is also good reason to think that he was not originally from Normandy but Brittany. The people living there, the Bretons, are close relatives of the Welsh and spoke (and still speak) a very similar language. If he truly was a Breton, then Turbeville would have been able to understand exactly what Morgan was proposing. In any event, he married the girl and in this way became Lord of Coity.

Now this marriage had profound and unforeseen consequences. Because Sir Paine received his Lordship as a marriage dowry and not as a gift from Fitzhammon, he was not legally obliged to pay taxes either to him or to the English Crown. Instead, he paid a token amount of one gold coin a year to a neighbouring Welsh prince, another descendant of Iestyn's. This tax-free status for Coity endured until about 1405.*

* See Chart 13: The Royal Lords of Coity to the First Gamage, page 236

The Turbeville family retained the Lordship of Coity until 1360, when Sir Richard II de Turbeville died without leaving issue. As he was the last surviving male of his family, he was succeeded as Lord of Coity by Sir Lawrence Berkerolles, the son of his sister Katherine. Then, in 1400, Wales was convulsed by the Owen Glendower rebellion. During this time, virtually all the castles of South Wales, with the notable exception of Coity, were put to the torch. Sir Lawrence, who was still the local Lord, sat out a long siege. He was eventually rescued by a force commanded by Prince Hal, the future Henry V. After this, Coity lost its tax-free status, becoming in this respect like any other small Lordship in England and Wales.

Sir Lawrence Berkerolles died in 1411, allegedly murdered by his wife Mathilde le Despencer. The story goes that she confessed and was punished by being buried alive, with just her head above ground. Left there to die slowly, her sister, Isabel, visited her daily. She would wear a dress with a long train and allow this to drag along the ground so that it would collect dew. As they talked, Mathilde, dying from thirst, could then suck the dew from the hem of the dress and get some small relief from her raging thirst. When, eventually, she did die, her ghost remained earthbound. Local legends call her the 'White Lady', and evidently she still haunts the crossroads by St Athans, where she was buried.

As she and Sir Lawrence had no children, a tussle now took place over who should inherit Coity. Eventually it passed to Sarah, the youngest of the late Richard II de Turbeville's sisters, who was married to William Gamage of Rogiate in Gwent. The Lordship then stayed in the Gamage family until 1584 when John Gamage, the father of Lady Barbara Gamage, died. As his only legitimate heir, she inherited the Lordship, its castle, lands, coal mines and other properties. Following her marriage, all this wealth came with her to her husband, Robert Sidney.*

---

* See Chart 14: The Gamages of Coity, page 238

CHAPTER 35

Coity and the Church on the Hill

During the late Medieval period (and probably long before this), the church of St Peter's-on-the-hill was also under the jurisdiction of the Lords of Coity. This means that the upkeep of this church would have been the responsibility of first the Turbevilles, then the Berkrolles and finally the Gamages, before, following the Reformation of the 1530s, it passed into the hands of the Church of England in Wales. Even then, as the local nobility, the Lords of Coity were expected to look after it as its patrons. This long association means they would surely have known all about any Arthurian connections the church may have had. In any case, the Gamages had family actually living in the village of *Llanbedr*. A distant cousin of Lady Barbara Gamage, the poet William Gamage was born there. He wrote a long poem, *Linsey-woolsie*, and dedicated this to the Sidneys.

The facts, therefore, are clear. For hundreds of years, Coity Castle was the administrative centre of a largely wooded area. Included in the territory and ruled by the Lordship was *Mynydd-y-gaer*, with its 'Arthurian' church of St Peter's-on-the-hill.

This connection made me suspect there might be more secrets associated with Coity. Therefore, I was keen to carry out further investigations to see if I could work out just what these might be. In our book *The Holy Kingdom*, my co-authors and I presented evidence showing that the Glastonbury of

Arthurian legend could not have been located in Somerset. We concluded that this was a myth spread around by medieval monks to attract pilgrims (with their cash!) to visit Glastonbury Abbey. My co-authors proposed that the real 'Glastonbury' was near Lichfield in the West Midlands. They were very keen on this idea; however, I had my reservations. As a result of my current researches, I was beginning to suspect that the original 'Glastonbury' was much closer to Somerset, being located in Glamorgan. The question was: where?

William of Malmesbury, a medieval historian whose work we have already encountered, suggests that the name Glastonbury was derived from *ynys witrin* or 'glassy island'. Although I don't speak Welsh, I know enough to realize that this is nonsense. According to several books in my possession, the Welsh name for Glastonbury was *Aberglaston*. When I analysed this name, it became clear that, contrary to what William of Malmesbury surmised, the root word *glas* has nothing to do with the English word 'glass' or its Latin equivalent '*vitrum*'. In actuality, *glas* means blue or green-grey, the colour of either the sea or a woodland canopy. The Welsh word *Glaston* is possibly derived from *glastennen*, which is still used in the closely related Cornish language as the name of a certain type of oak tree. The literal meaning of *glastennen* would appear to be 'blue tanning', which would be because oak trees of this variety were used for tanning leather (*tennen*), while a blue dye (*glas*) was also produced from their galls. Since *aber* means the confluence or exit point of a river, it follows that the place name *Aberglaston* must have referred to a wooded district with oak trees, close to a confluence of two rivers. This is patently not true of Glastonbury in Somerset, which, in ancient times, was marshland with a few hilltops standing proud as islands. There may have been a few oak trees growing on these islands, but the area was not woodland as such. Also, there is no river in the vicinity of Glastonbury. What appears to be a small river today is actually a drainage ditch which dates back only as far as the 17th century when the fenland swamp was drained so that there would be more arable land available for crops or cattle. It follows, therefore, that there could be no confluence of rivers either at or near Glastonbury, and neither was there an estuary. Thus, the appellation *aber* would have been entirely inappropriate.

At Coity, the situation was quite the opposite. As we have seen, the name means 'wooded land', and even today there are a substantial number of oak trees growing in the area. Although not exactly an *aber* (confluence) itself, it is placed midway between the Rivers Ogmore and Ewenny. Furthermore, the Ewenny (the 'Whitened River') has its sources on *Mynydd-y-gaer*, one of these fairly close to the Church of St Peter's-on-the-hill. There is also a recorded connection in the area with St Joseph of Arimathea, the supposed founder of the church at Glastonbury. As we have seen, he is usually called St Ilid in Welsh texts, and the Ewenny River has its sources close to Llanilid ('enclosure or church of Ilid'). Here, there is an ancient earth-bank circle called *y gaer gron*, 'the circular fortress'. In fact, this was not a defensive ring but rather a henge monument or 'sacred circle'. It is of a type that can be seen at other places in the British Isles such as Avebury and Stonehenge in Wiltshire and Knowlton Rings in Dorset. In pre-Christian times, such rings were used as open-air churches. Our word 'church', of course, comes from the Latin word *circus*, which means circle. In those days, it was believed that all religious ceremonies should be conducted in the open during daylight hours. This was so that God, whose 'eye' was the Sun, could watch proceedings. Welsh tradition states that Joseph of Arimathea preached to the early Christians of Britain within this circular monument that predates the church building next to it by many centuries.

Less than a mile from *Llanilid* is *Trevran*, which means 'Manor of Bran'. Again, Bran *Fendigaid* ('the Blessed') is listed in many genealogies as the father of Caradoc, the famous 'Caractacus', who for nine years (*c.*AD 43–52) fought against the invading Romans. Their principal historian during these times, Tacitus, tells us how Caractacus was eventually captured and, along with his entire family, taken as a prisoner back to Rome. He also relates how he made an impassioned speech to the Senate. This moved the Emperor Claudius so much that he released him from custody on condition that he stay in Rome and never again bear arms against the Romans. Welsh sources pick up the corollary to this story. They tell us that seven years later, which would be around AD 59, Bran and Eurgain, one of Caradoc's daughters, returned to Glamorgan with Joseph of Arimathea. The latter helped Eurgain establish a Christian college at what is now called Llantwit Major, but was then named the *Coreurgain* or 'Choir of Eurgain'. Meanwhile, Bran retired to Trevran, while his mentor, St Ilid, began his preaching at the 'Giant's Circle' at Llanilid.

All this further evidence linking Joseph of Arimathea to the Greater Coity area reinforced the idea that the real Glastonbury must have been somewhere in the vicinity too. However, the straight identification of *Aberglaston* with Coity was not wholly convincing. Firstly, it is stretching a point to say that Coity Castle stands at a confluence of rivers. Although it lies between the Rivers Ogmore and Ewenny, their confluence is some miles further south – at Ogmore Castle, to be precise. In any case, what we call Coity Castle today is Norman in origin. While it is possible that it stands on the site once occupied by Morgan's earlier fortress, this no longer exists. What remains of it, if anything, is another circular, grassy bank. This is several feet high and surrounds most of the castle. It is possible that this bank predates the Norman Castle, which is also circular in the main. In any event, the Turbevilles demolished whatever castle existed before their arrival and built most of what we see today. So could this earlier castle or hillfort be the real Glastonbury? Might it be the legendary Grail Castle, where, according to the Grail legends, Sir Percival was served a sumptuous banquet but failed to ask his host, the Rich Fisher King, the important question: whom does the Grail serve?

Poring over a detailed map of the area, I was inclined to think this might be so, but then I noticed something else. With its source not far from the castle was another, smaller stream. Called the *Nantbrynglas*, it flowed around a grassy eminence on which stands a woodland area called *Coedbrynglas*. More importantly, it flowed into the River Ewenny. Now, in Welsh, the place where two rivers form a confluence (*aber*) is normally named after the lesser one. Thus, Abergavenny is where the Gavenny river joins the much larger River Usk, and Abercynon is where the Cynon runs into the River Taff. By the same token, the place where the Brynglas stream (*nant* in Welsh) joins the River Ewenny should be called *Aberbrynglas*. I looked to see where this was. To my surprise, it was in a field very close to the village of Coychurch. Realizing that this might be important, I went to pay the village a visit.

Coychurch itself turned out to be ancient, apparently founded in the 6th century AD. Therefore, it was much older than the Norman church of St Mary's, which stands next to Coity Castle. The church was allegedly founded by a 'St Crallo', who, it is claimed, was the son of a Breton princess, St Canna. Her first husband (and Crallo's father) is said to have been her cousin, St Sadwrn, who conveniently deserted her to become a hermit in Anglesey. Other than his parentage, nothing else seems to have been recorded concerning this St Crallo. This made me suspicious that he was really no more than an invention intended to explain the church's name of *Llangrallo*. The involvement of St Canna could be explained by the fact that, not many miles from Coychurch is *Llangan*, a church said to have been founded by her. What seemed peculiar was that Crallo's alleged father, the hermit St Sadwrn, was both much older than she and was associated with North rather than South Wales. His only involvement in the life of St Canna seems to have been to father the boy Crallo and then to desert her. She, meanwhile, is credited with marrying a second husband by whom she became the mother of St Elian.

The more I looked at this, the more I became convinced that the 'St Crallo' story was an invention. I suspected that the real meaning of *Llangrallo* was probably 'Church of the Grail'. This, of course, would fit perfectly with all the other evidence linking this area of Glamorgan with Joseph of Arimathea, the uncle of Jesus, who is supposed to have brought the Holy Grail or cup containing Christ's blood to Britain. *Llanilid*, where he is said to have preached, is only three miles from Coychurch. Flowing through Coychurch itself is the *Nantbrynglas*, which joins the River Ewenny just a

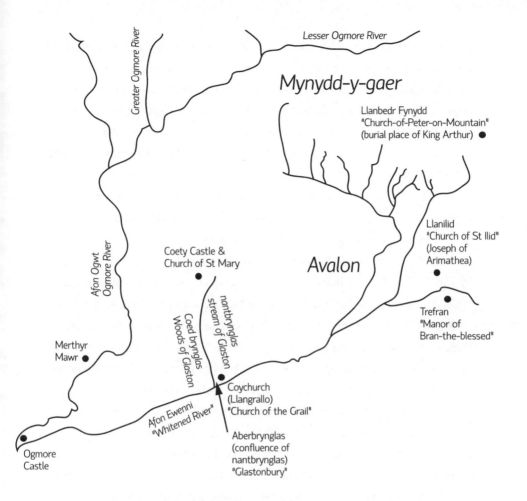

Map 6. The real 'Glastonbury' – in Glamorgan

couple of hundred yards from the church. To call the village of Coychurch *Aberbrynglas* would not be in error, and this is sufficiently similar to *Aberglaston* to be identified as such. (Map 6)

This, I was now suspecting, was at least part of the secret preserved by the Turbevilles, Berkrolles and Gamages: they were Lords not only of Coity but also of Coychurch, the original 'church in the woods (*coed*)'. This, I felt sure, was the real Glastonbury, its church presumably having once housed the Holy Grail. There was, however, another surprise in store when I proceeded to visit the church. I found a large, carved pillar inside that, like so many others in Wales, was once part of what was probably a wheel cross. This pillar had the single word 'Ebissar' carved on it.

When I looked into this, I discovered once more that there was a misleading story to explain this word. According to this legend, 'Ebissar' was a person's name: he was a pagan Saxon who was captured in battle. Given the choice of death or becoming a Christian monk, he took the latter option. Accepting the tonsure, he then lived out the remainder of his life as a Christian, and it was he who raised this cross.

When I considered this story further, it didn't seem to hold water. To begin with, 'Ebissar' doesn't sound at all like an Anglo-Saxon name. It does, however, sound as though it could be Hebrew in origin. *Ebenezer*, for example, is a Jewish name, *eben* meaning 'stone' in Hebrew and *Ebenezer* 'stone of help'. Lose the '-en-' and you have *Ebezer*, which phonetically is not much different from *Ebissar*. Alternatively, *-issar* could be a variant of the Welsh name *Assar*, meaning Sarah, which is the name of Abraham's wife in the Bible. This would be further evidence of Jewish influences in the area during the early centuries AD. If true, then the presence of the Ebissar stone would seem to support the legend of Joseph of Arimathea, who was Jewish himself, bringing Christianity to Wales. Of course, this evidence was anything but conclusive, so I now wanted to see if I could find anything else to support my new theory that Coychurch was the real Aberglaston, while the Lordship of Coity as a whole was the real Vale of Avalon.

CHAPTER 36

The Castle of the Holy Grail

The following day I drove to Coity itself, for the most part a rather charming suburb of Bridgend. These days, the castle, having been abandoned as a habitation in the 18th century, is little more than a romantic ruin. Standing at a distance, however, it is still just about possible to imagine how it must have looked at the time of Sir Lawrence Berkrolles, when it withstood the siege of Owen Glendower and his men. Nevertheless, it was not a big castle, so it was difficult to see how it could have survived such a prolonged siege without outside help. I was inclined to think there might be some truth to a story contained in the *Iolo Manuscripts* concerning a meeting between Sir Lawrence Berkrolles and Glendower. According to this story, the latter, in disguise, was entertained at the castle for four days with the utmost courtesy. Not knowing who his guest really was, Sir Lawrence boasted that he had sent out his men to scour the district for Glendower. The other agreed that apprehending him would be a good thing. However, as he left, Glendower shook Sir Lawrence's hand and, revealing his true identity, promised that he would never seek to harm him. Sir Lawrence Berkrolles was left speechless and, indeed, never spoke again.

I don't know if this story is true, but certainly Owen Glendower, while he may have wanted to capture the castle, would have had good reason not to harm either it or its Lord. He would have known that Coity was the last

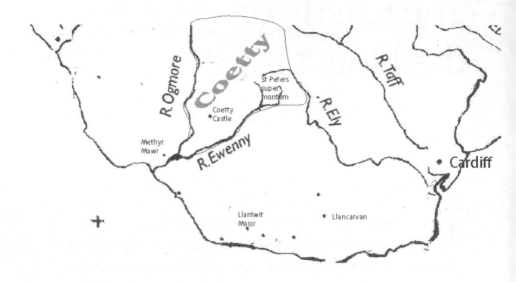

Map 7. The Royal Lordship of Coetty in Glamorgan

fragment of the earlier kingdoms of Wales, and that because it had never been conquered by the Normans – it was given in dowry – it still retained its independence from both the Crown of England and the Lordship of Glamorgan. This made it, potentially, a very special prize, but one that needed to be preserved intact if it was to have any meaning. In the event, the siege of Glendower had the opposite effect to that intended: it led directly to the ending of Coity's independence. Thus, we read the following lament in another of the *Iolo MSS*:

> '*One thousand four hundred and twelve – sway became extinct in Coetty [Coity]. Then vanish'd all semblance of justice to Cambria devoted.*'

Glendower must have known that Coity was a royal town whose lords claimed descent from the line of Iestyn, but did he know something else that he kept secret? Looking for an answer to this question, I left the ruined castle and made my way through a kissing gate into the churchyard. It was late afternoon by now and the sun was shining low along a path flanked by yew trees. These seemed old, but not old enough to prove there had been a church on the site prior to the Norman building we see today.

Once inside the church, my first impression was that there was little there of antiquarian interest, apart, that is, from a couple of small effigies lying on the floor, close to the altar. One of these represented the third Sir Payne de Turbeville who died in the early 14th century; the other was a memorial to one of his children who had died in childhood. I walked back down the central aisle feeling somewhat dejected, but then my attention was caught by something else. Pressed up against the south wall of the church was a curious piece of furniture that resembled a small wardrobe. Curious as to what it was, I walked over to examine it more closely. Standing about five feet in height and width but not much more than a foot in depth, it had a gabled roof that gave it the appearance of a rather large dolls' house. The church guidebook, however, said it was probably an 'Easter Sepulchre' and was meant to symbolize the tomb in which the body of Jesus was laid after the Crucifixion. As such, it would be brought out into the middle of the church on Good Friday to act as a focal point for devotions throughout the Easter Weekend.

While this seemed an entirely plausible explanation for such a curious object, I was not fully convinced. With its gabled roof, it looked to me more like a large reliquary, ie a closed box in which the bones of a saint could be kept. Furthermore, it bore little or no relation to the description of Jesus' tomb in the Bible. For one thing, there was no door to this Easter Sepulchre, so that on Easter Sunday there could be no rolling back of a stone to reveal it was empty. On the other hand, I could imagine it housing the bones of a prominent saint. If this were so, then the question was: whose bones might these have been?

The only clues to this were provided by a collection of carved panels on its front. These panels (though not the whole chest) are said to date from around AD 1500, which, if true, means they were carved during the reign of Henry VII. A date range of between 1490 and 1510 would put them after the Wars of the Roses but a generation or more before the Reformation. I found the choice of symbols depicted on these panels very interesting in that they formed a visual link between the stone plaques I had previously seen in the Mathew Chapel of Llandaff Cathedral, and the similar symbols on the font in Penshurst Church.

In all there were six panels. These were arranged in two rows of three, one row above the other. The top right-hand panel depicted the pillar onto which Jesus was tied and flogged. Also included on this panel were the whips used and a crowing cock, a reference to Jesus' own prophecy that Peter would betray him thrice before the cock crowed. The designs on the top left-hand panel were very like those on the shield placed over the tomb of St Dyfrig in Llandaff Cathedral. At its centre was an empty calvary cross as it might have looked after the Crucifixion. Leaning against it was a ladder and also shown were other implements used in the Crucifixion and its aftermath, including the spear and three pots containing burial spices that were brought to the tomb by Mary Magdalene and the other women. Just as on the Dyfrig shield and on the plaque at the foot of the tomb of Bishop Marshall (also in Llandaff), the Crown of Thorns was shown hanging over the central area of the cross. This is a familiar representation that seems to have both echoed the older wheel crosses and been a forerunner of the familiar crucified rose of the Rosicrucians.

Between these two panels there was a third that was more abstract in nature. It showed a floriated cross with a pierced heart at its centre. Around the cross, representations of the pierced hands and feet of Jesus were arranged in its quadrants, with the heart making five wounds in all. The floriated cross with the heart at its centre seemed directly related to the other version of the Rosicrucian cross, the one with a single rose (symbolizing the heart?) at the centre of a floriated cross.

On the bottom row, the two side panels were simply decorated with carvings of vines and flowers. The central panel, however, was again much more interesting. Carved on it was a shield emblazoned with three nails. As we have seen, it was common practice in Medieval times for noblemen to have their tombs embellished with at least one shield depicting their family's coat of arms. When dealing with legendary figures who either didn't have a family shield or whose arms were unknown, they would give them attributed arms: for example, Brutus, the legendary founder of the British nation, was attributed a shield bearing three crowns, while King Arthur was given a shield that was green with a white cross and with a picture of the virgin and child in the top right-hand corner. The attributed shield of Edward the Confessor, who lived before the standardization of coats of arms, is still used to this day. It is blue with a golden, floriated cross and five golden martlets (small birds). Taking all this into account, it would seem that the shield with three nails was also emblazoned with attributed arms. But whose arms were they?

The simplest answer to this question would be to say that the three nails represented the attributed arms of Jesus Christ. After all, tradition states that he was crucified using just three nails: one through each hand; a third passing through both feet. Yet there are difficulties with this interpretation. The oldest symbols for Jesus were the fish and then, later on, the *Chi-Rho* symbol ☧ which some people believe evolved into the familiar wheel cross. If the attributed arms on the shield were intended to be his, then it would make more sense to use one of these symbols. There is, however, another alternative. This is that the arms with their three nails' device were not attributed to Jesus but to someone else. But who could this possibly be?

Like the symbols on the other panels, they clearly refer to the aftermath of the Crucifixion rather than to the event itself. Thinking about this, I reasoned that simply removing the nails (a necessary task if the body of Jesus were to be brought down from the cross intact) would have been difficult to do. If the three nails, which were arranged in the form of the mystic Awen symbol, were not meant to be the attributed arms of Jesus, then the obvious alternative was that they were attributed to the man who succeeded in removing them. This man was, of course, Joseph of Arimathea. Furthermore, the Bible tells us that the stone-cut grave in which Jesus' body was laid to rest belonged to Joseph and had been intended for his own use. Thus, if the wooden chest as a whole was indeed an Easter Sepulchre, as the guidebook claimed, then it symbolized Joseph's family tomb. What could be more natural than that it should be decorated with a shield bearing his family's attributed arms?

There is a tradition that states that Joseph was either the uncle or brother of the Virgin Mary. If this is the case, then Joseph's family was the same as Mary's. The legends claim that Joseph, by then an old man, settled in Wales and established the first Christian college at Llantwit Major. This implies that he eventually died in Britain, perhaps leaving other members of his family to carry on his good work. All this reasoning, however, poses another question: is there any evidence, other than legends, that might link the family of the Virgin Mary with South Wales? If so, what was the family's relationship, if any, to the descendants of King Caractacus, ie such later Kings of Glamorgan as Maurice and Arthur? With these questions in mind, I felt instinctively that I was getting closer to the deepest secret of Coity and its connections with the inner teachings of Rosicrucianism.

CHAPTER 37

The Genealogy of Avallach

W hen Alan Wilson, Baram Blackett and myself wrote *The Holy Kingdom*, we made much use of respected genealogies. Foremost among these are contained in the Harley 3859 MS (today kept in the British Library) and the Jesus College 20 MS (today held at that college in Oxford). Both these manuscripts have some surprising things to say about a marriage involving a 'cousin' of the Virgin Mary. According to these sources, this cousin or blood relative is said to have married someone called Beli, the couple being ancestors of the later Kings and Saints of Glamorgan.

As we have noted, the genealogies contained in the Harley 3859 MS were originally compiled for the Wedding of Howell Dda's son Owen. Howell ruled over Deheubarth (southwest Wales) from AD 950–987, so these genealogies, which are the oldest of their kind to survive intact, predate the Norman invasion by about a century. The first list of Owen's ancestors contains the following: '...*Eugein map Aballac map Amalach, qui fuit beli magni filius et Anna mater eius quam dicunt esse consobrina* MARIÆ *uirginis matris d'ni n'ri ih'u xp'i.*' Translated from the Latin this says: '... Eugein, son of Aballac, son of Amalach, who was the son of Beli the Great and Anna his mother. Who they say to be the cousin of Mary the Virgin mother of our Lord Jesus Christ.' A similar genealogy is recorded in list 10, which ends with: '... Eudos, son of Eudelen, son of Aballac, son of Beli and Anna.'

'Eudos', of course, is Jude, a name which is Jewish in origin and must have been quite rare in Britain at the time.

There are equivalent listings in the Jesus College 20 MS, which give the ancestry of St Cadoc. These also speak of a marriage between Beli and Anna, again asserting that she was a cousin of the Virgin Mary. Meanwhile, in Geoffrey of Monmouth's *History of the Kings of Britain* – and also in the Welsh text, the *Brut Tyssilio*, from which it was derived – there is another story of a royal wedding from the same period: the mid 1st century AD. According to Geoffrey, a King of Britain called Arviragus married a lady called Genuissa who, it is claimed, was a daughter of the Emperor Claudius. The question is: could there be any connection between these two marriages? I believe there is but, unfortunately, the situation has been mixed up by modern historians who have relied too much on what was recorded by Roman historians writing long after the events in question. The following analysis is based on British accounts which were included in various Chronicles (Bruts) and also reflect what is written in various genealogies as preserved in Wales.

According to Geoffrey and others, Arviragus was the brother of Guiderius (*Gweirydd*) and both were the sons of Cunobelinus (*Cynfelin*), the high-King of South East Britain prior to the Roman invasion. The death of Cynfelin in around AD 40 seems to be what triggered the invasion in AD 43. He was succeeded by his eldest son, Guiderius, who was killed in battle with the Romans soon afterwards. This left his brother, Arviragus, to carry on the fight; however, in open ground his forces were no match for the Roman army, which included elephants to scare the Britons' chariot ponies. Arviragus had to abandon the South East and adopt guerilla tactics in defence of other, more mountainous parts of the island. According to Geoffrey, he eventually made peace with the Romans and married the Emperor's daughter Genuissa. As a wedding present, the Romans built the city of Gloucester for them, named after Claudius (*Gloyw* in Welsh).

So who, then, was this Arviragus and why do we find no mention of him in the preserved genealogies? Well, if we look again at this appellation, it becomes clear that it is really a title rather than a proper name. The Latin word *arvus* means 'low country' or 'ploughed land', while the suffix -*ragus* would appear to be derived from *Rex* (*regis*), Latin for 'king'. Thus, Arviragus means 'King of the low country' or 'King of the ploughed land'. This would be an appropriate title for a king ruling over southeastern England which is relatively flat and, long before the Romans arrived, was rich in plough land. However, this poses another question: if Arviragus was his title, what was this King's actual name?

I found a clue to solving this mystery in the Welsh triads. These are collections of triple-themed poems, many of them going back to the very earliest times. Triad 79 of the set published in an 18th-century book called *Myfynian Archaiology* records the names of three 'generous hosts', ie armies that did not require payment. One of these, we are told, was active at the time Caradawg (Caradoc or Caractacus) was fighting the Romans:

> '*The three generous hosts of the Isle of Britain: the host of Belyn son of Cynvelyn [Cunobelinus], in the warfare of Caradawg ap Bran [Caradoc son of Bran the Blessed]; the host of Mynyddawg Eiddin in the battle of Cattraeth [fought at the time of King Arthur]; and the host of Drywon son of Nudd the Generous, in the defile of Arderydd in the North [fought against Aidan, King of Scots, in AD 577 near Carlisle]. That is, everyone marched at his own expense, without waiting to be summoned, and without demanding either pay or reward of the country or the prince; and because of this they were called the three generous hosts.*'

What is said here is unequivocal: Cunobelinus had a son called Belyn (Beli), who fought in the wars of Caradoc. As we have seen, Cynvelin (Cunobelinus) died around AD 40. The Romans invaded in AD 43, and Tacitus records that their principal enemy thereafter was Caractacus, the King of the Silures. It looks as though Cunobelinus' son Belyn took a contingent of men from South East England and they placed themselves, voluntarily, under the banner of Caractacus so that they could carry on the fight against the Romans.

This deduction is derived from a passage in Tacitus taken from when Caractacus stood before the Roman Senate pleading for his life. Here, he told them that he was the 'ruler of many nations'. This would only have been true if he had been recognized as the overking of Britain and not just King of the Silures tribe alone. It follows that, after the death of Guiderius and the subsequent Roman conquest of his homeland in South East England, his younger brother, Belyn (the same person Geoffrey calls 'Arviragus'), joined forces with Caractacus and the Silures.

This Arviragus, still the titular King of South East England, was descended from Cunobelinus (*Cynfelin*) and his father Teneuvantius (*Teneufan*), who was a son of the famous King Ludd, who was the elder (deceased) brother of the war-leader Cassivelaunus (*Caswallon*), who fought against Julius Caesar in 55 and 54 BC. Clearly, then, the choice of a marriage partner for Arviragus was an important matter, as it had dynastic consequences. As we have seen, according to Geoffrey's *History of the Kings of Britain*, he married a lady called Genuissa. However, this name too seems to conceal rather than reveal her true identity. If we break it down into its roots, then '*genu-*' would seem to be derived from the Greek word *genus*, meaning family. It is then linked to '*Issa*', the feminine form of '*Issus*', meaning Jesus. Genuissa, therefore, translates as 'woman from the family of Jesus'.

As for the connection with the Emperor Claudius, he had two daughters but there is no record of either of them marrying a British king. However, it is possible that 'Genuissa' was his daughter by adoption. This was a frequent practice of Roman emperors when dealing with important heiresses, as adoption gave them control over who they married.

Tacitus tells us that the capture of Caractacus and his family did not bring the war in Britain to a conclusion. In fact, the Britons continued to fight just as strongly, defying Roman power with guerrilla tactics. Under these circumstances, it is not unreasonable to assume that Claudius may have seen the advantage of allowing a captive Jewish girl from the family of Jesus to be freed and allowed to marry the leader of the continuing British resistance, Belyn/Arviragus. If we assume that Belyn had, by now, been converted to Christianity, then marriage to a 'cousin' of the Virgin Mary (and, therefore, of Jesus himself) would have seemed an attractive proposition. If Claudius knew of this, he may well have arranged such a marriage as a means of gaining a peaceful outcome in Britain.

This, I believe, is the truth behind those genealogical records that speak of a marriage of Beli and Anna. The likely scenario is that she was either a daughter or granddaughter of Joseph of Arimathea, who tradition tells us was either an uncle or brother of the Virgin Mary. This also explains why the Romans allowed Bran and Eurgain to return to Glamorgan with Joseph. The intention would have been for them to negotiate the marriage between Beli and Anna in return for allowing them to preach Christianity in Siluria.

Some evidence that an understanding of this sort was reached is provided circumstantially by the subsequent history of South East England. In AD 60, Queen Boudicca of the Iceni, the tribe who lived in Norfolk, launched a rebellion against Roman rule. The Iceni and their allies burned the three major Romanized cities of the region to the ground – Colchester, St Albans and London. It was only with great difficulty and after receiving substantial losses that the Romans eventually succeeded in putting down this rebellion. However, there is no record of the Silures, possibly the most powerful tribe militarily in the whole of Britain, joining the rebellion. It seems likely that they were indeed holding to a treaty with Rome, one which guaranteed them religious freedom to be Christians in exchange for keeping the peace with Rome.

There is a further twist to this story, though. In the genealogies, we are told that Beli and Anna had either a son or grandson called Aballach, which is also written as Avallach in some sources. Avallach is also the Welsh form of Avalon, the place where King Arthur is said to have been taken for burial. Avalon was supposed to be an island, *ynys Avallach*, but the word *ynys* can mean a 'river meadow' as well as 'island' (for example, *ynysybwl*). It was also common in Wales to name districts and even whole countries after the nobles who ruled over them. Thus, Glamorgan or *Morganwg* is named after 'Morgan the Courteous', the King who ruled this region after the death of his father Arthur son of Maurice; while *Ceredigion* or Cardiganshire is named after Ceredig, one of the sons of a Prince of North Wales called Cunedda. Thus, it is not unreasonable to think that the river-meadow land of Avallach was once ruled by Avallach, the son or grandson of Beli and Anna. Very likely, his territory was the area embraced by the Greater and Lesser Ewenny rivers. This encloses Mynydd-y-gaer, the 'fortress mountain' on which stands the old church of St Peter's (where the Arthurian relics were found) as well as Llanilid and most of the rest of what later became the Lordship of Coity.*

With this discovery, my quest for the real Glastonbury seemed to have reached a successful conclusion. I was now pretty certain that originally Avallach/Avalon had been understood as being located in this part of Glamorgan. Then, perhaps in the 10th century and largely at the instigation of St Dunstan, King Edgar of England laid claim to the legend on behalf of the new monastery he and Dunstan founded in the marshlands of Somerset. As this fitted well with the Normans' plans, they went along with the charade that King Arthur and virtually all the most famous Celtic saints were buried there. William of Malmesbury, either out of gratitude or for some other reason, overlooked the total lack of evidence for Glastonbury being as old as was claimed. Later on, Edward I ordered the construction of a shrine in which to keep the supposed bones of Arthur, and after that there was no looking back. Glastonbury grew to be the richest abbey in England, which meant that, even after its destruction, no one was in a position to question the authenticity of its claims. It was not until Frederick Bligh Bond began to dig there during the First World War that the real truth was finally exposed. Alhough he, too, sought to conceal the painful facts, he found nothing on site to suggest there was or ever had been any church buildings there prior to Edgar's chapel of rest.

This could have been the end of the story had not Wilson and Blackett found Arthurian relics on the other side of the River Severn in South Wales. For the simple truth seems to be one of mistaken geography. King Arthur

---

* See Chart 15: The Avallach or Avallon Dynasty, p.239

was indeed buried in Avalon, though this was not in Somerset but rather Glamorgan, the true location of Joseph's mission among the Silures.

Once I realized this, everything else in the Glastonbury legends fell into place. St Dyvan and Fagan were sent to baptize King Lucius in AD 125, but as he was the King of Siluria (Glamorgan), they went to South Wales rather than Somerset. Accordingly, they founded a church for Lucius at Llandaff and built two churches of their own, both in Glamorgan. I also understood that the Medieval Welsh, those in the know, had little incentive to alert the Normans to the true situation. Instead, they kept the knowledge of the real locations of Avalon and Glastonbury to themselves, passing this information down the generations as a family secret.

There was, however, another dimension to all of this. Many of the Welsh saints, including St Dyfrig (who was crowned Arthur at Caerleon), St Cadoc (who was the principle of Llancarvon Abbey), St David (who moved the archbishopric of Wales from Caerleon to Dyfed) and many others, are recorded as being descendants of Beli and Anna. A lineage going back to them can also be found in the Harleian 3859 'wedding lists' of Owain the son of Hywel Dda. This one is particularly important, as Owain is recorded as being an ancestor of Rhys ap Tewdwr. He, in turn, is recorded as an ancestor of both King Henry VII (and hence Elizabeth I) and also of William Herbert, Earl of Pembroke. Therefore, I began to suspect that this information concerning the Beli and Anna lineage, with all that it implies, was the real secret of Rosicrucianism. At root it was not really a philosophy; this was just a contemporary cover adopted in the 17th century. The real Rosicrucianism was about 'rose culture', ie the grafting of bloodlines onto older root stocks. There could be only one reason for this, but before I explain this, we must first return to England, where more surprises were in store.

CHAPTER 38

The Mystery of the Grail

Returning to Kent, it was clear to me now that the Vale of Glamorgan and most particularly its northern fringe – roughly from Coity to Llanharan – was the real 'Vale of Avalon'. Included in this territory, which was an independent Lordship in the Middle Ages, was Llanilid, where there is a large *cor* or religious circle that was used by Joseph of Arimathea when he first started preaching to the local people, the Silures. Close by, near the crown of a hill called *Mynydd-y-gaer*, was the old church of *Llanbedr-fynydd* (St Peter's-on-the-hill), where my colleagues, Alan Wilson and Bram Blackett, found the memorial stone of Arthur son of Maurice and the silver votive cross with the legend '*pro anima Artorius*'. It seems likely that the Welsh name *Bedwyr*, which we translate into English as Bedivere, is actually a variant on *Pedr* or Peter. It seems reasonable to assume that the church was named after him rather than the Apostle Peter. In Malory's *Le Morte d'Arthur*, Bedwyr ends his days living as a hermit where King Arthur is buried. Curiously, Wilson and Blackett's dig revealed the foundations of a 6th-century, 'beehive' structure of the type used by hermits of that period, and it was right at the centre of this that the silver cross was discovered. As the centre of this structure would have been unknown to people using the later, rectangular church built on the site, the inference had to be that the cross was placed there at the time of Bedwyr, perhaps by him personally.

All this was evidence for an Arthurian connection with the eastern extremity of the Lordship. In the west there was the little brook called the *Nantbrynglas* or 'Stream of the *glas* (blue-green) hill'. It runs into the *Afon Ewenny* or 'Whitened River' close to Coychurch (Church in the wood). Using the accepted way of naming it, this confluence should be called *Aberbrynglas*. Since *bryn* can translate as 'bury' in English – and this in some circumstance is a cognate of *-ton* (for example, Shaftesbury, also known as Shafton, and Glastonbury as Glaston) – so *Aberbrynglas* could be written as either Aberglaston or as Glastonbury.

As if to confirm this identification, Coychurch is also called *Llangrallo*. Although it is supposedly named after a 'Saint Crallo', this appears to be invention after the fact. It seems more likely to me that this should be understood as 'Church of the Grail (Grallo)', the sacred cup or dish that Joseph of Arimathea is said to have brought to Britain. Perhaps this church – or rather one on this site – is where this treasure was once housed. Here, too, is the *Ebissar* stone which seems to be somehow connected with either Jesus himself or, more likely, with his family.

The subject of the Holy Grail, what it might have been and what it signifies, has been much discussed ever since the publication of Lincoln, Baigent and Leigh's book *The Holy Blood and Holy Grail* in 1982. Their idea, at the time deeply controversial, that the Grail was really a bloodline – Jesus having married Mary Magdalene and their having had at least one child – is now well known since the publication of Dan Brown's novel *The Da Vinci Code*. The idea that 'san graal' (holy grail) could be a code for 'sang raal' (royal blood) is now almost a cliché. Thus, today, based on very little or no evidence, it is assumed by many people that the marriage of Jesus and Mary is a fact and that a secret bloodline stemming from them infused the stock of the Merovingian Kings of France – and still endures to this day.

I have to say that back in 1982, when I first read *The Holy Blood and Holy Grail*, I found this an intriguing possibility. However, it does seem to confuse two separate issues that are both symbolized by the Holy Grail. First of all, there was the question of what was represented by the Holy

Grail. Secondly, what might it have contained? Now, in my opinion, the original 'Holy Grail' was not Mary Magdalene nor any bloodline stemming from her: it was a vessel used at the Last Supper, which was the Passover meal held by Jesus with his twelve disciples immediately prior to his arrest, trial and Crucifixion.

Joseph of Arimathea was not himself one of the twelve disciples. However, the Bible tells us that he was a secret follower of Jesus, although he was also a member of the Sanhedrin, the Jewish council of elders. This is hardly surprising. If Jesus were indeed his nephew, Joseph would have known him personally and may indeed have had a hand in his education. Furthermore, tradition tells us that Joseph was a wealthy trader in metals, principally tin and lead (which he would have obtained from the British Isles), but maybe also copper and silver as well. As a wealthy man, he would have qualified to be on the highest councils of the Jews. It is also said that Jesus used the Holy Grail when turning wine into his blood at the Last Supper, and this transformation (which is regularly re-enacted at the Mass) took place in Joseph's house. Again, if he really was Jesus' maternal uncle, then it is not at all unlikely that the latter held his Passover meal in his house. If this is so, then the 'Grail' was probably a *crater* or large 'punch bowl'; for in those days it was customary to dilute wine with water in just such a bowl prior to drinking it. This bowl would have belonged to Joseph too as part of his dinner set. Given that he was a trader in metals, it seems not unlikely that this bowl was metallic and may even have been made of silver. At any rate, after the supper it would have been a very treasured object and one that he would have doubtless brought with him to Britain.

This is one interpretation of the Holy Grail: that it was an actual vessel that Jesus used and Joseph treasured. The other alternative is that this vessel was a symbol for something else. Given that the wine it contained symbolized the blood of Jesus Christ, the most obvious allusion is to his body. We could say that Christ himself was the vessel of the Last Supper, an allusion that is reinforced by the story in the Bible that when a Roman Centurion stabbed him with a spear, what issued from the wound in his side was blood mixed with water. However, unless we choose to believe that Joseph brought the living body of Jesus to Britain, this line of reasoning does not get us very far. In my opinion, it seems more likely that the Grail was always a symbol for something more numinous than either a cup or the body of Jesus Christ: it symbolized a container for spiritual forces.

Following this line of reasoning, the content of the Grail is a metaphor for a special energy, understood by Christians as the manifestation of the Holy Ghost. This energy was present in the blood of Jesus and gave him the power to perform his miracles. Just as a car requires petrol or a computer electricity, so a developed human being or 'saint' needs this 'higher energy' in order to manifest powers that we would regard as supernatural.

It was this energy, which Jesus refers to as the Holy Breath or Holy Ghost, that he promised he would send to his apostles once he was no longer with them in person. On the first Whitsun, which took place seven weeks after Easter, it is said to have descended onto them like tongues of fire. Then, charged as it were with this 'force', they found they had the courage to preach without fear and the ability to speak in foreign languages (tongues) they had never learnt. Some of them also developed, or so we are told, the ability to carry out miracles of their own, even raising the dead on occasion. In other words, they were able to manifest supernatural abilities that had previously belonged solely to Jesus.

This much now seemed obvious. However, the symbol of the rose continued to elude me. What was its inner mystery and why was it so important to the Rosicrucians? Unlocking this mystery would prove to be the final piece of the jigsaw puzzle.

CHAPTER 39

The Rose of Sharon

These are just some of the possible interpretations of the Grail legend, but, as we have seen, there is another. The idea of an important bloodline is not limited to whether or not Jesus was married to Mary Magdalene and had children. He himself was a member of his mother Mary's family, which, of course, included her brother, Joseph of Arimathea and his family. Joseph's children were cousins of Jesus and, therefore, from the same family tree. I was beginning to understand that this was probably what the inner mystery of the Rosy-cross was originally all about. The rambling rose of the ancient British Royal family had been grafted with the genetic stock of Mary's family at the time Beli (Arviragus) married Anna (Genuissa). Jesus had been one bloom from the stock of Mary, but the hope was always that the 'rose bush' of Britain, ie the royal family tree, would bear further roses of this type. These would not be the red roses of the *Rosa gallica* that came from the grafting of the Norman lineage onto the ancient bloodstock of England nor, indeed, the white roses-of-the-field that were from the native briar stock of the old British. The rose of Mary, celebrated by the Rosicrucians, would be golden – the Rose of Sharon.

The hope was that blooms from this stock would manifest to produce saints and saintly kings. Such people would prove worthy to be custodians of the 'Grail', ie the Holy Ghost force that was originally manifested by Jesus and was later poured out on his apostles. However, it was also understood that only those people with the right blood – that is, descended from the family of the Virgin Mary – could safely handle such a force. In addition, they first had to prove their worthiness by undergoing trials and tribulations that would put off other men. If they passed these tests, then they were shown the Holy Grail itself: not a silver dish this time but rather a numinous vision of a cornucopia. This, at least, is how it appears in the medieval Grail legends.

It seemed to me now that this understanding of the Grail mystery and its connection with rose symbolism was the deepest secret preserved at Coity. The medieval Lords of this tiny Principality – the Turbevilles, Berkrolles and Gamages – knew that they were descended from Iestyn ap Gwrgan, the last King of Glamorgan; they were aware that through him they could trace their family tree back to Caractacus and the other pre-Roman kings of Britain. However, they also seem to have known that they carried the genes of Joseph of Arimathea, the Virgin Mary's brother, who brought the Holy Grail to Coychurch, the real Glastonbury in the real Vale of Avallach.

Throughout the 14th and 15th centuries, the Welsh aristocracy worked hard at rebuilding the fortunes of their families. Prominent among these were the Herberts of Abergavenny and the Mathews of Llandaff, who also claimed descent from Iestyn. For these lords of the Welsh Renaissance, their moment came in 1485. In that year, history took one of its more unexpected detours and Henry VII, Welsh by birth but only part Welsh by ancestry, took the throne of England.

Henry VII opened the door to a new understanding between England and Wales that was to have profound consequences. However, his son, Henry VIII, took things much, much further. Aware of how the pre-Augustine Church in Britain had been independent of Rome, he had few qualms about defying the Pope and declaring himself Head of the Church of England. It is doubtful that he would have dared do this had he not believed that the ancient British Church, as founded by Joseph of Arimathea, had primacy.

During the reign of Elizabeth I, men of Welsh descent, such as Sir Henry Herbert and Dr John Dee, were able to formulate a new kind of philosophy that was both patriotic in an Arthurian way and progressive in that it favoured science, exploration and a more open-minded attitude towards religion. One strand of this philosophy was the idea of personal development through one's own efforts rather than relying on the intervention of Jesus Christ as saviour. These ideas had their roots in Pelagianism. This was a 'heresy' that was formulated in the late 4th and early 5th centuries by a British monk called Pelagius. He taught that as there was no Original Sin as such, Christians did not need saving from it. In his opinion, sacraments administered by others were of little use, and Jesus Christ was to be viewed as a guide and example rather than a saviour. Salvation could not be attained by piggy-backing on his achievements: rather, it was the individual's responsibility to carry his or her own cross and walk the path to calvary for him- or herself. Pelagianism was declared a heresy by the Council of Carthage of AD 418, but this carried little force in Britain, where teachers such as Pelagius derived their authority from their own achievements rather than their ranking in the Church hierarchy.

These ideas fitted well with the new Protestantism sweeping Europe in the 16th century, and they found their focus in the Rosicrucian pamphlets of the early 17th century. By now, James VI of Scotland had been crowned James I of England, heralding another major change. A descendant of Robert the Bruce, James was aware of an ancestry that claimed he was himself descended from Kings David and Solomon of ancient Israel. There is also good evidence to suggest that, like Elizabeth I, he believed that the British nations were descended from the Lost Tribes of Israel. He was also an initiated Freemason and believed that he ruled by Divine Right. As I have written about all of this extensively in my books *Secrets of the Stone of Destiny* and *London: A New Jerusalem*, I will not go further into these subjects here. However, this is the milieu that Sir Robert Sidney and his wife Lady Barbara found themselves immersed in, and it fitted well with ancient teachings about a Welsh King Arthur.

Although the marriage of Robert Sidney and Barbara Gamage took place in 1584, it was not until the accession of James in 1603 that he was raised to the peerage as Baron Sidney of Penshurst. James favoured the Sidneys in a

Figure 6: Wounds panel from the Coity Chest.

way that Elizabeth never had, giving Robert his uncle's extinct titles. Was this because, whereas Elizabeth was somewhat jealous of the Sidneys and resented their getting married without her permission, James recognized something else: Divine Right? (Figure 5)

This seems to me to be the hidden message of the Lady of Penshurst stone. The cross on it is similar in shape to the one with the pierced heart at its centre on the panel of the Coity Chest. This is exactly the same as the one on the Edward IV Roll mentioned earlier that is now kept in a library in Philadelphia. This cross is part of the attributed arms of King Arthur – a white floriated cross on a green background with a picture of the Virgin and child charged in the chief corner dexter. Seeing this gave me another idea:

Figure 7: Attributed arms of King
Arthur (after Edward IV Roll).

what if the Lady on the stone was also meant to represent the Virgin Mary?

In that case, maybe the design on the stone as a whole was a covert representation of the attributed arms of Arthur. That made sense; for the way the cross emanated from her heart could be a symbol for the emergence of the family of the Virgin. The stone could have been yet another secret symbol for the descent of the Coity Lords from both King Arthur and the blood of the Virgin's family. This raised another question: why was the stone in Penshurst?

According to the booklet on sale in Penshurst church, the two memorial stones now hanging in the bell tower were found in 1854 buried under the north aisle. It has been suggested that they are somehow connected with the French Huguenots. On the other hand, because the stones are reckoned by some to be 13th century, a more recent theory is that they are connected to the Albigensian crusade, which took place in Southern France between 1209 and 1229. In fact, there is no evidence for either of these theories. It seems much more likely to me that the stones were brought to Penshurst from Coity, either by Lady Barbara herself or later on in the 17th century. As the Lady of Penshurst stone is only part of a coffin lid, we can infer that this was broken at a time when iconoclasm was widespread. In this context, it is significant that the parish guide to St Mary's Church of Coity reveals that following the Reformation, a 'commission' of local nobles robbed Coity of many of its treasures. It lists Robert Gamage, Esq. among the Commissioners, so it seems likely that it was at this time that the Lady of Penshurst stone came into possession of the Gamage family, then Lords of Coity. As to its burial under the north aisle, we can assume this was done during the period of Puritan rule during the 1640s and 1650s that followed the Civil War between Crown and Parliament. At that time it was commonplace for Parliamentarian soldiers to smash images of the Virgin Mary and other saints in an orgy of iconoclasm that has left most older churches disfigured to this day. It seems likely that the stone was buried to preserve it, perhaps on the orders of Algernon Sidney, who was an officer in Cromwell's New Model Army, and the younger son of the 2nd Earl of Leicester. Algernan was eventually executed in 1683, and it is possible that the secret of the stone's hiding place went with him to the grave.

Returning to Penshurst Place, as I browsed the shelves of the gift shop, I came across something else that seemed important. It was a simple postcard printed from the portrait of a young woman. Her name was Dorothy and she was the eldest daughter of the 2nd Sidney Earl of Leicester, and therefore a granddaughter of the 1st Earl and his wife Lady Barbara Gamage. Dorothy was by all accounts a very attractive lady, so much so that the poet Edmund Waller wrote poems to her, addressing her as 'sacharissa' or 'most sweet'. Enjoying the attention, she flirted for a while with his affections, but eventually she turned down his proposal of marriage as he was simply too poor and too lacking in social skills. When she eventually did marry in 1639, it was to a fellow aristocrat, Henry Spencer, 3rd Baron Spencer of Wormleighton. In the Civil War that followed shortly afterwards, he was an ardent royalist, distinguishing himself well in 1642 in the Battle of Edgehill. For his services to the Crown, he was rewarded with the title of Earl of Sunderland, making his wife, Dorothy, a Countess like her mother. This was about as good as it would get for Dorothy, for in the following year her young husband was killed in the First Battle of Newbury. He was only 23 years old, and his widow was not yet 26.

This might have been the end of the story had not their short marriage produced two children. Their son, the 2nd Earl of Sunderland, was very prominent in the Government of Charles II, although less so with his brother James II, whose Catholicism he disapproved of. He regained his position of influence at the court of William and Mary, reconciling them to

Mary's sister Anne. His son, the 3rd Earl of Sunderland, was another Robert Spencer. He made an advantageous marriage to Lady Ann Churchill, the younger daughter of John Churchill, Duke of Marlborough, who famously led the army that defeated the forces of Louis XIV in 1704 at the battles of Blenheim. Their second son, Charles Spencer, eventually inherited both the Dukedom of Marlborough and the Earldom of Sunderland. From him are descended all the later Dukes of Marlborough and also Sir Winston Churchill, Britain's most famous Prime Minister.

This was quite an eye-opener for me, for it meant that Sir Winston Churchill had been a man 'of the blood'. Like King Arthur, who also rescued Britain at a most dangerous time, he was descended from Anna, the cousin of the Virgin Mary, who was most likely the daughter or granddaughter of Joseph of Arimathea. This was startling enough, but there was more to come. The third son of Sir Robert Spencer, 3rd Earl of Sunderland, and Lady Ann Churchill was the Honourable John Spencer. He too had a son, another John Spencer, who was raised to the peerage in 1761 and, in 1765, was created 1st Earl Spencer. Descended from him are all the later Earls Spencer and, of course, Lady Diana Spencer, Princess of Wales, who was the daughter of the 8th Earl Spencer. This means that her sons, Prince William, Earl of Cambridge, and Prince Harry, are also descended from the Coity/ Avallach lineage. Furthermore, as I write this, it has been announced that William's wife, Catherine Middleton, Duchess of Cambridge, is expecting a baby. This child, who should live well into the 22nd century, represents yet another rung in the Avallach-Coity descent.*

If you follow down all the generations descended from Beli and Anna, they must have millions of descendants, some aristocratic but many more who are commoners. Because of the major migrations from Britain that took place in the 18th, 19th and 20th centuries, many of these will be living in diverse places such as the USA, Canada and Australia. However, what is special about Prince William is that he is in the direct line of succession to

---

* See Chart 16: The descent of Diana, Princess of Wales, from Barbara Gamage, page 240

the throne of Great Britain. When and if he is crowned, he will be the first known descendant of the Avallach Dynasty to rule over Britain since the death of King Cadwallader in AD 689. It is curious, therefore, that one of his names is Arthur, for if he chooses to use this, he will be the first king of this name to sit on the throne of Britain since the death of the famous King Arthur of legend. In a very real sense he will be the 'Once and Future King': probably a descendant of King Arthur son of Maurice and of Beli and Anna.

Thus it is that, through the hastily arranged marriage of Prince Charles and Lady Diana Spencer, there was a fresh grafting of the Damascene rose onto the briar stock of the Royal family. That the marriage itself ended in disaster cannot take away the significance of this. With her genes, Lady Diana brought something of significance to the House of Winsor: a deeply emotional nature that expressed itself as extraordinary empathy for the world's poor and dispossessed. These qualities seem to have passed on to the next generation, for Prince William, the Earl of Cambridge, and his wife have made clear their determination to carry on Diana's charitable work. Because of this, it is just possible that she unwittingly saved the British monarchy through the power of love. Of course, we have yet to see if William will turn out to be a second Arthur. However, as his grandmother Queen Elizabeth II entered Westminster Abbey for his marriage, she could be forgiven a moment of self-congratulation. Diana, now the Lady of the Lake, might have gone to her island in Althorp Park, her coffin draped in the fateful arms of le Despencer, but the Blood of Avalon flows now in the next generation. In that fateful crash in the Paris tunnel, the rambling rose may have been pruned at an inopportune moment. However, it is resilient and ready to produce more blooms. Some are white, some red, but who knows, maybe soon there will be one of the kind we have all been waiting for: a golden Rose of Sharon.*

---

* See Chart 17: The Coity 'Rosicrucian' lineage in brief, page 242

CHAPTER 40

Epilogue

I t is now nearly four years since I began writing this book, and even more since I carried out the bulk of the research on which it is based. Therefore, I thought it would be interesting to see what happened to the various families who, together, made up the 'Welsh Renaissance' of the 15th and 16th centuries and who laid the bedrock for the 'Rosicrucian Enlightenment' (as Dame Francis Yates called it) of the 17th century.

The marriage of Prince William to Kate Middleton – now known as the Duke and Duchess of Cambridge – went smoothly and according to plan. However, as he was still a serving officer in the RAF – one who flies air-sea rescue helicopters – they chose a cottage in Wales for their first married home, positioned not far from the airbase from which he operated.

Already, in 2013, the Duchess has shown herself to be a natural at handling both the protocols of royalty and the demands of the media. To date, her only major mistake was to be photographed topless while on honeymoon at a private residence in France. These pictures which, although not published in the UK, appeared in a number of European papers and magazines and caused major embarrassment to the Royal family, reminding them that, like Diana, this potential future queen has a price on her head. As far as the paparazzi are concerned, she is a meal ticket and, therefore, fair game. If she had thought it would be life as usual when out of the public spotlight, she has been disabused of this illusion. From now on, unless she and her Prince take active measures to secure it, she has no private life. At all times she must behave as though she is being watched by a camera lens, for all too often she will be.

A somewhat similar fate has befallen her brother-in-law, Prince Harry. He, like William, is a helicopter pilot, but in an attack rather than a rescue role. From October 2012 to March 2013, he was serving with British forces in Afghanistan, his task being to act as 'shotgun' on an Apache helicopter. His job is to fly higher than helicopters sent to rescue wounded troops and, from this vantage point, attack and take out any enemy forces that seek to hinder such operations. This, press reports point out, is not an easy option, but is somewhat similar to being a Spitfire or Hurricane Ace in World War II. Thus it is that the third in line to the throne is following a very active military career, one wholly in line with his Arthurian ancestors.

APPENDIX 1

The Curse on the House of Clare

In 1066, when William the Conqueror invaded England, he had his two half-brothers among his knights, Richard of Bienfaite and Orbec, and Baldwin, Lord of LeSap and Meulles. These two noblemen were legitimate sons of Gilbert of Brionne by William's mother Herleva (he himself was illegitimate). The brothers were well rewarded for their efforts at Hastings. Baldwin was made hereditary Sheriff of Exeter and given large land holdings in Devon. Meanwhile, Richard received Tonbridge and also Clare. Situated on the borders of Essex and Suffolk, today Clare is not much more than a village, but in those days it was a wealthy Lordship. Richard built castles at both these locations, but with Clare he also received large land holdings in the east of England. Accordingly, 'de Clare' now became the family patronym for his branch of the family.

Richard of Tonbridge and Clare was an important baron with ambitions. He married Rohese, the daughter of Walter Giffard, the father of the 1st Earl of Buckingham. Following Walter's death, a large part of the Giffard estate passed to the de Clare family. This, however, was just the beginning.

Richard and Rohese had five sons, Roger, Walter, Richard, Robert and Gilbert, as well as two daughters. Roger and Gilbert were present at the hunting accident which killed King William II 'Rufus'. This occurred while he was out riding in the New Forest in 1100. While it was called a 'hunting accident', there is little doubt that, in reality, it was an assassination, for William Rufus was deeply unpopular with his barons and with the people of England. The fatal arrow was fired by Walter Tirel, the husband of Rohese de Clare. She was a sister of Roger and Gilbert de Clare and, at the very least, they were complicit in the cover-up. As it worked out, their involvement in the assassination did the de Clare family no harm at all in the eyes of the King's successor, his brother Henry I – quite the reverse. In due course,

Roger inherited his father's lands in Normandy, while Walter received lands on the fringes of Wales, around Chepstow and Nether Gwent; he went on to found Tintern Abbey in the valley of the River Wye. Meanwhile, their brother Richard became a monk, while the fourth brother, Robert, received the forfeited lands of the Baynards in the eastern counties.

Gilbert de Clare was particularly favoured by King Henry I. He was wounded during a siege of his castle at Tonbridge by William Rufus, but, following the latter's death, was granted Cardiganshire by Henry I. As this county of West Wales was anything but conquered, this was really more of an invitation to carve himself an earldom than a gift of existing territory. Accordingly, Gilbert took his arms into Wales. It would be the beginning of the de Clares' long involvement in Welsh affairs.

At around the same time as Fitzhammon was extending his overlordship into Glamorgan, other Marcher Lords were pushing forward into the rest of South Wales. As early as 1088, a lesser-ranked Norman nobleman, Bernard of Neufmarché, pushed his way into Breconshire to create a small Marcher lordship there, but the death of Rhys ap Tewdwr left a vacuum that others were keen to exploit. Around 1093, Roger of Montgomery, Earl of Shrewsbury, led an army from Shropshire down through Cardigan to Pembroke. Here he built the original Pembroke Castle, and although the Welsh were later able to expel the Normans from most of South West Wales, this castle proved impregnable. The Normans, therefore, retained a foothold and were later able to retake the whole area of South West Wales that had at one time been the Principality ruled by Rhys ap Tewdwr.*

Meanwhile, the Clares pressed on with their own claims to a piece of Wales. Gilbert de Clare, son of Richard of Tonbridge, had three sons. The eldest, another Richard, was slain by the Welsh in 1135 or 1136 on his way to Pembroke. The second, another Gilbert, inherited Chepstow Castle and Nether Gwent from his uncle Walter (founder of Tintern Abbey). In 1138, he was created Earl of Pembroke by King Stephen, the title having lapsed.

---

* See Chart 18: The family of the Dukes of Normandy and the early Lords of Clare, page 243 & Chart 19: Early Earls of Pembroke, page 244

His son Richard 'Strongbow' de Clare, the 2nd Earl of Pembroke, led a Norman invasion of Ireland. He was invited over by Dermot McMurrogh, King of Leinster, who was in deep trouble. Strongbow both defeated McMurrogh's opponents and married his daughter Aoive, thereby becoming the *de facto* ruler of Ireland. From these beginnings grew the Clare holdings in Ireland, which included the present-day County Clare.

As Strongbow's son Gilbert died while still a minor, he had no male heir. Thus, upon his own passing, his lands and titles passed to his daughter Isabella and hence to her husband, William Marshal, who became the 3rd Earl of Pembroke of this dispensation.

William Marshal was probably the greatest knight of his age, certainly in England. Although they didn't always deserve it, as Marshal of England, he served four kings loyally: Henry II, Richard I, John and Henry III. He also went on crusades and was a close friend of the Knights Templar, joining their order shortly before he died in 1219. However, it is said that a curse was put on him by the Bishop of Ferns, County Wexford, that William Marshal's sons should have no children and consequently his estates would be broken up. As it turned out, although he had four sons, who each, in turn, inherited the Pembroke title, none of them produced legitimate offspring. On the death of the last (in 1235), the lands and wealth of the Marshals was shared between the husbands of his five daughters. The Pembroke title itself passed to William de Valence, the husband of William's daughter Joan. With the death of their son Aymer de Valence (in 1324) the Pembroke title went vacant. There would be three further creations of the Pembroke Earldom, all of which became extinct, before (in 1452) the title was eventually given to a Welshman, Jasper Tudor. Today it resides with the Herbert family, the current Earl being the 18th of his line.*

A similar fate, perhaps the result of another curse, befell the main branch of the de Clare family. Richard de Clare, the 3rd Earl of Hertford, who was the son of Roger de Clare, brother to Gilbert and Rohese and son of Richard of Tonbridge, married Amice FitzWilliam. Through her, he gained

---

* See Chart 20: The Marshal Earls of Pembroke and the House of Clare, page 245

possession of the Earldom of Gloucester and Lordship of Glamorgan, the old titles of Sir Robert Fitzhammon. Three further generations of Clares inherited the titles of Earl of Gloucester and Lord of Glamorgan, including the famous 'Red Earl', Sir Gilbert de Clare. He was a formidable baron who built a number of castles to extend his power base, including Caerphilly. He married Joan, the daughter of Edward I, so that their son, another Gilbert de Clare, was the first cousin of Edward II. Yet there seems to have been a curse on the progeny of the Red Earl. His son, the last male de Clare, was killed in the Battle of Bannockburn while he was still without an heir himself. Following his demise, the immense family fortune, which became the subject of much argument and litigation, was shared among his three sisters. However, the husband of the eldest, Sir Hugh le Despencer the Younger, was hanged, while the husband of the second, Sir Piers Gaveston, was beheaded by Welsh knights. The two ladies married again, but the de Clare family was finished as a political force.

There were a couple of attempts to revive the Clare/Clarence title in the form of a Dukedom. Lionel of Antwerp, the third son of Edward III, was given the title of Duke of Clarence, but as he only had a daughter, his title died with him. A second attempt was made when George Plantagenet, the brother of Edward IV, was made Duke of Clarence. He was later murdered – drowned in a barrel of Malmsey wine according to some accounts – so, again, the title died. The most recent Duke of Clarence was Prince Albert Edward, son of Edward VII when the latter was Prince of Wales. However, he died from pneumonia in 1892, and the title again became extinct.

Clarence House is currently the home of Prince Charles, and there is some speculation that his younger son, Prince Harry will, in time, be given the Dukedom of Clarence. It may, however, be decided that this is a dangerously poisoned chalice that he would be better off not receiving. After all, it has proved an unlucky title to hold since Bannockburn in 1314; why take the risk?

The Houses of Spencer and Churchill

As for the Spencers, Diana's brother Charles, now twice divorced (and married for the third time), continues to be the 9th Earl Spencer. By no means an idle aristocrat, he was pursuing a promising career in the media prior to his father's death. Since then he has followed this by writing books and inaugurating the Althorp Literary Festival. Althorp House itself has been much improved since he took over its management. Gone is the tacky décor of Raine Spencer, and the house has had its biggest restoration since the 18th century. To date, he has six daughters but only one son (from his second marriage), so the Spencer succession has been secured for another generation at least.*

The other great family descended from the marriage of Lady Dorothy Sidney to the Earl of Sunderland is the Marlborough branch of the Spencer/ Churchills. John Churchill, England's pre-eminent soldier in the late 17th and early 18th centuries, was created Duke of Marlborough for his great victory over the French at the Battle of Blenheim (1704). Further victories followed: Ramilles (1706), Oudenarde (1708) and Malplaquet (1709). A grateful nation rewarded their hero with a palace, Blenheim, which was built between 1705 and 1724. It is a huge building and the only palace in the UK that is not home to royalty. John Churchill had two daughters, the younger of whom married Sir Robert Spencer, 3rd Earl of Sunderland. They had three sons, the second of whom, Lt General Sir Charles Spencer, 3rd Duke of Marlborough, carried on the Marlborough title, while the third, the Honourable John Spencer, gave rise to the line of the Earls Spencer. The Dukedom of Marlborough has carried on through the centuries and is today held by John George Spencer-Churchill, 11th Duke of Marlborough and 13th Earl of Sunderland.

---

* See Chart 21: Dukes of Marlborough and Earls of Sunderland, page 246

His son and heir apparent is Charles James Spencer-Churchill, Marquis of Blandford. He attained unwanted notoriety in the 1990s when it was revealed he was a drug addict; he was sent to prison in 1995 for forging prescriptions and again in 2007 for driving offences. As a result of this behaviour, his father disinherited him for a time so that, although he would still inherit the title Duke of Marlborough, the family properties, including Blenheim Palace, would pass to his brother George on whom has already been bestowed the title of Earl of Sunderland. However, the Marquis of Blandford has managed to stay clean from drugs for five years and to rebuild both his life and his reputation with his father. As a result, in November 2012 it was announced by the Duke that he is restoring Lord Blandford's inheritance; he will, after all, succeed to the Blenheim estate when he becomes the 12th Duke of Marlborough.

A second important line of Spencer-Churchills descends from Lord Randolph Spencer-Churchill (d.1895), younger son of the 6th Duke of Marlborough. He was a Member of the House of Commons and, for a short time, held the post of Chancellor of the Exchequer. However, he overplayed his hand by resigning from this post and never achieved the position he really wanted, that of prime minister. He died from syphilis contracted from a prostitute at the relatively young age of 46.

Lord Randolph's eldest son, Winston, was half American, with his mother, Jenny Jerome, coming from New York. Winston was born in Blenheim Palace, but as the son of a younger son he had no title. Even so, he was able to serve as Prime Minister as a commoner from 1940–45 (and again from 1951–6) and is credited with steering Great Britain safely through the critical years of the Second World War. Sir Winston Churchill was also a prolific writer as well as soldier and politician. What for other, lesser men would have been an entire life's work was, for him, a part-time occupation to fill in the hours when he was not actively engaged in politics. This does not mean his writing was second-rate – far from it. His historical works, especially his magnum opus, the four volumes of his *History of the English Speaking Peoples*, won him the 1953 Nobel prize for literature. As if this were not enough, he was also a talented artist and even engaged in some brick-laying at Chartwell, his home near Westerham in Kent. As it happens, that is not as surprising as it at first seems. Winston Churchill, like his father Randolph, was a Freemason whose original function was building castles and cathedrals out of blocks of stone. Whether or not he attained the rank of rose-croix is a secret known only to his fellow freemasons, but it would be very surprising if he hadn't.

Like his father and grandfather, Winston's son, another Randolph, also went into Parliament. He did not achieve very much, but his first wife, the socialite Pamela Digby (who was later known as Pamela Harriman), achieved notoriety as the 'greatest courtesan of the 20th century'. Not only was she married three times – her third husband being Averell Harriman, the former Governor of New York and US ambassador to first the USSR and then Britain – but she had numerous affairs with other, powerful men. Her son by Randolph Churchill was another Winston, who also went into Parliament. He did not attain high office, though, generally regarded as a lightweight if right-wing Conservative. He died in 2010, leaving behind two sons and two daughters to carry on the legacy.

More interesting due to her flamboyance was Winston's half-sister, Arabella Churchill. One of the most famous hippies in Britain, she was the joint founder and organizer of the Glastonbury Festival of Rock Music. A peace crusader and charity fundraiser, she embraced Tibetan Buddhism. What her grandfather, Sir Winston Churchill, the Prime Minister, would have made of this we will never know, but he would surely have been much more upset to hear that her son, Jake, was jailed for three years in Australia on drug charges. She died from cancer in 2007.

APPENDIX 3

The House of Sidney

The Spencers and Churchills are not, of course, the only descendants of Sir Robert Sidney and his wife Barbara Gamage. He gave active military service in the Netherlands, so naturally many of his descendants in the Sidney family followed in his footsteps as military men and Netherlandophiles. His son, Sir Robert Sidney, 2nd Earl of Leicester, commanded a regiment in the Netherlands for a time, but is better remembered as a politician than a soldier; he was a Member of Parliament for, successively, Wilton (where his aunt, the Countess of Pembroke, held sway), Kent and Monmouthshire (twice). The latter, of course, is in Wales on the border with England. As Lord of Coity, he was continuing the family's involvement with Wales as well as England. Perhaps more memorable, though, was his building of Leicester House, a magnificent mansion in the very heart of what is now Soho. Except for the square's name, nothing now remains of this building. The Sidney connection is hinted at, though, by the name of Lisle Street that runs to its north: Viscount De L'Isle being one of the Earl's titles and now again held by the Sidneys of Penshurst today.*

The children of the 2nd Earl were even more involved in military action than either their father or grandfather. As we have seen, Lady Dorothy Sidney (Sacharissa) married Henry Spencer, 1st Earl of Sunderland, who was killed in 1643 at the First Battle of Newbury. A Cavalier, he was fighting on the side of King Charles I, so, at first, it is surprising that two of his bothers-in-law, Philip Sidney (who became the 3rd Earl of Leicester) and Algernon Sidney (Dorothy's brothers), were on the opposing side. The latter was a Colonel in Cromwell's New Model Army ('Roundheads') and served as MP for Cardiff in the Long Parliament which sat throughout the tumultuous period of the Civil War. However, he did fall out with Cromwell

---

* See Chart 22: Earls of Leicester and Viscounts De L'Isle, page 247

and soon came to regard the Lord Protector as a tyrant who had betrayed the Parliamentarians. After Cromwell died and Charles II was restored to the throne (1660), both brothers made their peace with the new King. However, Algernon later fell out with Charles II, who he again regarded as insufficiently respectful of the wishes of Parliament. He subsequently became implicated in the Rye House Plot (1683) to assassinate both the King and his brother, the Duke of York (later to be crowned James II); he was arrested, tried and executed for treason that same year. Because of his principled stand against what he perceived as Royalist tyranny, he is regarded by many as a Republican martyr.

A third son of the 2nd Earl, Henry Sidney, had better fortune. Born in 1641, he was 20 years younger than Algernon and therefore too young to be involved in the Civil War. He too, however, turned out to be no friend to James II. Entering Parliament in 1679, he wrote and was one of the signatories of the letter sent to William of Orange in 1688 inviting him to come to England to take the throne. In 1690, he was at the new King's side at the Battle of the Boyne. William's victory effectively ended James II's rule and is still celebrated by Ireland's Orangemen to this day.

The new King, William III, rewarded him successively with the titles Baron Milton, Viscount Sydney and, finally, Earl of Romney. He is best remembered, however, for his period from 1693 to 1702 when he was Master of the Ordnance. This was a highly important position that put him in charge of ordering and maintaining the Royal Ordnance of cannons and other weapons. During this time, he caused all the royal weaponry (and even items such as prison clothing) to be marked with the Sidney coat of arms, the Broad Arrow. This still applies to this day and is used more broadly by the Ordnance survey when marking sighting plinths on the tops of mountains and all of their maps. Curiously, this mark is very similar to the old symbol of Awen (/I\), which, as we have seen, was emblazoned on the arms of Sir Guy de Bryan (who lies buried in Twekesbury Abbey). It is Welsh in origin and is said to go back to Druidic times. Perhaps this is why the King allowed the use of the Broad Arrow – ostensibly the Sidney coat of arms – on royal property.

Following the death in 1698 of Philip Sidney, the 3rd Earl of Leicester, the title passed successively to three of his sons, Philip (d.1705), John (d.1737) and Jocelyn (d.1743). At this point there was a problem with the succession. Jocelyn didn't have any sons, but he did have an illegitimate daughter, Anne. However, an elder brother of his, Thomas Sidney, who had died in 1728 without ever having a chance to hold the Leicester title, had left behind him two legitimate daughters, Mary and Elizabeth. This caused legal wrangles, which eventually led to the splitting up of the Sidney estates. Penshurst Place and the bulk of the Sidney wealth passed to Elizabeth and Mary, while the Welsh possessions (including Coity) went to Jocelyn's daughter Anne. Because none of the heirs were male, the family titles became extinct.

This is a fate that all British aristocratic families fear, for not only does it mean a loss of status, but it can also mean destitution. Elizabeth Sidney married a Mr William Parry. The Sidney name as well as the titles were lost, and her daughter was plain Elizabeth Jane Parry. She married Sir Bysshe Shelley, the famous poet, who was his grandson by an earlier marriage, but he and Elizabeth Jane did have a son, John, who took the surname Shelley-Sidney in honour of his illustrious ancestors. He had a son, Philip Charles, who dropped the 'Shelley' part of the surname and went back to Sidney. He made what turned out to be a fortunate marriage to Sophia FitzClarence, an illegitimate daughter of King William IV.

This brought the Sidneys back into royal circles, and he was rewarded with a baronetcy as Baron De L'Isle and Dudley. Three generations later, William Philip Sidney, the 6th Baron De L'Isle and Dudley, won a VC for bravery in defending the Anzio Beachhead during the Battle for Italy in the Second World War. It was awarded to him by General Alexander in 1944, the ribbon for the medal being taken from the VC belonging to Sidney's father-in-law, General Gort. In 1956 he was created 1st Viscount De L'Isle of Penshurst, and, in 1961, he took up the post of Governor General of Australia – the last non-Australian to hold this office. In 1966, he was made a Knight of the Garter, only the second person ever to hold the twin honours of VC and KG. Thus, by the end of his life (he died in 1991), he put the Sidney family back into the higher echelons of the peerage. He would no doubt have been created Earl of Leicester, too, were not this title now held by the Coke family. As it was during the time of the 1st Viscount De L'Isle, when the Penshurst church was refurbished and the Sidney chapel painted with ancestral shields on the ceiling, we must assume that he had an interest in these matters. Whether he was an active Rosicrucian or Freemason has not been disclosed. He was succeeded by his son, Philip John Algernon Sidney, who is the 2nd Viscount De L'Isle and 7th Baron De L'Isle and Dudley. Under his guidance, Penshurst has continued to prosper, finding a balance between being a family home and a tourist attraction. Famed for its gardens as well as its ancient buildings, it has so far managed to stay in private hands and out of the National Trust's.

The House of Mathew/Matthews

To find out more about the Mathew/Matthews family and Earls of Llandaff, I went to the British Library, which houses a large number of Welsh genealogies. It soon became clear that the family was very large, with members scattered all over the territories that were once part of the British Empire, notably Canada and Australia. To my surprise, I also discovered that the title of Earl of Landaff was held by a branch of the family that lived in Ireland. In fact, it was a title held under the peerage of Ireland and not, as was implied by the name, of Wales and England. The family seat of the Earls of Landaff was actually at Thomastown Castle in the County of Tipperary, a property that now lies in ruins. The 1st Earl of Landaff was Francis Matthews, who was born in 1738 and died in 1806. He was succeeded by his son, Francis James Matthew, who was a member of Parliament and died in 1833. He was the last to hold the title of Earl of Landaff, which then became extinct.

There were, however, other descendants who are of interest, notably Theobald Mathew (1790–1856). He was born at Thomastown, but achieved prominence not in politics but the Temperance Movement. For a short time he was a Capuchin monk, but he abandoned the cloistered life, instead making the war against alcohol consumption his life's work. From small beginnings in Cork in 1838, he won over millions of people to 'take the pledge' and give up drinking alcoholic beverages completely. The movement spread quickly to Britain and to America, where he gave sermons up and down the country. Soon, almost every town in both countries had its Temperance Society.

A descendant of Theobald Mathew was Arnold Harris Mathew (1852–1919), who founded the Old Roman Catholic Church of Great Britain. Born in France, he was baptized twice: once into the Catholic Church and then again into the Church of England. This sort of religious dual identity was prophetic of his life. Initially, he went into the Roman Catholic priesthood and received his Doctorate of Divinity from the hands of Pope Pius IX himself. He then went on to become a Dominican friar, historically the order most closely linked to the Spanish Inquisition. However, Arnold Mathew was too much of a rebel to be constrained by hierarchies or ortho-doxies, and, in 1889, he left the Roman Catholic Church as a matter of conscience. In 1908, after years of soul-searching, he joined the breakaway Old Catholic Church of Utrecht; in due course, he was consecrated as its first Bishop in Great Britain. Still unhappy, he did not stay in this church either, but soon formed his own 'Old Roman Catholic Church' of which he was Archbishop. Despite its name, this was – and is – independent of both the Roman Catholic Church and the Old Catholic Church of Utrecht. For one thing, it had a different attitude to certain dogmas, and it allows its priests to marry. To safeguard what he saw as his line of apostolic succession, Archbishop Mathew consecrated a number of bishops and was unwittingly instrumental in the founding of the Liberal Catholic Church, a strange amalgam of Catholic rituals, theosophical ideas and Rosicrucianism.

We can only guess what David Mathew, the giant hero of the Battle of Towton and patriarch of the family, would have made of this. However, seen objectively, Mathew's Old Roman Catholic Church was somewhat analogous to the pre-Norman *clas* church. Like those earlier churches, it had little connection with the establishment, but revolved around the personality and charisma of its founding 'saint': Arnold Mathew. Also, like a typical *clas* church, Mathew's Old Roman Catholic Church gave rise to satellites, some in America and others in Europe. The Liberal Catholic Church, which even Mathew considered heretical, went much further and openly embraced continental Rosicrucianism. Unwittingly, this Mathew at least seems to have maintained the connection to certain 'Rosicrucian' ideals he may not have even known his family held 500 years ago.

The Many Houses of Herbert

Besides the Mathews, the other great family to gain from the Wars of the Roses was undoubtedly the Herberts. As we have seen, Henry Herbert, the 2nd Earl of Pembroke, married Mary Sidney, the sister of Sir Philip and Sir Robert Sidney. She was a rather amazing woman who, it has been suggested, was very likely the author of the plays we attribute to Shakespeare. As the evidence for this is presented very well by Robin P Williams in her book *Sweet Swan of Avon*, I won't go into it here. What I will say is that Mary, Countess of Pembroke, is one of the very few people with the poetic skills, education and access to source materials to be considered as candidates for this ultimate accolade. Also, if it was her who wrote the plays, it would explain why Ben Jonson, a friend of hers, referred to Shakespeare as 'Sweet Swan of Avon', for the Hampshire/Wiltshire Avon flowed through her lands at Wilton and there is a portrait of her wearing an elaborate lace collar embroidered with swans. Coincidence? I think not. As further evidence for the family connection, Mary, Countess of Pembroke, had two sons, William and Philip. It was they who, following her death, arranged and paid for the publication of the first folio of Shakespeare's plays without which they may have disappeared from memory. So, at the very least, we have the Herbert family to thank for the preservation of the greatest literary corpus in the whole of English literature.*

Mary's eldest son, William, inherited his father's title of Earl of Pembroke. However, his brother Philip is said to have caught the eye of the bisexual King of England and Scotland, James I (formerly King James VI of Scotland), who thought he had attractive dancing legs.

Accordingly, he was awarded (for what services we can only guess at) the title of Earl of Montgomery. Then, following the death of his brother without

---

* See Chart 23: Herbert Earls of Pembroke, Montgomery and Carnarvon, page 248

an heir, he took over the Pembroke title, too. The two titles have continued to run together in this family ever since. The 17th Earl of Pembroke (14th Earl of Montgomery), who died in 2003, was a film director. His most famous movie was *Emily* (1976), an erotic, 'coming of age' film that starred Koo Stark in the title role. Her subsequent affair with Queen Elizabeth's second son, Prince Andrew, gave the film some notoriety which it probably didn't deserve. The present holder of the earldoms is the 17th Earl's only son, William Alexander Sidney Herbert. He seems to have inherited his father's artistic bent and has a first class degree in Industrial Design. However, a promising career in this line was cut short by the death of his father and the need for him to take charge of the Pembroke Estate. This includes Wilton House, where there is a statue of Shakespeare and where Mary Sidney Herbert, the Countess of Pembroke, once lived.

At present, the Earl of Pembroke has no male heir, which means that should anything happen to him, the family's titles and properties would go to Henry George Reginald Herbert, the 8th Earl of Carnavon. This title dates back to the mid-18th century when it was given to Major General William Herbert, younger brother of the 10th Earl of Pembroke. The most famous holder of the Carnarvon title is the 5th Earl, George Stanhope Molyneux Herbert, who sponsored Howard Carter's dig for the tomb of Tutankhamen. The Earl died in 1923 as a result of a mosquito bite he received in Egypt when he went there to view the tomb of King Tut. Naturally, this was put down to the pharaoh's curse on whoever would disturb his final resting place, even though Howard Carter, who actually excavated the tomb, lived on for many years. Nevertheless, curse or no curse, the 5th Earl brought back many treasures from Egypt, and these today, perhaps including some small items from the tomb of Tutankhamen, are held in a private museum in the family seat of Highclere Castle.

This huge, imposing mansion is near Newbury in Berkshire. It stands on earlier structures going back to the 9th century, but was largely rebuilt by Sir Charles Barry, the architect who designed the current Houses of Parliament in London. It is in the Jacobean style, which was popular in the early Victorian period. Currently, it is being used as the set for the successful TV series *Downton Abbey*. There is an irony here, for the main plot of the first series of this upstairs/downstairs soap opera centred on the risk that the fictional Earl of Grantham has no son, and there is a risk that his daughters will lose the family home and estates to a cousin. In real life, it is the Pembrokes who face this risk, while the Earl of Carnarvon, who lives in the real Downton Abbey, is the titular heir to Wilton House and will remain so unless the present Earl of Pembroke produces a son.*

Three earldoms in one family might seem sufficient; however, Sir William Herbert, the 1st Earl of Pembroke, married Anne Parr, the sister-in-law of Henry VIII, and had a second son, Sir Edward Herbert. Descended from him are the Earls of Powis, a title that has been restored to the family on more than one occasion after the extinction of the male line. The family seat of this branch of the Herbert family is Powis Castle, a magnificent building near Welshpool in mid Wales. Without going into details, the family had many ups and downs before eventually, in 1801, the heiress, Henrietta Herbert, married Edward Clive, who was re-created as a new 1st Earl of Powis by George III. Edward Clive was the fabulously rich son of Robert Clive ('Clive of India'), who established British supremacy in Bengal for the East India Company. Using the Clive fortune, the new Earl of Powis and his wife were able to renovate Powis Castle and its gardens to become one of the greatest houses of the 19th century. Today it has been taken over by the National Trust, and the gardens have recently been restored back to their days of baroque glory. Meanwhile, visitors to the house are able to catch a glimpse of 18th-century India in the Clive Collection. This includes textiles, armour, silver, jade and ivory – in fact, everything one associates with India in the very earliest days of the British Raj.

Another line of Herberts culminated in the Marquises of Bute, who, in Victorian times, became the richest family in Britain. As Philip Herbert, the 7th Earl of Pembroke and 4th Earl of Montgomery, had no son, his titles passed to his brother Thomas. However, he did have a daughter, Charlotte,

---

* See Chart 24: The Herbert Earls of Powis, page 250

and she inherited family property in Wales, principally in Cardiff. She married Thomas Hickman, 1st Viscount Windsor, and they had a son who later only had a daughter, Charlotte Jane Hickman. She, however, married John Crichton Stuart, 1st Marquis of Bute. Their grandson was John Crichton-Stuart, 2nd Marquis of Bute. It was he who appreciated the importance of Cardiff as a port for shipping coal and steel to the British Empire. Accordingly, he built the Bute Docks, which at the time was a licence to print money.*

His son, the 3rd Marquis of Bute, was quite different in character. A devout Roman Catholic, he rebuilt Cardiff Castle and Castel Coch (near Merthyr Tydfil) as Gothic follies. The décor of Cardiff Castle celebrates the Welsh heritage of the Arthurian Age, while Castel Coch, a more personal family retreat, focuses on his family's descent from King Lucius and the early Christians of the Glamorgan Dynasty. Although still very wealthy by ordinary standards, the Marquises of Bute lost much of their legendary fortune over the succeeding generations. The present holder of the title, the 7th Marquis of Bute, prefers not to use it and is generally known instead as 'Johnny Dumfries' or 'Johnny Bute'. Now retired, he is a former racing driver who is most famous for winning the Formula 3 championship in 1984 and the Le Mans 24 Hours in 1988. He also drove for Lotus in Formula 1 in 1986 alongside Ayrton Senna.

As for Raglan Castle, the original family seat of the Herberts at the time of the Wars of the Roses, this was inherited by Elizabeth Herbert, the granddaughter of William Herbert, the 1st Earl of Pembroke, who was beheaded in 1469. She married Sir Charles Somerset, who was descended from John Beaufort, 1st Earl of Somerset, in turn descended from John of Gaunt, Earl of Lancaster and third son of Edward III. The Somersets, therefore, were minor royalty and could trace their line back to William the Conqueror. Charles Somerset was awarded the title Earl of Worcester, and Raglan became the seat of this branch of the family. In the 1630s, Edward 'Lord Herbert', the son of the 5th Earl of Worcester, built a machine that

---

* See Chart 25: The Herbert ancestry of the Marquises of Bute, page 251

used steam power to pump water to make a fountain from the moat. The invention was never taken further, but this is the earliest known use of what was obviously a steam engine.

During the Civil War of the mid-17th century, Raglan suffered badly. The Worcesters were on the side of the King and refused to surrender the castle to Parliamentary forces. It was sieged and eventually surrendered to General Fairfax and the Roundheads. He ordered that the castle be slighted, ie made uninhabitable. Charges were placed and considerable damage done to the walls, but the main loss was the library. This was either burned or looted, and as a result many valuable Welsh manuscripts were lost. In the ancestry tracing series *Who Do You Think You Are?* it was revealed that the comedian Alexander Armstrong is directly descended from the Earls and Marquises of Worcester. He is, therefore, not only of royal, Norman descent, but also from the Herberts. Clearly, this family is full of surprises!

The Stradlings and St Donats

When John Gamage died in 1584, his daughter Barbara Gamage was still a minor. Consequently, she was put under the guardianship of a cousin, Sir Edward Stradling, and went to live in his house, St Donat's Castle. It was here that shortly afterwards (and much to the annoyance of Queen Elizabeth) she married her childhood sweetheart, Sir Robert Sidney.

The Stradlings were an old family who had come to Wales at the time of the Norman Conquest. Indeed, the founding patriarch of the family, Sir William le Esterling, was one of Fitzhammon's 'Knights of Despoilation'. He was given the Lordship of St Donat's as his reward. The Stradlings, like most of the other noble families in the area, married ladies from equivalent or sometimes higher levels of the aristocracy. History is silent about the first seven generations from William le Esterling, but then Sir Peter Stradling (from the time of Edward I), married Eleanor, the daughter of Richard 'Strongbow' de Clare.*

Their son, another Sir Edward Stradling, was Viscount of Glamorgan in 1367. He was married to Gwenllian, the sister of Sir Lawrence Berkrolles, who was both Lord of East Orchard Manor and of Coity. Following the death of Sir Lawrence, they contested his will, believing that Coity should pass to his sister and thus into the Stradling family. This case went to Chancery, and in the end it was decided that while East Orchard should pass to Gwenllian, Coity should go to Sir Gilbert Gamage, who was directly descended from the Turbevilles.

Beginning what was to become a family tradition, Sir Edward's son, Sir William Stradling, went on pilgrimage to Jerusalem and enrolled as a Knight of the Holy Sepulchre. This was a good and usually painless way of getting yourself a knighthood without having to rely on the patronage of

---

* See Chart 26: The Stradlings of St Donats, page 252

the local senior nobility and the favour of the monarch. His son, Sir Edward Stradling III, did the same thing and, in c.1423, married Jane, the illegitimate daughter of Bishop (later Cardinal) Henry Beaufort. The Beauforts were descended from John of Gaunt, Duke of Lancaster and the third son of Edward III by his mistress (and later second wife) Katherine Swinford. Although born before the Duke's marriage, the Beauforts were legitimized by Act of Parliament. Bishop Henry Beaufort was a powerful man in court and was Chancellor of England under both Henry IV and V. Meanwhile, Jane's mother was said to be Alice, daughter of Richard FitzAlan, Earl of Arundel. This was another powerful family from the 1st league. Thus, by virtue of this marriage, Sir Edward Stradling found himself connected to those close to the centre of power.

His son, Sir Henry Stradling, followed the by now routine path of going on pilgrimage to Jerusalem, although he died on the return journey. Prior to this unfortunate event, he was married to Elizabeth Herbert. She was the sister of Sir William Herbert, the Yorkist Earl of Pembroke, who was beheaded in 1469. The most startling event of Sir Henry Stradling's life occurred in 1455 when he was captured by pirates. This was a fairly frequent incident even in those days, as the coasts of England and Wales were not protected as they are now by coastguards. Pirates could, and did, raid from North Africa as well as France, taking people away either for ransom or as slaves. In Sir Henry's case, a ransom was paid to his captor, Colyn Dolphin. Later, this notorious pirate was shipwrecked near St Donats. He and his gang were captured and all of them hanged by order of Sir Henry.

Sir Henry's son, Thomas Stradling, married Jenet, daughter of Thomas Mathew of Radyr. As her brother fought alongside Henry Tudor at the Battle of Bosworth, the Stradlings found themselves well placed with the new Tudor Dynasty.

Thomas Stradling's grandson, another Sir Thomas Stradling, married Catherine Gamage of Coity. It was through this connection that his son, Sir Edward Stradling, was related to Lady Barbara Gamage, who was herself a great-granddaughter of Sir Thomas Gamage. Sir Edward Stradling was a noted antiquarian and bibliophile. He compiled a family history and also wrote a history of the Norman invasion of Glamorgan. As he was closely linked with them by virtue of interests as well as family, it would be true to say that Sir Edward was a member of the Dee circle and very probably a 'Rosicrucian' in the generic sense of the term, meaning an enlightened, Christian mystic.

After the Reformation, the Stradlings continued to be a Roman Catholic family, which cost them a great deal. The line eventually died out in 1728, and St Donats Castle was sold. In 1925, it was bought and restored by the American media mogul Randolph Hearst. He spent a fortune on the castle, refurbishing it with entire rooms taken from other castles and ancient buildings. In the 1930s, he held lavish parties there where he entertained film stars and senior politicians such as Winston Churchill and the young John F Kennedy. After he died, the castle was sold and, in 1962, taken over by Atlantic College, a trust set up to promote internationalism in education. Run on progressive, liberal ideas, Lord Louis Mountbatten of Burma was made its President in 1967. It is still functioning today, and so the castle, although in good order, is not open to the general public.

The Fate of Coity, the Welsh Avalon

As we have seen, Coity Castle fell to the portion of Anne, the illegitimate daughter of Jocelyn Sidney, 7th Earl of Sidney. He died in 1728, and the castle was subsequently bought by the Edwin family of Llanfihangel. By this time, the castle itself was already in ruins; it was the lands that went along with it that were valuable. Llanfihangel means 'Church of St Michael' and is the name of a parish near Cowbridge in the Vale of Glamorgan. The patriarch of the family was Humphrey Edwin, a wealthy hatmaker who was Sheriff of Glamorgan in 1689 and Lord Mayor of London in 1697. He was a dissenter, which is to say a Puritan; an interest in Protestant esotericism seems to have been something of a family tradition.

Humphrey Edwin died in 1707 and was succeeded to the family properties by his eldest son, Samuel (d.1722), who had three children. The eldest of these, Catherine Edwin, remained unmarried, but joined a Christian sect called the Moravian Church of Bedford. This was an offshoot of the Unity Brtheren, a German Protestant organization that many believe was closely connected with German Rosicrucianism.

Samuel's son Charles added to the estate by buying the manor of Coity and other lands. He was also highly politically active, being MP for Glamorgan in 1738 and for Westminster in 1742–7. His wife, Lady Charlotte Edwin, was the daughter of the Duke of Hamilton and was a prominent early member of the Methodist Church, which gained enormous popularity during this period.

Charles Edwin was succeeded by his other sister, Ann, who married Thomas Wyndham, heir to the Dunraven Estate. In 1642, the Wyndhams acquired lands at Dunraven. This is on the coast of the Vale of Glamorgan, close by where the waters of the Ogmore River and its tributary, the Ewenny river, enter the Severn Estuary. He died in 1751, and she followed him 1758.

Their son, Charles Wyndham, who was MP for Glamorgan from 1780–9, inherited the family estates.

He was followed by his son, Thomas Wyndham. In 1802, he built a magnificent house called Dunraven Castle. Used as a hospital in the Second World War, it was demolished in 1960. All that remains now are the walled gardens and one or two other, outdoor fragments of walls and stairways. In 1810, his daughter Caroline married Henry Quin, the son of an Irish aristocrat. Her father-in-law, when raised to the peerage of England, took the title of Earl of Dunraven, presumably in anticipation of his son's inheritance. Thus it was that, on his death, Lady Caroline became the 2nd Countess of Dunraven.

She was an important benefactor to the Coity area and in Bridgend, close to the law courts, there is still the remnants of a water fountain that she had installed for the public good of the town. On it there is an inscription: 'Erected by Caroline, Countess of Dunraven, in memory of her friend John Randall esq, who for thirty-three years managed her estates. AD 1860.' Those estates would have included Coity Castle.

The last Earl of Dunraven (the 7th) died in 2011. As he had no male progeny, his titles went extinct with him. The former Dunraven estates, however, had already been broken up. Today, Coity Castle, like many other important sites in Wales, is administered by Cadw, the Welsh Heritage trust. The ruined church of *Llanbedr-fynydd* (St Peter's-on-the-hill) remains the property of Alan Wilson and Baram Blackett, although they have issued many shares certificates to spread the ownership to their supporters in the quest for the real King Arthur project.

For latest news and links, visit Adrian on his Facebook 'club' page at: www.facebook.com/AGGilbert1

APPENDIX 8

Charts of family trees

CHART 1

Courtship, First Marriage
and Progeny of Prince Charles

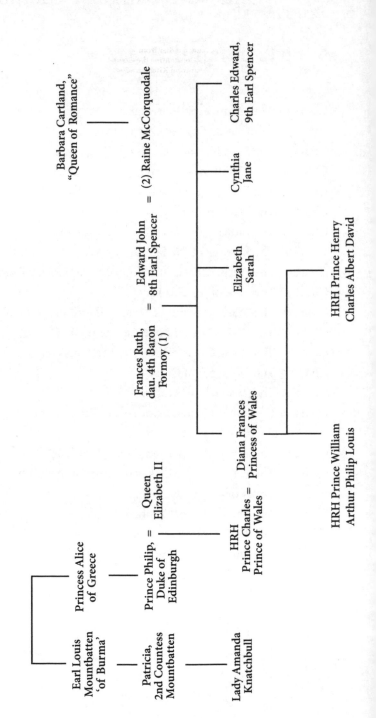

CHART 2

Saints and Kings of Glamorgan

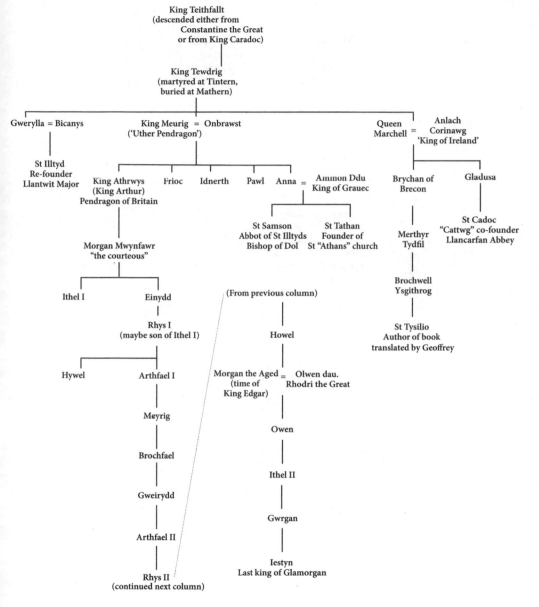

King Teithfallt
(descended either from
Constantine the Great
or from King Caradoc)

King Tewdrig
(martyred at Tintern,
buried at Mathern)

Gwerylla = Bicanys

King Meurig = Onbrawst
('Uther Pendragon')

Queen
Marchell =

Anlach
Corinawg
'King of Ireland'

St Illtyd
Re-founder
Llantwit Major

King Athrwys
(King Arthur)
Pendragon of Britain

Frioc   Idnerth   Pawl   Anna =

Ammon Ddu
King of Grauec

Brychan of
Brecon

Gladusa

St Samson
Abbot of St Illtyds
Bishop of Dol

St Tathan
Founder of
St "Athans" church

Merthyr
Tydfil

St Cadoc
"Cattwg" co-founder
Llancarfan Abbey

Morgan Mwynfawr
"the courteous"

Brochwell
Ysgithrog

Ithel I   Einydd

(From previous column)

St Tysilio
Author of book
translated by Geoffrey

Rhys I
(maybe son of Ithel I)

Howel

Hywel   Arthfael I

Morgan the Aged =
(time of
King Edgar)

Olwen dau.
Rhodri the Great

Meyrig

Owen

Brochfael

Ithel II

Gweirydd

Gwrgan

Arthfael II

Rhys II
(continued next column)

Iestyn
Last king of Glamorgan

CHART 3

The First Norman Lords of Glamorgan

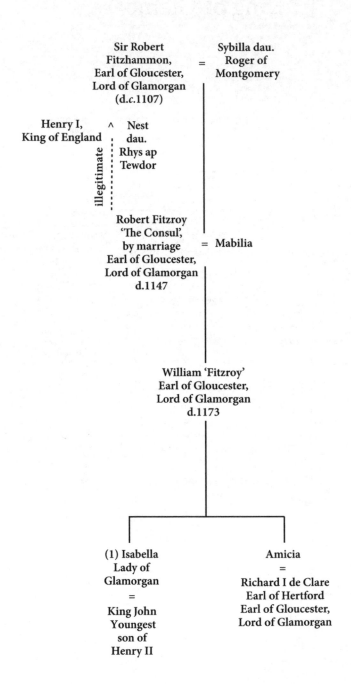

Sir Robert
Fitzhammon,
Earl of Gloucester,   =   Sybilla dau.
Lord of Glamorgan   Roger of
(d.*c.*1107)   Montgomery

Henry I,   ∧   Nest
King of England ⦙   dau.
                 ⦙   Rhys ap
illegitimate   ⦙   Tewdor

Robert Fitzroy
'The Consul',
by marriage   =   Mabilia
Earl of Gloucester,
Lord of Glamorgan
d.1147

William 'Fitzroy'
Earl of Gloucester,
Lord of Glamorgan
d.1173

(1) Isabella   Amicia
Lady of   =
Glamorgan   Richard I de Clare
   =   Earl of Hertford
King John   Earl of Gloucester,
Youngest   Lord of Glamorgan
son of
Henry II

CHART 4

The Children of Iestyn ap Gwrgan,
Last King of Glamorgan

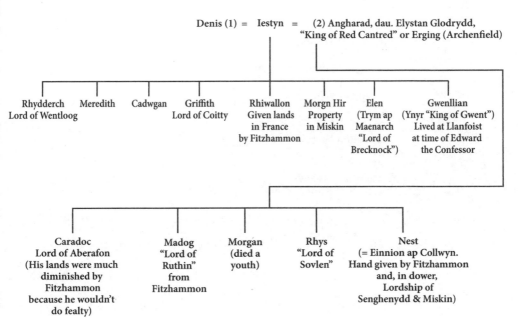

Denis (1) = Iestyn = (2) Angharad, dau. Elystan Glodrydd,
"King of Red Cantred" or Erging (Archenfield)

Rhydderch Lord of Wentloog	Meredith	Cadwgan	Griffith Lord of Coitty	Rhiwallon Given lands in France by Fitzhammon	Morgn Hir Property in Miskin	Elen (Trym ap Maenarch "Lord of Brecknock")	Gwenllian (Ynyr "King of Gwent") Lived at Llanfoist at time of Edward the Confessor

Caradoc Lord of Aberafon (His lands were much diminished by Fitzhammon because he wouldn't do fealty)	Madog "Lord of Ruthin" from Fitzhammon	Morgan (died a youth)	Rhys "Lord of Sovlen"	Nest (= Einnion ap Collwyn. Hand given by Fitzhammon and, in dower, Lordship of Senghenydd & Miskin)

CHART 5

The Dark Age Dynasty of North Wales

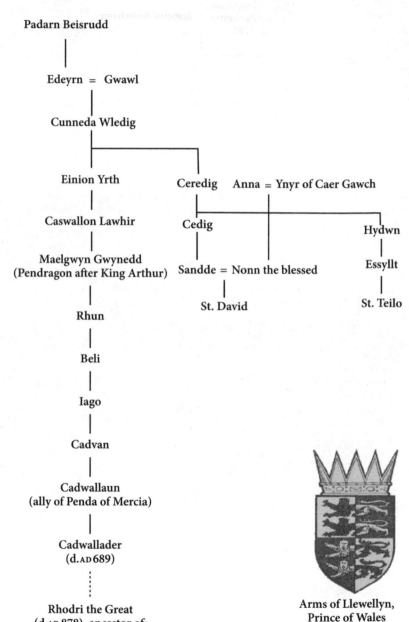

Padarn Beisrudd

Edeyrn = Gwawl

Cunneda Wledig

Einion Yrth   Ceredig   Anna = Ynyr of Caer Gawch

Caswallon Lawhir   Cedig   Hydwn

Maelgwyn Gwynedd
(Pendragon after King Arthur)   Sandde = Nonn the blessed   Essyllt

St. David   St. Teilo

Rhun

Beli

Iago

Cadvan

Cadwallaun
(ally of Penda of Mercia)

Cadwallader
(d.AD 689)

Rhodri the Great
(d.AD 878), ancestor of:
Llewellyn the Great "Prince of Wales" (d.1240),
ancestor of: Roger Mortimer, ancestor of: Edward IV,
maternal grandfather of Henry VIII

Arms of Llewellyn,
Prince of Wales

CHART 6

The Despencer Lords of Glamorgan

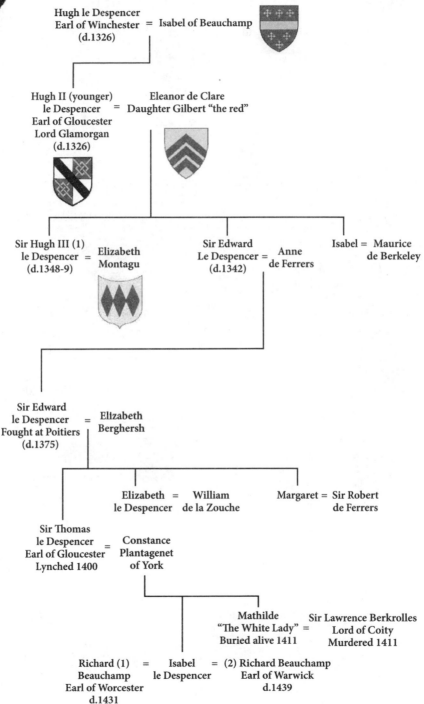

Hugh le Despencer
Earl of Winchester = Isabel of Beauchamp
(d.1326)

Hugh II (younger)   Eleanor de Clare
le Despencer   =   Daughter Gilbert "the red"
Earl of Gloucester
Lord Glamorgan
(d.1326)

Sir Hugh III (1)   Sir Edward   Isabel = Maurice
le Despencer = Elizabeth   Le Despencer = Anne   de Berkeley
(d.1348-9)   Montagu   (d.1342)   de Ferrers

Sir Edward
le Despencer = Elizabeth
Fought at Poitiers   Berghersh
(d.1375)

Elizabeth = William   Margaret = Sir Robert
le Despencer   de la Zouche   de Ferrers

Sir Thomas
le Despencer = Constance
Earl of Gloucester   Plantagenet
Lynched 1400   of York

Mathilde   Sir Lawrence Berkrolles
"The White Lady" =   Lord of Coity
Buried alive 1411   Murdered 1411

Richard (1)   =   Isabel   = (2) Richard Beauchamp
Beauchamp   le Despencer   Earl of Warwick
Earl of Worcester   d.1439
d.1431

CHART 7

The Lineage of the
House of Lancaster

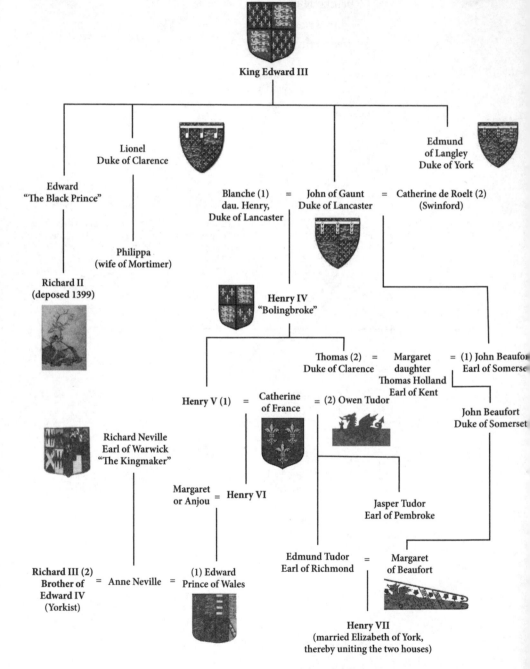

King Edward III

Lionel
Duke of Clarence

Edmund
of Langley
Duke of York

Edward
"The Black Prince"

Blanche (1) = John of Gaunt = Catherine de Roelt (2)
dau. Henry,   Duke of Lancaster   (Swinford)
Duke of Lancaster

Philippa
(wife of Mortimer)

Richard II
(deposed 1399)

Henry IV
"Bolingbroke"

Thomas (2) = Margaret = (1) John Beaufort
Duke of Clarence   daughter   Earl of Somerset
                  Thomas Holland
Henry V (1) = Catherine   Earl of Kent
                of France = (2) Owen Tudor

John Beaufort
Duke of Somerset

Richard Neville
Earl of Warwick
"The Kingmaker"

Margaret
or Anjou = **Henry VI**

Jasper Tudor
Earl of Pembroke

Richard III (2)   (1) Edward
Brother of = Anne Neville = Prince of Wales
Edward IV
(Yorkist)

Edmund Tudor = Margaret
Earl of Richmond   of Beaufort

Henry VII
(married Elizabeth of York,
thereby uniting the two houses)

CHART 8

The Lineage of the House of York

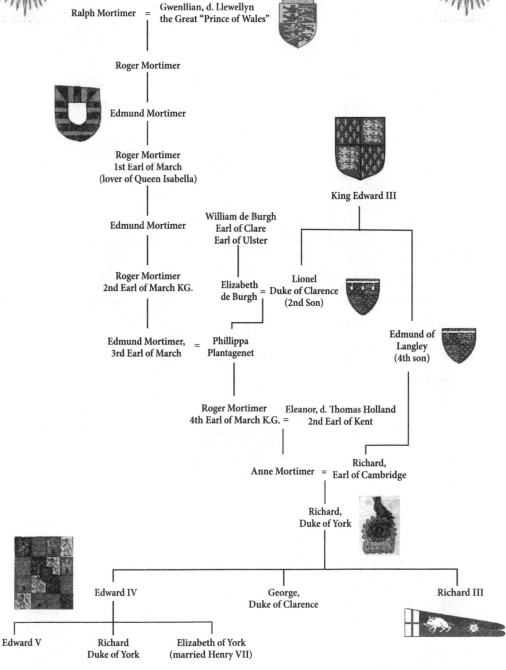

Ralph Mortimer = Gwenllian, d. Llewellyn the Great "Prince of Wales"

Roger Mortimer

Edmund Mortimer

Roger Mortimer
1st Earl of March
(lover of Queen Isabella)

King Edward III

Edmund Mortimer

William de Burgh
Earl of Clare
Earl of Ulster

Roger Mortimer
2nd Earl of March KG.

Elizabeth de Burgh = Lionel Duke of Clarence (2nd Son)

Edmund Mortimer,
3rd Earl of March = Phillippa Plantagenet

Edmund of Langley (4th son)

Roger Mortimer
4th Earl of March K.G. = Eleanor, d. Thomas Holland 2nd Earl of Kent

Anne Mortimer = Richard, Earl of Cambridge

Richard, Duke of York

Edward IV

George, Duke of Clarence

Richard III

Edward V

Richard Duke of York

Elizabeth of York
(married Henry VII)

CHART 9

Herbert Earls of Pembroke
and the Sidney Family

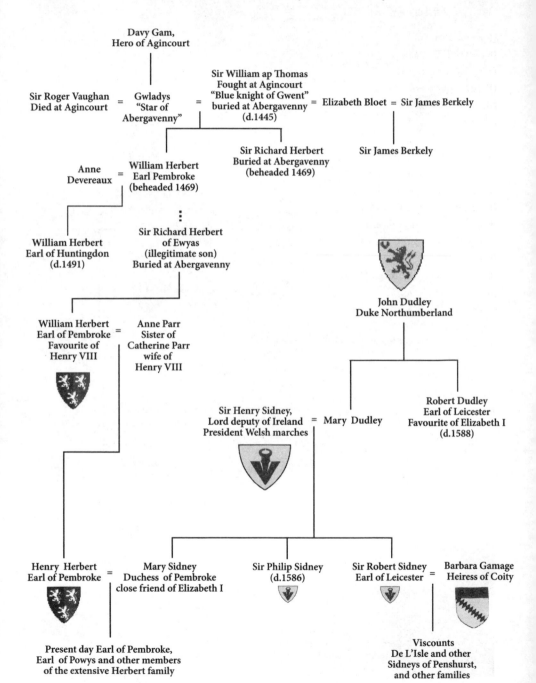

Davy Gam,
Hero of Agincourt

Sir Roger Vaughan
Died at Agincourt
= Gwladys
"Star of
Abergavenny"
= Sir William ap Thomas
Fought at Agincourt
"Blue knight of Gwent"
buried at Abergavenny
(d.1445)
= Elizabeth Bloet = Sir James Berkely

Sir Richard Herbert
Buried at Abergavenny
(beheaded 1469)

Sir James Berkely

Anne
Devereaux
= William Herbert
Earl Pembroke
(beheaded 1469)

William Herbert
Earl of Huntingdon
(d.1491)

Sir Richard Herbert
of Ewyas
(illegitimate son)
Buried at Abergavenny

John Dudley
Duke Northumberland

William Herbert
Earl of Pembroke
Favourite of
Henry VIII
= Anne Parr
Sister of
Catherine Parr
wife of
Henry VIII

Robert Dudley
Earl of Leicester
Favourite of Elizabeth I
(d.1588)

Sir Henry Sidney,
Lord deputy of Ireland
President Welsh marches
= Mary Dudley

Henry Herbert
Earl of Pembroke
= Mary Sidney
Duchess of Pembroke
close friend of Elizabeth I

Sir Philip Sidney
(d.1586)

Sir Robert Sidney
Earl of Leicester
= Barbara Gamage
Heiress of Coity

Present day Earl of Pembroke,
Earl of Powys and other members
of the extensive Herbert family

Viscounts
De L'Isle and other
Sidneys of Penshurst,
and other families

CHART 10

The Tree of Jesse to Jesus

Old Testament	St Matthew Gospel	St Luke Gospel
(Jesse d.*c.*1000 BC)	Jesse	Jesse
(King David d.*c* 965 BC)	David	David
(King Solomon d.*c.*931 BC)	Soloman	Nathan
(King Rehoboam d.913 BC)	Roboam	Mattatha
(King Abijah d.911 BC)	Abia	Menan
(King Asa d.870 BC)	Josaphat	Melea
(King Jehoshaphat d.848 BC)	Joram	Eliakim
(King Jehoram d.841 BC)	Ozais	Jonan
(King Joash/Jehoash d.796 BC)		Joseph
(King Amaziah d.767 BC)	Achaz	Juda
(King Uzziah/Azariah d.740 BC)		Simeon
(King Jotham d.732 BC)	Joatham	Levi
(King Ahaz/Jehoahaz I d.716 BC)	Ezechias	Matthat
(King Hezekiah d.687 BC)	Manasses	Jorim
(King Manasseh d.643 BC)	Amon	Eliezer
(King Amon d.641 BC)	Josias	Jose
(King Josiah d.609 BC)		Er
(King Jehoahaz II d.609 BC)	Jechonias	Elmodam
(King Jehoiakim d.598 BC)	Salatjiel	Cosam
(Jeconiah)	Zorobabel	Addi
(Shealtiel born in Babylon)	Abiud	Melchi
(Zerubbabel 'Shoot of Babylon'	Eliakim	Neri
began to restore temple 520 BC)	Azor	Salathiel
	Sadoc	Zorobabel
	Achim	Rhesa
	Eliud	Joanna
	Eleazer	Juda
	Matthan	Joseph
	Jacob	Semei
	Joseph	Mattathias
	Jesus	Maath
		Nagge
		Esli
		Naum
		Amos
		Mattathias
		Joseph
		Janna
		Melchi
		Levi
		Matthat
		Heli
		Joseph
		Jesus

CHART 11

The Mathew Family of Llandaff
and the Relic of St Teilo

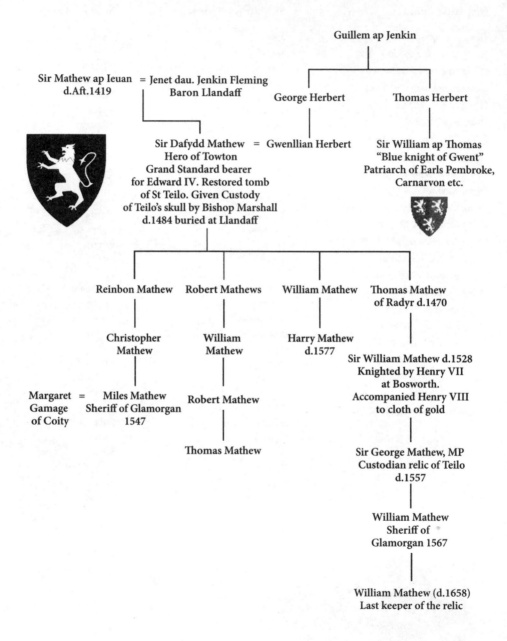

Guillem ap Jenkin

Sir Mathew ap Ieuan = Jenet dau. Jenkin Fleming
d.Aft.1419   Baron Llandaff

George Herbert

Thomas Herbert

Sir Dafydd Mathew = Gwenllian Herbert
Hero of Towton
Grand Standard bearer
for Edward IV. Restored tomb
of St Teilo. Given Custody
of Teilo's skull by Bishop Marshall
d.1484 buried at Llandaff

Sir William ap Thomas
"Blue knight of Gwent"
Patriarch of Earls Pembroke,
Carnarvon etc.

Reinbon Mathew

Robert Mathews

William Mathew

Thomas Mathew
of Radyr d.1470

Christopher
Mathew

William
Mathew

Harry Mathew
d.1577

Sir William Mathew d.1528
Knighted by Henry VII
at Bosworth.
Accompanied Henry VIII
to cloth of gold

Margaret = Miles Mathew
Gamage   Sheriff of Glamorgan
of Coity   1547

Robert Mathew

Thomas Mathew

Sir George Mathew, MP
Custodian relic of Teilo
d.1557

William Mathew
Sheriff of
Glamorgan 1567

William Mathew (d.1658)
Last keeper of the relic

CHART 12

The Welsh Descent of King Henry VII

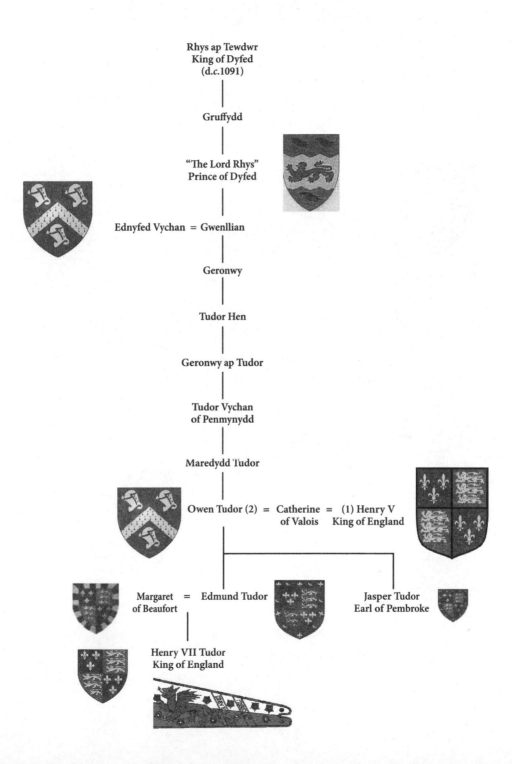

Rhys ap Tewdwr
King of Dyfed
(d.c.1091)

Gruffydd

"The Lord Rhys"
Prince of Dyfed

Ednyfed Vychan = Gwenllian

Geronwy

Tudor Hen

Geronwy ap Tudor

Tudor Vychan
of Penmynydd

Maredydd Tudor

Owen Tudor (2) = Catherine = (1) Henry V
of Valois   King of England

Margaret = Edmund Tudor   Jasper Tudor
of Beaufort   Earl of Pembroke

Henry VII Tudor
King of England

CHART 13

The Royal Lords of Coity
to the First Gamage

Arms of Iestyn

Arms of Turbeville

Morgan, son of Meyrig,
son of Griffith, son of Iestyn,
son of Gwrgan

Assar = Sir Pain
de Turberville

Sir Simmont
de Turberville

Sir Pain II = Matilde
de Turbeville

Sir Gilbert
de Turbeville

Sir Pain III
de Turbeville
(effigy in St Mary's
church Coity)

Sir Gilbert II = Meiwen
de Turbeville

Sir Gilbert III
de Turbeville

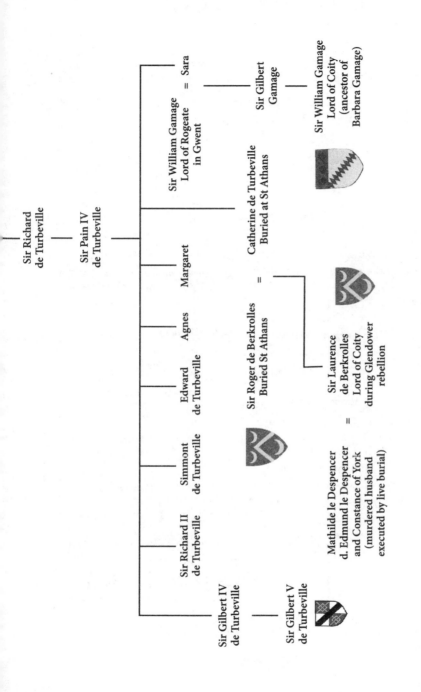

Sir Richard
de Turbeville

Sir Pain IV
de Turbeville

Sir Gilbert IV
de Turbeville

Sir Gilbert V
de Turbeville

Sir Richard II
de Turbeville

Simmont
de Turbeville

Edward
de Turbeville

Agnes

Margaret

Catherine de Turbeville
Buried at St Athans

Sir William Gamage
Lord of Rogeate
in Gwent

= Sara

Sir Gilbert
Gamage

Sir William Gamage
Lord of Coity
(ancestor of
Barbara Gamage)

Sir Roger de Berkrolles
Buried St Athans

Mathilde le Despencer
d. Edmund le Despencer
and Constance of York
(murdered husband
executed by live burial)

=

=

Sir Laurence
de Berkrolles
Lord of Coity
during Glendower
rebellion

CHART 14

The Gamages of Coity

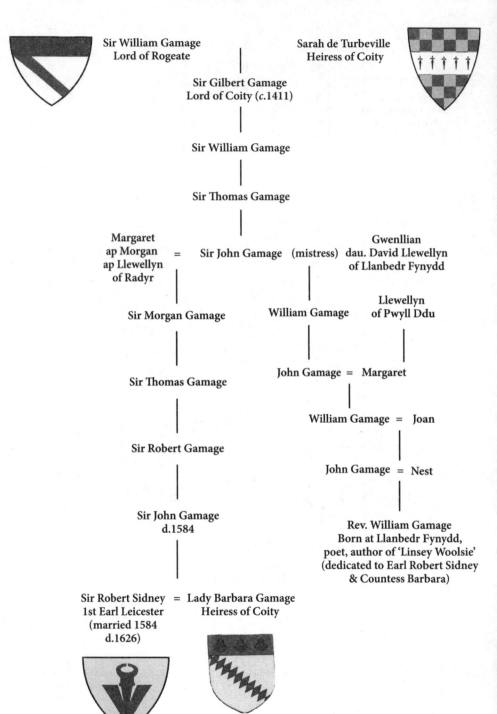

Sir William Gamage
Lord of Rogeate

Sarah de Turbeville
Heiress of Coity

Sir Gilbert Gamage
Lord of Coity (*c.*1411)

Sir William Gamage

Sir Thomas Gamage

Margaret
ap Morgan
ap Llewellyn = Sir John Gamage (mistress) Gwenllian
dau. David Llewellyn
of Llanbedr Fynydd
of Radyr

Sir Morgan Gamage William Gamage Llewellyn
of Pwyll Ddu

Sir Thomas Gamage John Gamage = Margaret

Sir Robert Gamage William Gamage = Joan

John Gamage = Nest

Sir John Gamage
d.1584

Rev. William Gamage
Born at Llanbedr Fynydd,
poet, author of 'Linsey Woolsie'
(dedicated to Earl Robert Sidney
& Countess Barbara)

Sir Robert Sidney = Lady Barbara Gamage
1st Earl Leicester   Heiress of Coity
(married 1584
d.1626)

CHART 15

The Avallach or Avallon Dynasty

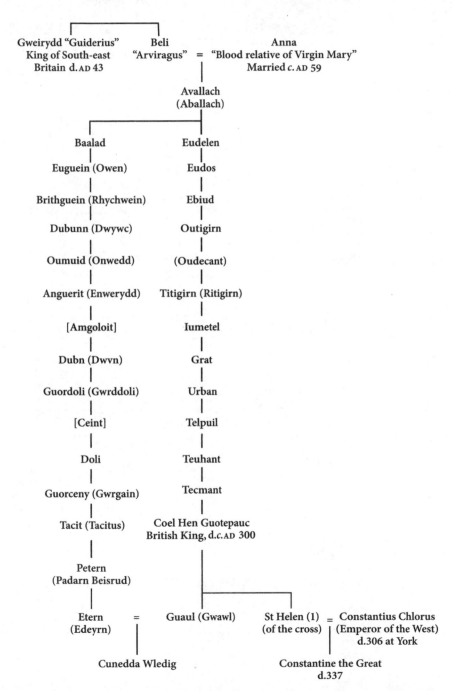

Cynfelyn Cunobelinus
King of South East Britain
d.*c.*AD 40

Gweirydd "Guiderius"
King of South-east
Britain d. AD 43

Beli
"Arviragus" = "Blood relative of Virgin Mary"
Married *c.* AD 59

Anna

Avallach
(Aballach)

Baalad

Eudelen

Euguein (Owen)

Eudos

Brithguein (Rhychwein)

Ebiud

Dubunn (Dwywc)

Outigirn

Oumuid (Onwedd)

(Oudecant)

Anguerit (Enwerydd)

Titigirn (Ritigirn)

[Amgoloit]

Iumetel

Dubn (Dwvn)

Grat

Guordoli (Gwrddoli)

Urban

[Ceint]

Telpuil

Doli

Teuhant

Guorceny (Gwrgain)

Tecmant

Tacit (Tacitus)

Coel Hen Guotepauc
British King, d.*c.*AD 300

Petern
(Padarn Beisrud)

Etern
(Edeyrn)   =   Guaul (Gwawl)

St Helen (1) = Constantius Chlorus
(of the cross) | (Emperor of the West)
d.306 at York

Cunedda Wledig

Constantine the Great
d.337

CHART 16

Descent of Diana, Princess of Wales, from Barbara Gamage

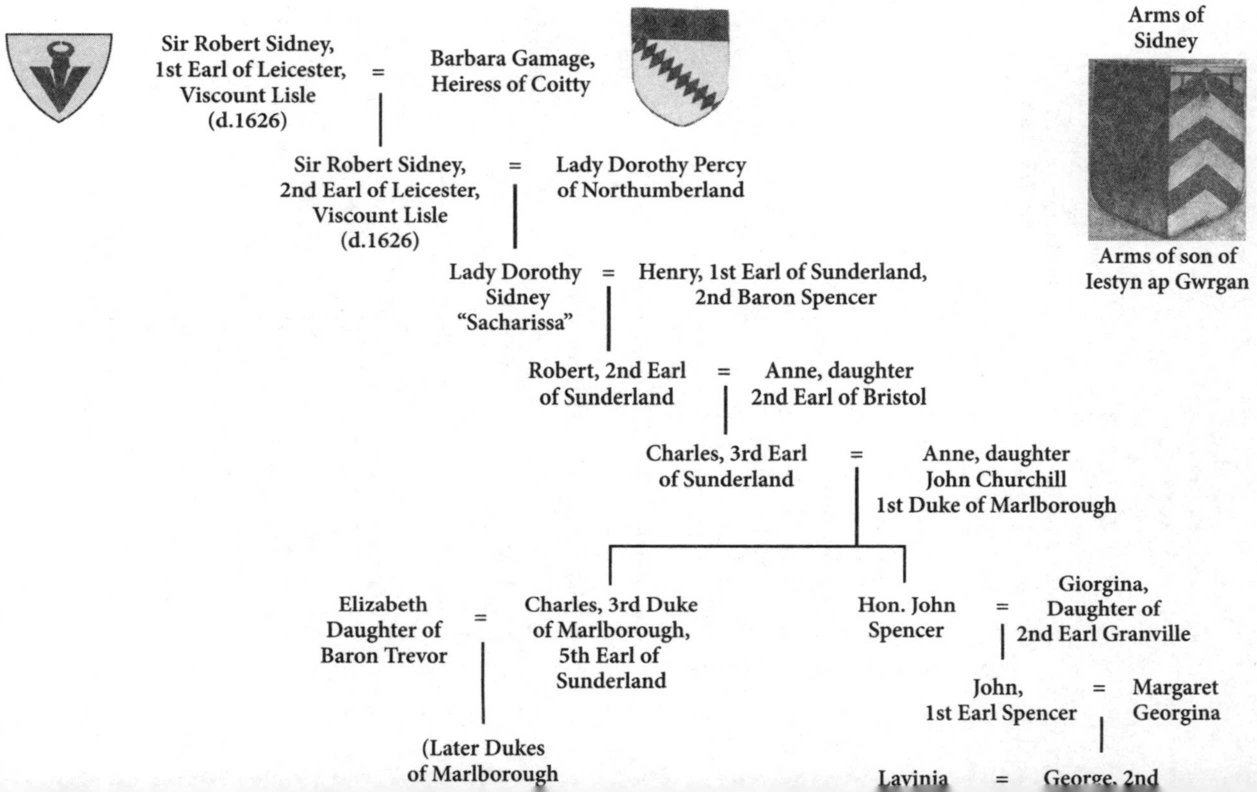

Arms of Sidney

Arms of son of Iestyn ap Gwrgan

Sir Robert Sidney, 1st Earl of Leicester, Viscount Lisle (d.1626) = Barbara Gamage, Heiress of Coitty

Sir Robert Sidney, 2nd Earl of Leicester, Viscount Lisle (d.1626) = Lady Dorothy Percy of Northumberland

Lady Dorothy Sidney "Sacharissa" = Henry, 1st Earl of Sunderland, 2nd Baron Spencer

Robert, 2nd Earl of Sunderland = Anne, daughter 2nd Earl of Bristol

Charles, 3rd Earl of Sunderland = Anne, daughter John Churchill 1st Duke of Marlborough

Charles, 3rd Duke of Marlborough, 5th Earl of Sunderland = Elizabeth Daughter of Baron Trevor

(Later Dukes of Marlborough)

Hon. John Spencer = Giorgina, Daughter of 2nd Earl Granville

John, 1st Earl Spencer = Margaret Georgina

Lavinia = George, 2nd

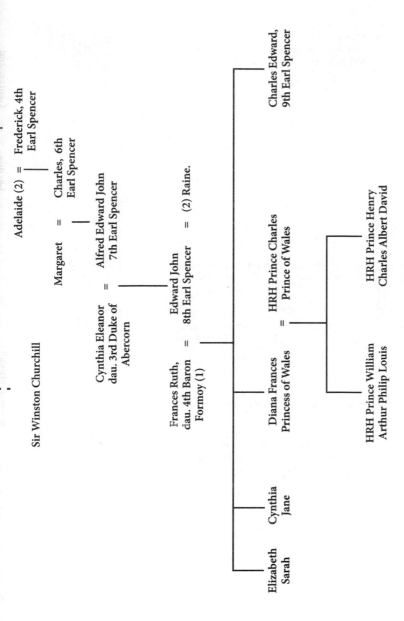

Adelaide (2) = Frederick, 4th
Earl Spencer

Sir Winston Churchill

Margaret = Charles, 6th
Earl Spencer

Cynthia Eleanor = Alfred Edward John
dau. 3rd Duke of   7th Earl Spencer
Abercorn

Frances Ruth,   = Edward John   = (2) Raine.
dau. 4th Baron   8th Earl Spencer
Formoy (1)

Elizabeth   Cynthia
Sarah   Jane

Diana Frances   = HRH Prince Charles
Princess of Wales   Prince of Wales

Charles Edward,
9th Earl Spencer

HRH Prince William   HRH Prince Henry
Arthur Philip Louis   Charles Albert David

Lady Diana Spencer was a 12th generational descendant of Barbara Gamage of Coity.
She therefore had the lineage of Iestyn ap Gwrgan of Glamorgan and King Arthur. Prince Charles
has the lineage of the North Wales kings. Their marriage brought these lines together.
Prince William will be the first King of Great Britain to be demonstrably a descendant
of King Arthur and the 'Holy Grail' dynasty of Coity.

CHART 17

The Coity 'Rosicrucian' Lineage in Brief

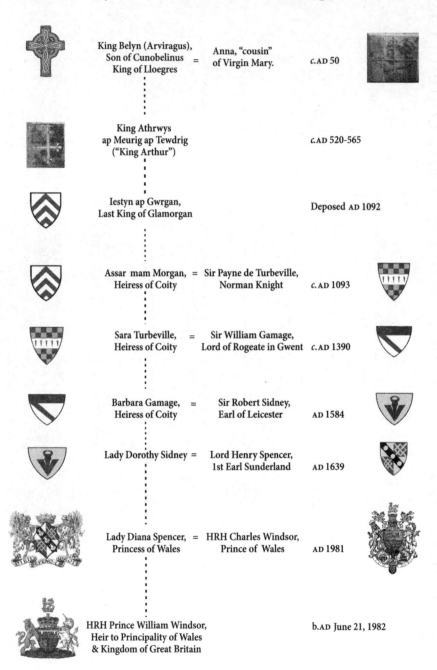

King Belyn (Arviragus),
Son of Cunobelinus = Anna, "cousin"
King of Lloegres   of Virgin Mary.   c.AD 50

King Athrwys
ap Meurig ap Tewdrig   c.AD 520-565
("King Arthur")

Iestyn ap Gwrgan,   Deposed AD 1092
Last King of Glamorgan

Assar mam Morgan, = Sir Payne de Turbeville,
Heiress of Coity   Norman Knight   c.AD 1093

Sara Turbeville, = Sir William Gamage,
Heiress of Coity   Lord of Rogeate in Gwent   c.AD 1390

Barbara Gamage, = Sir Robert Sidney,
Heiress of Coity   Earl of Leicester   AD 1584

Lady Dorothy Sidney = Lord Henry Spencer,
1st Earl Sunderland   AD 1639

Lady Diana Spencer, = HRH Charles Windsor,
Princess of Wales   Prince of Wales   AD 1981

HRH Prince William Windsor,   b.AD June 21, 1982
Heir to Principality of Wales
& Kingdom of Great Britain

CHART 18

The Family of the Dukes of Normandy and the Early Lords of Clare

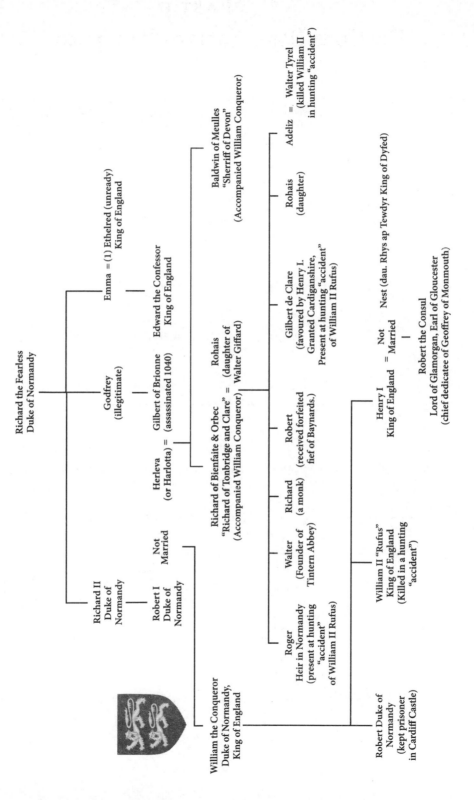

CHART 19

The Early Earls of Pembroke

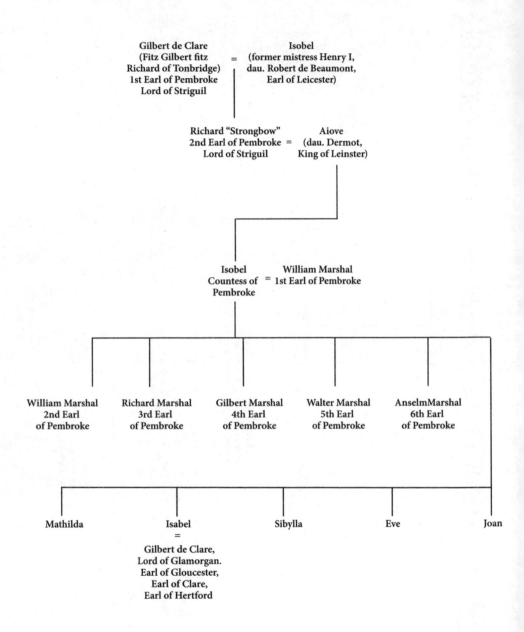

Gilbert de Clare
(Fitz Gilbert fitz
Richard of Tonbridge)
1st Earl of Pembroke
Lord of Striguil

=

Isobel
(former mistress Henry I,
dau. Robert de Beaumont,
Earl of Leicester)

Richard "Strongbow"
2nd Earl of Pembroke =
Lord of Striguil

Aiove
(dau. Dermot,
King of Leinster)

Isobel
Countess of =
Pembroke

William Marshal
1st Earl of Pembroke

William Marshal
2nd Earl
of Pembroke

Richard Marshal
3rd Earl
of Pembroke

Gilbert Marshal
4th Earl
of Pembroke

Walter Marshal
5th Earl
of Pembroke

AnselmMarshal
6th Earl
of Pembroke

Mathilda

Isabel
=
Gilbert de Clare,
Lord of Glamorgan.
Earl of Gloucester,
Earl of Clare,
Earl of Hertford

Sibylla

Eve

Joan

CHART 20

The Marshal Earls of Pembroke and House of Clare

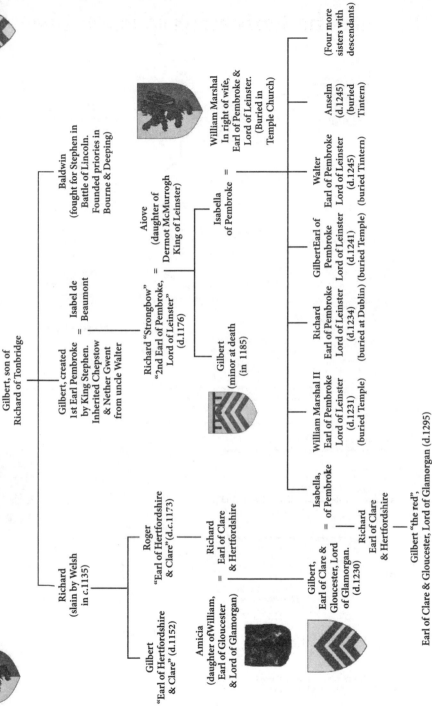

Gilbert, son of
Richard of Tonbridge

Richard
(slain by Welsh
in c.1135)

Gilbert, created
1st Earl Pembroke
by King Stephen.
Inherited Chepstow
& Nether Gwent
from uncle Walter

= Isabel de
Beaumont

Baldwin
(fought for Stephen in
Battle of Lincoln.
Founded priories in
Bourne & Deeping)

Richard "Strongbow"
"2nd Earl of Pembroke,
Lord of Leinster"
(d.1176)

= Aiove
(daughter of
Dermot McMurrogh
King of Leinster)

Gilbert
(minor at death
in 1185)

Isabella
of Pembroke

= William Marshal
In right of wife,
Earl of Pembroke &
Lord of Leinster.
(Buried in
Temple Church)

Gilbert
"Earl of Hertfordshire
& Clare" (d.1152)

Roger
"Earl of Hertfordshire
& Clare" (d.c.1173)

Richard
Earl of Clare
& Hertfordshire

Amicia
(daughter of William,
Earl of Gloucester
& Lord of Glamorgan)

= Gilbert,
Earl of Clare &
Gloucester, Lord
of Glamorgan.
(d.1230)

Isabella,
of Pembroke

Richard
Earl of Clare
& Hertfordshire

William Marshal II
Earl of Pembroke
Lord of Leinster
(d.1231)
(buried Temple)

Richard
Earl of Pembroke
Lord of Leinster
(d.1234)
(buried at Dublin)

Gilbert Earl of
Pembroke
Lord of Leinster
(d.1241)
(buried Temple)

Walter
Earl of Pembroke
Lord of Leinster
(d.1245)
(buried Tintern)

Anselm
(d.1245)
(buried
Tintern)

(Four more
sisters with
descendants)

Gilbert "the red",
Earl of Clare & Gloucester, Lord of Glamorgan (d.1295)

CHART 21

The Dukes of Marlborough and Earls of Sunderland

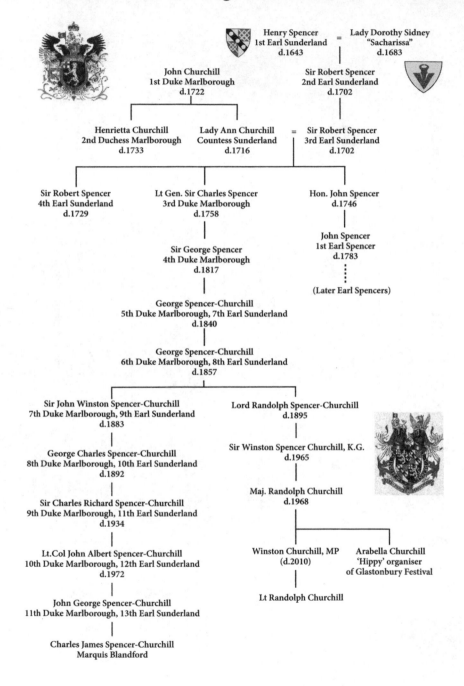

Henry Spencer
1st Earl Sunderland
d.1643
=
Lady Dorothy Sidney
"Sacharissa"
d.1683

John Churchill
1st Duke Marlborough
d.1722

Sir Robert Spencer
2nd Earl Sunderland
d.1702

Henrietta Churchill
2nd Duchess Marlborough
d.1733

Lady Ann Churchill
Countess Sunderland
d.1716
=
Sir Robert Spencer
3rd Earl Sunderland
d.1702

Sir Robert Spencer
4th Earl Sunderland
d.1729

Lt Gen. Sir Charles Spencer
3rd Duke Marlborough
d.1758

Hon. John Spencer
d.1746

Sir George Spencer
4th Duke Marlborough
d.1817

John Spencer
1st Earl Spencer
d.1783

(Later Earl Spencers)

George Spencer-Churchill
5th Duke Marlborough, 7th Earl Sunderland
d.1840

George Spencer-Churchill
6th Duke Marlborough, 8th Earl Sunderland
d.1857

Sir John Winston Spencer-Churchill
7th Duke Marlborough, 9th Earl Sunderland
d.1883

Lord Randolph Spencer-Churchill
d.1895

George Charles Spencer-Churchill
8th Duke Marlborough, 10th Earl Sunderland
d.1892

Sir Winston Spencer Churchill, K.G.
d.1965

Sir Charles Richard Spencer-Churchill
9th Duke Marlborough, 11th Earl Sunderland
d.1934

Maj. Randolph Churchill
d.1968

Lt.Col John Albert Spencer-Churchill
10th Duke Marlborough, 12th Earl Sunderland
d.1972

Winston Churchill, MP
(d.2010)

Arabella Churchill
'Hippy' organiser
of Glastonbury Festival

John George Spencer-Churchill
11th Duke Marlborough, 13th Earl Sunderland

Lt Randolph Churchill

Charles James Spencer-Churchill
Marquis Blandford

CHART 22

The Earls of Leicester and Viscounts De L'Isle

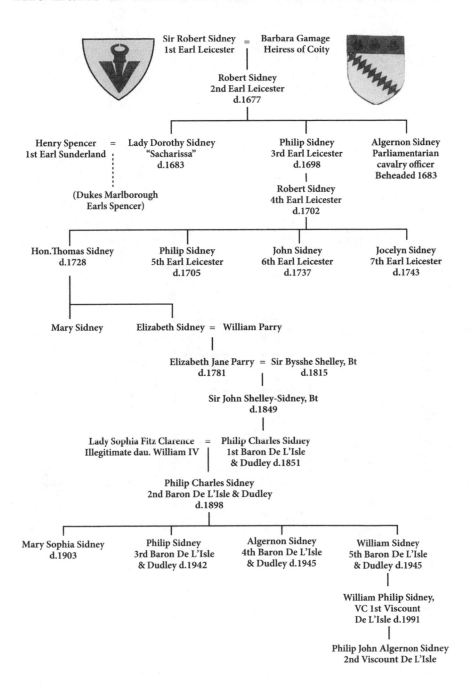

Sir Robert Sidney = Barbara Gamage
1st Earl Leicester   Heiress of Coity

Robert Sidney
2nd Earl Leicester
d.1677

Henry Spencer = Lady Dorothy Sidney
1st Earl Sunderland   "Sacharissa"
                       d.1683

(Dukes Marlborough
Earls Spencer)

Philip Sidney
3rd Earl Leicester
d.1698

Algernon Sidney
Parliamentarian
cavalry officer
Beheaded 1683

Robert Sidney
4th Earl Leicester
d.1702

Hon. Thomas Sidney
d.1728

Philip Sidney
5th Earl Leicester
d.1705

John Sidney
6th Earl Leicester
d.1737

Jocelyn Sidney
7th Earl Leicester
d.1743

Mary Sidney

Elizabeth Sidney = William Parry

Elizabeth Jane Parry = Sir Bysshe Shelley, Bt
d.1781   d.1815

Sir John Shelley-Sidney, Bt
d.1849

Lady Sophia Fitz Clarence = Philip Charles Sidney
Illegitimate dau. William IV   1st Baron De L'Isle
                                & Dudley d.1851

Philip Charles Sidney
2nd Baron De L'Isle & Dudley
d.1898

Mary Sophia Sidney
d.1903

Philip Sidney
3rd Baron De L'Isle
& Dudley d.1942

Algernon Sidney
4th Baron De L'Isle
& Dudley d.1945

William Sidney
5th Baron De L'Isle
& Dudley d.1945

William Philip Sidney,
VC 1st Viscount
De L'Isle d.1991

Philip John Algernon Sidney
2nd Viscount De L'Isle

CHART 23

Herbert Earls of Pembroke, Montgomery and Carnarvon

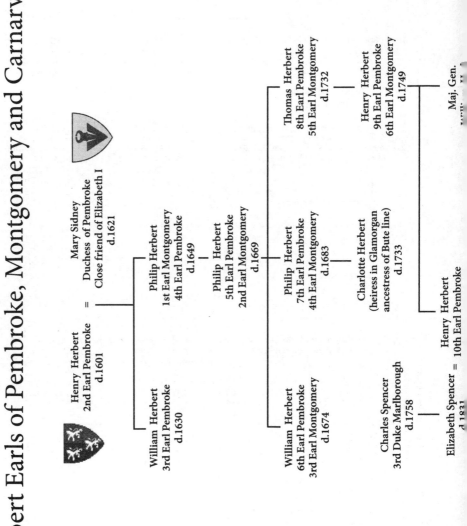

Henry Herbert
2nd Earl Pembroke
d.1601
=
Mary Sidney
Duchess of Pembroke
Close friend of Elizabeth I
d.1621

William Herbert
3rd Earl Pembroke
d.1630

Philip Herbert
1st Earl Montgomery
4th Earl Pembroke
d.1649

Philip Herbert
5th Earl Pembroke
2nd Earl Montgomery
d.1669

William Herbert
6th Earl Pembroke
3rd Earl Montgomery
d.1674

Philip Herbert
7th Earl Pembroke
4th Earl Montgomery
d.1683

Thomas Herbert
8th Earl Pembroke
5th Earl Montgomery
d.1732

Charlotte Herbert
(heiress in Glamorgan
ancestress of Bute line)
d.1733

Henry Herbert
9th Earl Pembroke
6th Earl Montgomery
d.1749

Charles Spencer
3rd Duke Marlborough
d.1758

Henry Herbert
10th Earl Pembroke

Elizabeth Spencer =
d.1831

Maj. Gen.

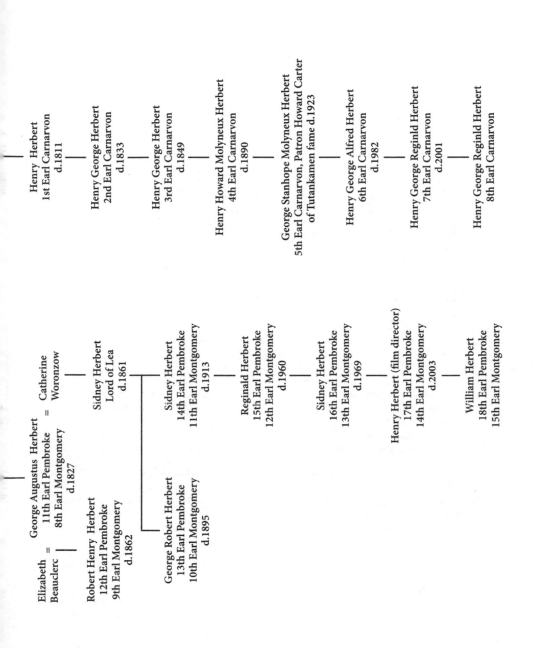

Henry Herbert
1st Earl Carnarvon
d.1811

Henry George Herbert
2nd Earl Carnarvon
d.1833

Henry George Herbert
3rd Earl Carnarvon
d.1849

Henry Howard Molyneux Herbert
4th Earl Carnarvon
d.1890

George Stanhope Molyneux Herbert
5th Earl Carnarvon, Patron Howard Carter
of Tutankamen fame d.1923

Henry George Alfred Herbert
6th Earl Carnarvon
d.1982

Henry George Reginld Herbert
7th Earl Carnarvon
d.2001

Henry George Reginld Herbert
8th Earl Carnarvon

Elizabeth = George Augustus Herbert = Catherine
Beauclerc   11th Earl Pembroke   Woronzow
             8th Earl Montgomery
             d.1827

Robert Henry Herbert
12th Earl Pembroke
9th Earl Montgomery
d.1862

Sidney Herbert
Lord of Lea
d.1861

George Robert Herbert
13th Earl Pembroke
10th Earl Montgomery
d.1895

Sidney Herbert
14th Earl Pembroke
11th Earl Montgomery
d.1913

Reginald Herbert
15th Earl Pembroke
12th Earl Montgomery
d.1960

Sidney Herbert
16th Earl Pembroke
13th Earl Montgomery
d.1969

Henry Herbert (film director)
17th Earl Pembroke
14th Earl Montgomery
d.2003

William Herbert
18th Earl Pembroke
15th Earl Montgomery

CHART 24

The Herbert Earls of Powis

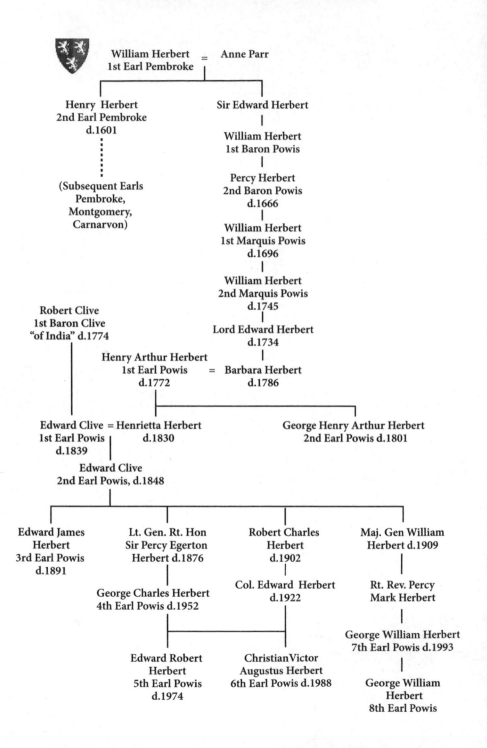

William Herbert
1st Earl Pembroke = Anne Parr

Henry Herbert
2nd Earl Pembroke
d.1601

Sir Edward Herbert

William Herbert
1st Baron Powis

(Subsequent Earls
Pembroke,
Montgomery,
Carnarvon)

Percy Herbert
2nd Baron Powis
d.1666

William Herbert
1st Marquis Powis
d.1696

William Herbert
2nd Marquis Powis
d.1745

Robert Clive
1st Baron Clive
"of India" d.1774

Lord Edward Herbert
d.1734

Henry Arthur Herbert
1st Earl Powis
d.1772   =   Barbara Herbert
d.1786

Edward Clive = Henrietta Herbert
1st Earl Powis   d.1830
d.1839

George Henry Arthur Herbert
2nd Earl Powis d.1801

Edward Clive
2nd Earl Powis, d.1848

Edward James
Herbert
3rd Earl Powis
d.1891

Lt. Gen. Rt. Hon
Sir Percy Egerton
Herbert d.1876

Robert Charles
Herbert
d.1902

Maj. Gen William
Herbert d.1909

George Charles Herbert
4th Earl Powis d.1952

Col. Edward Herbert
d.1922

Rt. Rev. Percy
Mark Herbert

George William Herbert
7th Earl Powis d.1993

Edward Robert
Herbert
5th Earl Powis
d.1974

Christian Victor
Augustus Herbert
6th Earl Powis d.1988

George William
Herbert
8th Earl Powis

CHART 25

The Herbert Ancestry of the Marquises of Bute

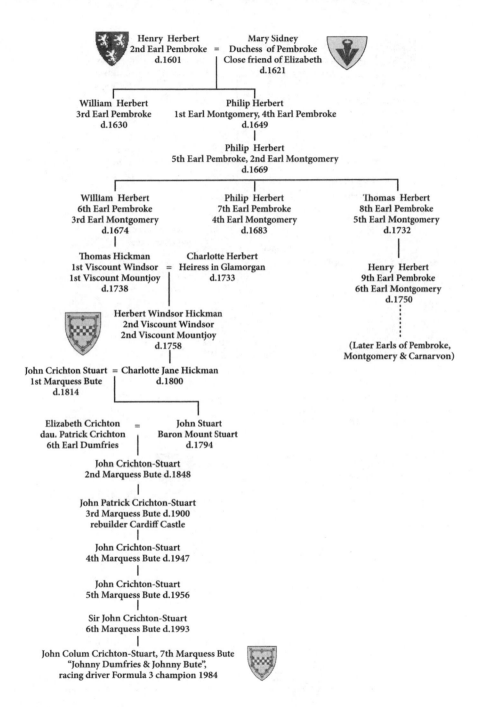

Henry Herbert
2nd Earl Pembroke = Duchess of Pembroke
d.1601 | Close friend of Elizabeth
d.1621

Mary Sidney

William Herbert
3rd Earl Pembroke
d.1630

Philip Herbert
1st Earl Montgomery, 4th Earl Pembroke
d.1649

Philip Herbert
5th Earl Pembroke, 2nd Earl Montgomery
d.1669

William Herbert
6th Earl Pembroke
3rd Earl Montgomery
d.1674

Philip Herbert
7th Earl Pembroke
4th Earl Montgomery
d.1683

Thomas Herbert
8th Earl Pembroke
5th Earl Montgomery
d.1732

Thomas Hickman
1st Viscount Windsor
1st Viscount Mountjoy
d.1738 = Charlotte Herbert
Heiress in Glamorgan
d.1733

Henry Herbert
9th Earl Pembroke
6th Earl Montgomery
d.1750

Herbert Windsor Hickman
2nd Viscount Windsor
2nd Viscount Mountjoy
d.1758

(Later Earls of Pembroke,
Montgomery & Carnarvon)

John Crichton Stuart = Charlotte Jane Hickman
1st Marquess Bute   d.1800
d.1814

Elizabeth Crichton
dau. Patrick Crichton
6th Earl Dumfries = John Stuart
Baron Mount Stuart
d.1794

John Crichton-Stuart
2nd Marquess Bute d.1848

John Patrick Crichton-Stuart
3rd Marquess Bute d.1900
rebuilder Cardiff Castle

John Crichton-Stuart
4th Marquess Bute d.1947

John Crichton-Stuart
5th Marquess Bute d.1956

Sir John Crichton-Stuart
6th Marquess Bute d.1993

John Colum Crichton-Stuart, 7th Marquess Bute
"Johnny Dumfries & Johnny Bute",
racing driver Formula 3 champion 1984

CHART 26

The Stradlings of St Donats

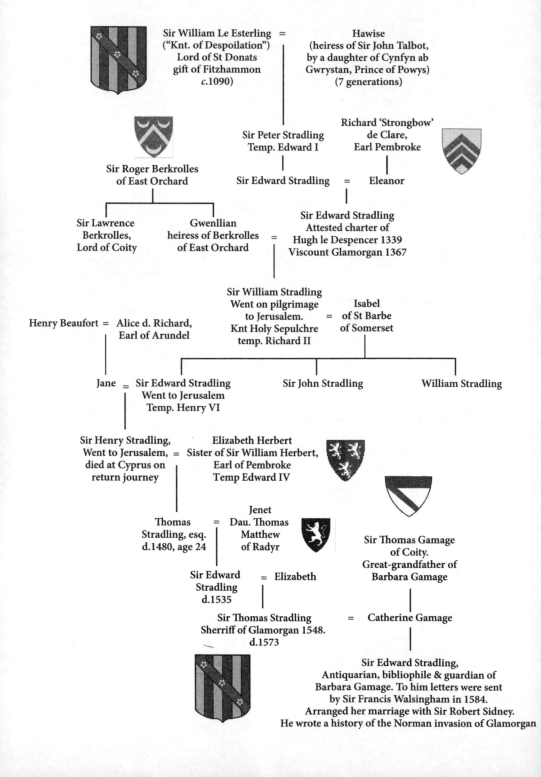

Sir William Le Esterling = Hawise
("Knt. of Despoilation") (heiress of Sir John Talbot,
Lord of St Donats by a daughter of Cynfyn ab
gift of Fitzhammon Gwrystan, Prince of Powys)
c.1090) (7 generations)

Sir Peter Stradling   Richard 'Strongbow'
Temp. Edward I   de Clare,
    Earl Pembroke

Sir Roger Berkrolles
of East Orchard

Sir Edward Stradling = Eleanor

Sir Lawrence   Gwenllian   Sir Edward Stradling
Berkrolles,   heiress of Berkrolles   Attested charter of
Lord of Coity   of East Orchard   =   Hugh le Despencer 1339
    Viscount Glamorgan 1367

Sir William Stradling
Went on pilgrimage   Isabel
Henry Beaufort = Alice d. Richard,   to Jerusalem.   =   of St Barbe
    Earl of Arundel   Knt Holy Sepulchre   of Somerset
    temp. Richard II

Jane = Sir Edward Stradling   Sir John Stradling   William Stradling
    Went to Jerusalem
    Temp. Henry VI

Sir Henry Stradling,   Elizabeth Herbert
Went to Jerusalem, = Sister of Sir William Herbert,
died at Cyprus on   Earl of Pembroke
return journey   Temp Edward IV

    Jenet
Thomas = Dau. Thomas
Stradling, esq.   Matthew
d.1480, age 24   of Radyr   Sir Thomas Gamage
    of Coity.
    Great-grandfather of
Sir Edward = Elizabeth   Barbara Gamage
Stradling
d.1535

Sir Thomas Stradling = Catherine Gamage
Sherriff of Glamorgan 1548.
d.1573

Sir Edward Stradling,
Antiquarian, bibliophile & guardian of
Barbara Gamage. To him letters were sent
by Sir Francis Walsingham in 1584.
Arranged her marriage with Sir Robert Sidney.
He wrote a history of the Norman invasion of Glamorgan

Index